Edith Sylla

SELECTED LETTERS OF PLINY

C. PLINI SECUNDI

EPISTULAE SELECTAE

SELECTED LETTERS OF PLINY

WITH AN INTRODUCTION AND NOTES BY J. H. WESTCOTT

UNIVERSITY OF OKLAHOMA PRESS

NORMAN

Library of Congress Catalog Number: 65-11225

New edition published by the University of Oklahoma Press, Publishing Division of the University, Norman, Oklahoma, from the original edition published by Allyn and Bacon, Boston. New edition first published 1965. Manufactured in the United States of America. Second printing of new edition, September, 1968.

PREFACE

My obligations, in the preparation of my Introduction and Notes, have been chiefly to Mommsen's important article on the Younger Pliny, in *Hermes,* III.; to Kraut's and Lagergren's dissertations on the language and style of Pliny; and in a more general sense to the various editors cited in the list on page xli of the Introduction and the Abbreviations on page 128. Indebtedness in detail I have been careful to acknowledge specifically.

The text is that of Keil, with a few changes.

I have to thank several of my colleagues for valuable information upon matters which come within the sphere of their special knowledge, but most of all the general editors for their faithful and sympathetic coöperation in all stages of my work. To them are due, in greater measure than they are willing to acknowledge, whatever merits the book may prove to possess.

J. H. W.

PUBLISHER'S FOREWORD

THE requirements of both teachers of Latin and their students in the United States have made imperative the revival of many of the texts which were at one time widely used. John Howell Westcott's *Selected Letters of Pliny,* first published in 1898, when that classical scholar was Musgrave Professor of Latin in Princeton University, has been brought back into print as part of an extended program of revivals developed by the Committee on Greek and Latin College Textbooks of the American Philological Association in co-operation with the University of Oklahoma Press. Other works which have appeared in this program are:

Tacitus: Selections from His Works, edited, with an introduction and notes, by Frank Burr Marsh and Harry J. Leon.

Selected Letters of Cicero, edited, with an introduction and notes, by Frank Frost Abbott.

Xenophon's Anabasis: Books I IV, edited, with an introduction, notes, and vocabulary, by Maurice W. Mather and Joseph William Hewitt.

Selections from Herodotus, selected and edited, with an introduction, notes, and vocabulary, by Amy L. Barbour.

The development of new texts is also envisaged by the American Philological Association, and these will be published in a series sponsored by that association, under the imprint of the University of Oklahoma Press.

SAVOIE LOTTINVILLE
for the University of Oklahoma Press

CONTENTS

INTRODUCTION

I

LIFE OF PLINY

WITH most of the classical writers we have no sense of personal acquaintanceship. But happily there are some exceptions to this rule. The man we know best among the ancients — and in fact there are few of any age that we know as well — is Cicero. This is because of his voluminous correspondence.[1] In a similar way, though in an inferior degree, we are acquainted with the Younger Pliny through his letters.

Cicero Seneca Pliny

When we hear of Roman letter-writers, three names at once occur to our minds: Cicero, Seneca, Pliny.[2] Cicero's are real letters; Seneca's are merely moral essays in epistolary form; Pliny's are letters, indeed, but each one is a literary unit, somewhat like an essay of the *Spectator*, dealing usually with a single theme, and carefully worked up to a high degree of stylistic perfection, with a view to publication.

Pliny portrays his own age

Cicero's letters are a far more complete revelation of the mind of their writer, but then there was in Cicero's nature far more to be revealed. Yet Pliny, while intellectually many degrees inferior to Cicero, was a good man and a clever one, whose acquaintance is well worth making. Moreover, he draws the most satis-

---

[1] Upwards of eight hundred letters, extending over twenty-six years.

[2] It has been observed that these three names well illustrate the progress from the purely Roman to the cosmopolitan point of view.

factory picture we have of the imperial age of Rome, at the beginning of the second century, when the empire was in its prime. Taking all its faults and limitations into account, it was still a great age, worthy of the canvas of an artist. The character of the last generation of the republic had been largely determined by Cicero's intellectual activity. Pliny was no epoch-maker, but he attained a rare success in portraying for the world of after times the happier, more cheerful, and more virtuous aspects of the age in which he lived. Juvenal and Tacitus, his contemporaries, were vastly superior to him in genius, but they were both pessimistic in tone; the grim narrative of the historian is an even more terrific indictment of the age than the diatribes of the satirist. Their pictures are all shadows. Pliny's are brighter, and we cannot escape the conviction that they are truer for the average of life.

Contrasted with Juvenal and Tacitus

Pliny's career was peaceful, busy, prosperous. He was favored by his circumstances, but his industry fairly earned the success which so richly rewarded it.

Period covered by his life

Born in 62 A.D., at the Cisalpine town of Comum, on the shore of the lovely Lacus Larius,[1] of a family which had long been one of local consequence, — like English landholders near a borough, — he passed his childhood in the later years of the last and worst of the Julian Caesars; his youth of study, in the reign of Vespasian; his young manhood of active participation in affairs, under Domitian; his prime, in important positions of trust, and in somewhat intimate relations with the great emperor Trajan. He lived under nine emperors.

Parentage and name

His father was L. Caecilius Cilo: he was probably the second son of his parents, and, as was not unusual at that period, probably took his *cognomen*

[1] The Lake of Como.

from his mother's family; his name, then, was P. Caecilius Secundus, his older brother bearing the name Cilo after their father.[1]

The Caecilii were a plebeian family of great antiquity. This branch of it had been settled at Comum for several generations. Catullus's thirty-fifth poem is an invitation to a poet Caecilius of Comum to visit him at Verona.[2] Pliny repeatedly speaks of Comum as his *patria*.[3] It was also the home of his mother's family, the Plinii.[4]

Adoption by his uncle, Pliny the Elder

When very young, our Pliny lost his father. He was afterward adopted[5] by the will of his mother's brother, Pliny the Elder, as he is called, who was not only the most learned man and the chief

---

[1] Take this instance by way of illustration:

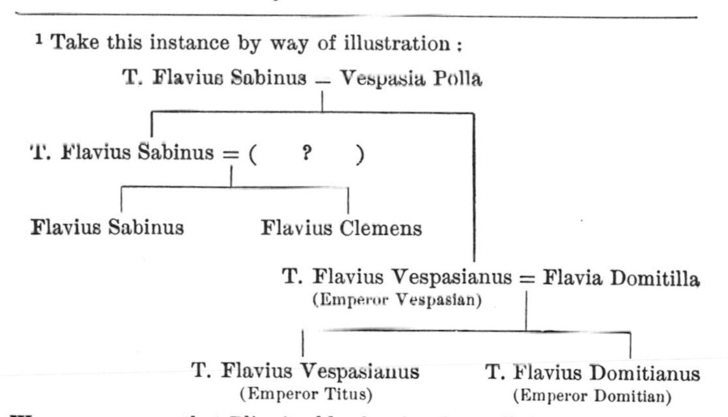

We may suppose that Pliny's elder brother bore all three names of his father: L. Caecilius Cilo. He himself was called Secundus, not because he was the second son, but because that happened to be the cognomen of his mother's family.

[2] This poem was written between 59 and 54 B.C., about 120 years before our author's birth. It contains a complimentary allusion to Caecilius's forthcoming poem, showing that Pliny was not the first literary man in his family.

[3] Epp. IV. 30. 1; V. 7. 2; VI. 24. 2; VII. 32. 1.

[4] Suet. *Vita Plinii;* several inscriptions; Ep. VII. 11. 5.

[5] Under the republic in cases of adoption, whether *inter vivos* or by

writer of his generation, but also a conscientious and ener getic official. Vespasian, rough soldier though he was, besides being a sagacious practical ruler, had the good sense to encourage literature. Among all his subordinates none was more trusted than the Elder Pliny, who, in 77 A.D., dedicated his encyclopaedic 'Natural History' to Vespasian's son Titus.

Doubtless the circumstance that Pliny was brought up by this uncle rather than by his father had an influence upon his after career. The uncle was a prodigy of industry, as we learn from a letter[1] of the nephew, describing his habits of study, which were such that in comparison the nephew, who to us seems painfully studious, might well call himself a mere idler. Yet the boy was distressingly precocious, according to modern notions; we are tempted to think him something of a prig. Bulwer has well described him as a "graceful pedant." In his maturity we pardon the pedantry for the sake of the grace. But there is no cause for regret that the Greek tragedy[2] which he composed at the age of fourteen has been lost. Doubtless it was no more than a school exercise, such as was done by many a youth who failed afterward to become famous in the literary world.[3]

Youthful character

---

testament, the adopted son assumed the three names of his adoptive father, adding his own gentile name, in the form of an adjective. Thus, e.g., the son of L. Aemilius Paulus, adopted by P. Cornelius Scipio, became P. Cornelius Scipio Aemilianus; young Octavius, adopted by the will of Julius Caesar, became C. Julius Caesar Octavianus. But great irregularity in the matter of proper names had grown up after the decay of the old *gentes* and of the *patria potestas*, so that we have no reason to be surprised at the form of our author's name, assumed after his testamentary adoption by the uncle who had been in many respects a father to him, viz., C. Plinius Caecilius Secundus.

[1] Ep. III. 5.

[2] Ep. VII. 4. 2.

[3] An English schoolboy of our day has sometimes, as a vacation task, to compose in heroic hexameters a Latin poem as long as a book of the Aeneid.

for some of the facts of Trajan's reign; but with its fulsome adulation and long-winded rhetoric, it is very tiresome reading — a great contrast to the letters in point of interest. After putting on the finishing touches, Pliny read it for three successive days to an audience of his friends, who professed to enjoy it. It was only fair on their part to say so, for he was always infinitely obliging about listening to the literary productions of other people. Except for this solitary extant specimen we might have entertained a higher opinion of his oratory. Public recitations, which had begun in the time of Augustus, had long been a recognized institution. Aspirants to literary fame hired a public room, filled it with an audience of their friends, and there recited and declaimed. The occupation of the real orator being taken from him by the changed political conditions of the age, the rhetorician had usurped his place. Reputation was measured by the size of audiences and the noise of their applause. The influence of sensationalism, invading all departments of literature, produced an era of false taste, of artificiality in both matter and expression. Epics, dramas, forensic speeches were equally labored and unnatural. Pliny was appreciably affected by the spirit of his time. At least he was an enthusiastic and indefatigable listener as well as performer at 'recitations.' There is evident sincerity in his complaint of the manner in which many openly neglected, while others attended with a perfunctory show of interest, these literary gatherings.[1] In 103 or 104 he became a member of the college of augurs, and was later appointed one of the commissioners of the Tiber.[2]

Public readings

Augur

During all these years Pliny had been growing in reputa-

[1] Ep. I. 13; on this general topic, see Robert, *Rome et l'Empire*, pages 322–327.

[2] *Curator alvei Tiberis et riparum et cloacarum urbis:* Inscriptions 1, 2, and 4, pages xxv and xxvi.

tion as an advocate. His earlier practice seems to have been mainly in the court of the *Centumviri*.[1]

The Court of the Centumviri

This tribunal was a very ancient one, the history of which is but imperfectly known. It was permanent, but its members were probably chosen annually from the tribes. The name was correct enough so long as there were 105 members, three from each tribe; but it was retained after the number was raised to 180. They sat in the Basilica Julia, with a spear (*hasta*), the ancient symbol of Quiritary ownership, planted before them. The court was divided into four chambers, which usually sat separately. But for cases of special importance they were combined, sometimes in one body (*quadruplex iudicium*), sometimes in two sections (*duplex iudicium; duae hastae*).[2] Cicero enumerates[3] the kinds of causes referred to this court, viz., disputes as to Quiritary ownership, including 'servitudes,' wills, intestate succession, guardianship, and questions of *status*, involving freedom or citizenship. In Pliny's time it was doubtless concerned chiefly, if not entirely, with questions of inheritance.

Even in his later years he did not entirely abandon this part of his practice, for he writes of being overworked with cases in this court,[4] and all through the letters are numerous anecdotes about it and familiar allusions to it.[5]

But the climax of an advocate's career was to be engaged in great state trials, such as those of provincial governors arraigned before the Senate for maladministration. In this respect also Pliny's ambition was gratified. He was engaged on behalf of the province of Baetica for the prosecution of Baebius Massa and of Caecilius Classi-

State trials

---

[1] Hunter, *Roman Law*, pages 49–51.

[2] Epp. I. 18; IV. 24; VI. 33; Quint. XII. 5. 6.

[3] *De Orat.* I. 38.

[4] Ep. II. 14. 1.

[5] Ep. IX. 23.

cus,[1] and on behalf of the province of Africa for the prosecution of Marius Priscus. In the last case he was associated with Tacitus. He was subsequently counsel for the defence of Julius Bassus and of Varenus Rufus, both ex-governors of Bithynia. These two cases were difficult and complicated. Their preparation necessitated a thorough acquaintance with the province in question, and it was possibly owing to the familiarity with Bithynian affairs which he then acquired, that Pliny was afterward[2] selected by Trajan for governor (*legatus pro praetore*) of Bithynia and Pontus.

Governor of Bithynia

Under the Empire the Roman provinces were divided into two classes. Those which had been long organized, which were tranquil and needed no military garrison, were administered by proconsuls sent out annually by the Senate. Those which were turbulent, or which lay on an exposed frontier, or which for any reason required a large military force, were governed by the emperor through *legati* appointed by himself, to serve during his pleasure. A province might at any time be transferred from one list to the other. Pontus and Bithynia had been senatorial provinces, but their administration had fallen into such disorder that Trajan found it necessary to take them over into his own hands, and to send out an imperial legate with extraordinary powers, to reorganize the government and restore order.

The provinces

The book containing the correspondence with Trajan consists (with the exception of the first fifteen[3] epistles) wholly of letters written during Pliny's tenure of this important post. It breaks off suddenly at Epistle CXXI, and of the rest of Pliny's life we know

The Trajan letters

---

[1] About the chronology of this case and that of Marius Priscus there has been much controversy. See Appendix I.

[2] Probably in 111 A.D.

[3] 1–14; there are two numbered 3.

nothing. Whether he died suddenly or not, whether in the province or after his return home, we cannot say. But his death probably occurred before 115, for in the great inscription to his memory in the wall of the Thermae at Comum, Trajan is mentioned without the titles — conferred in 114 — of Optimus and Parthicus.[1]

Date of death

Such was the public life of Pliny, — an admirable type of the successful and patriotic Roman gentleman of rank under the early Empire. But, after all, it is not so much 'Pliny the Consul' that interests us as Pliny the literary enthusiast, and still more Pliny the man, so admirable and lovable in all the manifestations of personal character. Little has yet been said of his private life.

Typical Roman gentleman

Though married certainly twice, and probably thrice, he was disappointed in the hope of children.[2] The daughter of Pompeia Celerina, who is addressed in Ep. I. 4, was probably his second wife. He was on the best of terms with his mother-in-law. She was a rich woman, who allowed him 'to treat her purse as his own.'[3] Not far from the year 100 he married his last wife, Calpurnia, much younger than himself. Their union was a happy one. His letters to her[4] and about her[5] are tender and lover-like, and it is evident that his affection was returned. His descriptions of her interest in his pursuits and her anxiety for his success, which led her to sit behind a curtain to hear him speaking at the bar, are very charming. A number of letters to her grandfather Fabatus and her aunt Calpurnia Hispulla put us in touch with the affairs of a harmonious family circle. The second letter

Marriages childless

His last wife

and her relatives

---

[1] Cagnat, *Épigraphie Latine,* page 182; Egbert, *Latin Inscriptions,* page 132.

[2] Ep. VIII. 10. *Ad Trai.* 2. 2.

[3] Ep. III. 19. 8.

[4] Epp. VI. 4; VI. 7; VII. 5.

[5] Epp. IV. 19; VIII. 10.

to Trajan expresses gratitude for the grant of the *ius trium liberorum*, the privileges of 'a father of three children.'[1]

He was perhaps unable to remember his father; at all events he does not speak of him. Toward his mother and uncle he was affectionate and dutiful.[2] In this respect his conduct was not exceptional. But in generosity toward his friends, in liberality toward worthy objects, in tireless public spirit, he has few equals among men known in ancient history. To quote from Mr. Hardy:[3] "At one time he gives a fellow-townsman 300,000 sesterces to make up the equestrian census;[4] at another time he contributed 100,000 towards the wedding-dower of a friend's daughter;[5] at another he helped Artemidorus the philosopher to satisfy his clamorous creditors.[6] The poet Martial received some help towards his journey home to Spain.[7] Quintilian was presented with a sum of 50,000 sesterces for his daughter's dower,[8] while an old nurse was settled comfortably on a little farm which Pliny bought for her."[9]

Filial conduct

Benevolence, private and public

Perhaps it is a stronger evidence of friendship to beg a favor for a man than to give him money. This depends upon whether one is more like Dickens or like Thackeray. Pliny was like both, and used his influence, as well as his property, without stint for the good of his friends. We find him asking, and obtaining, for one or another of them, a centurion's commission,[10] a military tribuneship,[11] the *latus clavus*,[12] the *ius trium*

Obliging disposition

---

[1] See the note on *iure trium liberorum*, page 121, line 9, for explanation.

[2] Ep. VI. 16 and 20.

[3] *Correspondence with Trajan*, page 26.

[4] Ep. I. 19. 2.

[5] Ep. II. 4. 2.

[6] Ep. III. 11. 2.

[7] Ep. III. 21. 2.

[8] Ep. VI. 32.

[9] Ep. VI. 3. 1.

[10] Ep. VI. 25. 3.

[11] Epp. III. 8; IV. 4. 2; VII. 22. 1.

[12] Ep. II. 9. 2; *ad Trai.* 4.

liberorum.[1] He was ever ready to assist his friends in a canvass for office, while his help and encouragement of young advocates was generous and unfailing.[2]

Social position

With such a character and social position, Pliny must have known everybody that was worth knowing. He loved and venerated such old men as Verginius and Spurinna; he took a kindly interest in his townsmen of Comum; he was on terms of easy equality with the prominent men of his generation in social and political life; he had some acquaintance with philosophers; and among men of letters he found his most congenial intimate friends.

His public liberality proved his hearty interest in all good causes: schemes for municipal improvement, charitable foundations, education, all found in him a sympathetic promoter.

Benefactions to Comum

For the benefit of his native town he endowed a foundation for the support of poor children[3] at a cost of 500,000 sesterces. Another sum of 1,000,000 founded a public library,[4] and 100,000 provided a fund for its maintenance. Finding that the boys went from Comum to school at Mediolanum (Milan), he offered to pay one-third of the salary of a teacher to be settled at Comum.[5] The town was further remembered in his will by the bequest of a sum of money for the construction and maintenance of a public bath,[6] and of 1,866,666 sesterces to provide an annual public banquet,[7] after the death of certain freedmen of the testator. Benevolence to his slaves was not left by him for merely posthumous expression, for it was his habit to manumit any who were

Kindness to slaves

[1] Ep. II. 13. 8; *ad Trai.* 94.
[2] Epp. VI. 12; VI. 23.
[3] Inscription, page xxvi; Epp. I. 8. 10; V. 7. 3.
[4] Ep. I. 8. 2.
[5] Ep. IV. 13. 5.
[6] Inscription, page xxvi.
[7] Inscription, page xxvi.

seriously ill,[1] so that if they died, they might die free and dispose by will of their small possessions. Comum was not the only place benefited by his liberality, for he built and dedicated a temple at Tifernum,[2] and restored a temple of Ceres on one of his estates, providing it with colonnades to shelter the worshippers, and with a new statue of the goddess.[3]

All this munificence implies wealth. Pliny was rich, but not extremely so. He sometimes had to complain of hard times or of poor vintages, and to hesitate about a desired purchase.[4] We know that he had estates from both his father and his mother,[5] and he must have inherited something from his uncle. Two of his villas, which overlooked the Lake of Como, he playfully called Tragedy and Comedy.[6] His Tuscan estate,[7] near Tifernum and the Apennines, yielded an income of 400,000 sesterces.[8] Besides country houses at Tusculum,[9] Tibur, and Praeneste,[10] he owned a splendid villa on the seashore at Laurentum, seventeen miles from Rome. This was evidently a favorite with him, for one of the longest of the letters gives an elaborate description of it.[11]

His large property

Country houses

Like most literary men who make a large figure in town, — always excepting Charles Lamb and Dr. Samuel Johnson, — Pliny is forever sighing for the country. Just how much of such sighing is genuine and how much is conventional is hard to determine.

Fondness for the country

O rus quando te aspiciam!

is always an eminently proper sentiment, and has the best

---

[1] Ep. VIII. 16.
[2] Ep. IV. 1.
[3] Ep. IX. 39.
[4] Epp. II. 15; III. 19; VIII. 2.
[5] Epp. II. 15; IV. 6; IX. 7. 2.
[6] Ep. IX. 7. 2.
[7] Epp. III. 4; IV. 6; V. 6. 1; IX. 15. 1.
[8] *Ad Trai.* 8. 5.
[9] Ep. IV. 13. 1.
[10] Ep. V. 6. 45.
[11] Ep. II. 17.

of authority. And it is clear that many Romans of that over-civilized age had a real taste for the enjoyment of country seats during a part of the year, and their literature from Catullus on is full of appreciation of the milder and lovelier aspects of nature. They delighted in a trim garden or well-kept park, in the soft, sweet beauty of a peaceful landscape, reminding us not a little in this respect of the English poets of the eighteenth century.

Roman view of nature

One so enthusiastic in his interest in literature as Pliny, may be supposed to have tried his hand at pretty much every sort of writing. He confesses, Ep. IV. 27: —

Wrote verses

Ego interdum versibus ludo.

More than once we find a mention of his 'hendecasyllabics,' which he appears to regard with a certain amount of indulgence, and which he hints, not without a suspicion of glee, are just a little naughty. One cannot help smiling at the care taken by so excellent a man to assure us that he was a wicked fellow after all in his lighter moments. He certainly had not the qualities of a poet, and the loss of his verses is not one to be deeply deplored. No doubt they were clever and ingenious, but wholly academic. Even Cicero, when he tried to write poetry, could only produce admirable prosody.

Pliny's extant works are the Panegyric and the two collections of letters, viz.: nine books of general correspondence, and one containing the letters to Trajan. These last are, in most cases, accompanied by the emperor's replies. The dates of the several books are discussed in Appendix I. Suffice it to say here, that the selection of the letters[1] and their arrangement were the work of the author himself. It is

Extant works

Was his own editor

[1] I.e., the nine books.

not a case of haphazard survival, nor yet of posthumous editing by a stranger. We have the satisfaction of knowing that the collection contains just what the writer intended it should. We are not troubled with misgivings, therefore, in forming our estimate of him. As he tells his own story, we may take him at his word. It is eminently fitting that such a man, and the representative of such an age, should appear before the world in a literary toilet thus carefully arranged. Letters which showed him *en déshabillé,* so to speak, or betrayed him at an unguarded moment, when he forgot his pose, if he ever had such a moment, would be out of keeping. Pliny in a state of nature would not be the real Pliny. He is least artificial in the letters to Trajan, but he is not there at his best. We appreciate his abilities and his conscientious endeavors as an administrator. But he is out of his element at such a post as the governorship of a troublesome province. No doubt he was proud to be trusted, but the position clearly worried him, and in his heart he pined for the brilliant society of Rome or the calm literary repose of his villas.

Artificiality

Pliny's chief excellence as a writer is his *clearness,* and the chief element of his charm is his *modernness,* of thought and expression. One evidence of this is the singular felicity of Melmoth's translation in 'Johnsonese.' Warton said of this version that it bettered the original. While we might not be willing to go so far as that, we do feel that the extraordinary appropriateness of its eighteenth century English to the Latin of the original letters stamps Pliny as in many respects a kindred spirit with the English authors of that time.

Modernness of spirit

To sum up our impressions, — Pliny is the most amiable of the ancient writers. Not only is he admirable in all private relations, but nothing unkind is said by him of any contemporaries while they live, except of Regulus and other equally infamous representatives of

Amiability

the class of informers. His facile disposition enabled him to get on with Domitian and with Trajan. He goes to the public games, though they bore him and though he does not approve of them. He goes hunting, but does not really care for it, and takes his writing-tablets along with his hunting-gear. He does not object to a little indecency in verse, but in his conduct there is no trace of anything impure. He is not the only man who has "admired the contrast between a strict life and a wanton muse." His denunciations of the wicked are so beautifully expressed that we cannot help feeling that he took a good deal of satisfaction in the style of his invective, and that the iniquity of evil-doers did not make him really unhappy. It must have been difficult for him to be stern. When his support of friends under a cloud was really brave and unselfish, the complacency with which he tells of it afterward robs it of much of its heroic flavor.

Easy-going disposition

Conventionality

Vanity

It is a pity that one so kindly should appear in history as a persecutor of Christians, but it is evident that he had no liking for the *rôle*. And his letter of intercession for the ungrateful freedman has been compared without striking impropriety to St. Paul's Epistle to Philemon.

Not a hearty persecutor

His 'calculated sensibility,' which reminds Mr. Mackail of Rousseau, and his elaborate simplicity, come dangerously near provoking a patronizing smile; yet, when we have read all he has to say for himself, we cannot deny that, with all his weaknesses and affectations, the main stuff of his character is thoroughly good, and we find ourselves able to award him that respect which it would be painful to withhold from a man so genial and so attractive.

His character essentially noble

INSCRIPTIONS RELATING TO PLINY

These are collected in Mommsen's article in *Hermes,* III.

1.

C · PLINIO · L · F
OVF CAECILIO
SECVNDO COS
AVG · CVR ALVEI · TIBER
ET RIP*ar et cloac*A*r* VRB

Found in a small house in Como, on a stone which served as a step.

2.

C · PLINI*o l. f.*
*o*VF · CAEC*ilio*
SECVNDO *c*OS
AVGVR · CVR · ALV · TIB
*et ripa*R ET CLOAC · VRB
raef · *a*ER SAT PRAEF
AER · MIL *pr. tr. pl.* ↄ · IMP
SEVIR · EQ · R · TR · M*i*L
LEG · III · GALL · X · VIRO
STL · IVD · FL · DIVI · T · AVG

VERCELLENS

This was discovered at Fecchio, a village not far from Comum.

3.

A small fragment of the pavement of a church in Como.

4.

C · PLINIVS · L · F · OVF · CAECILIVS *secundus cos.*
AVGVR · LEGAT · PROPR · PROVINCIAE · PON*ti et bithyniae*
CONSVLARI · POTESTA*t* · IN · EAM · PROVINCIAM · E*x s. c. ab*
IMP · CAESAR · NERVA · TRAIANO · AVG · GERMAN*ico dacico missus*
CVRATOR · ALVEI · TI*b*ERIS · ET · RIPARVM · E*t cloacar. urb.*
PRAEF · AERARI · SATV*r*NI · PRAEF · AERARI · MIL*it. pr. trib. pl*
QVAESTOR · IMP · SEVIR · EQVITVM *romanorum*
TRIB · MILIT · LEG · *iii* · GALLICA*e xuir stli*
TIB · IVDICAND · THERM*as ex iis* . . . . . . ADIECTIS · IN
ORNATVM · HS · $\overline{CCC}$ . . . . *et eo amp*LIVS · IN · TVTELA*m*
HS · $\overline{CC}$ · T · F · I *item in alimenta* LIBERTOR · SVORVM · HOMIN · C
HS · $\overline{XVIII}$ $\overline{LXVI}$ ƆCLXVI · REI*p. legauit, quorum inc*REMENT · POSTEA · AD · EPVLVM
*pl*EB · VRBAN · VOLVIT · PERTIN*ere* . . . . . *item uiuu*S · DEDIT · IN · ALIMENT · PVEROR
ET · PVELLAR · PLEB · VRBAN · HS *$\overline{d}$ item byhliothecam et* IN TVTELAM · BYBLIOTHE
CAE · HS · $\overline{C}$

This is the great inscription which was graved on the wall of the Thermae which Pliny gave to Comum. The marble slab was broken into six pieces, of which four were built into a tomb in St. Ambrose's Church. These four subsequently disappeared, and only the first one has been rediscovered. By its aid and that of written records Mommsen reproduced the whole inscription.

II

PLINY'S STYLE

The style of Pliny may be generally characterized by two statements which at first seem inconsistent. He was undoubtedly an imitator of Cicero, and at the same time he was a true representative of the Silver Age.

In his smooth, copious fluency he is like his avowed master and model, Cicero: in his diction, his forms of expression, his syntax, he shows a striking affinity with the chief prose writers of his own time, Quintilian, his teacher, and Tacitus, his friend.

Compared with the men of his own generation, he is freer than any from the peculiar faults of the Latinity of the time, and exhibits the least departure from the language in its strictly classical forms. Yet no man can escape the influence of his age and environment, and it is therefore only natural that even in Pliny we find many neologisms, many words the sense of which has been altered, many poetic expressions transferred to prose, many rare and far-fetched constructions, over-frequent figures of speech, and, in general, a style marked by somewhat excessive antithesis, and not free from artificial conceits. And yet it is, withal, a good style, always interesting, sometimes beautiful, here and there exhibiting a nervous vigor worthy of Tacitus.

Following are some of the features of Pliny's diction and style, which, though not necessarily peculiar to him, may be fairly regarded as characteristic. The examples under each head are to be taken merely as illustrative, not as an exhaustive list. No examples have been given which do not occur in the letters of this collection.

§ 1. Vocabulary

a. Among newly formed words may be cited:

capitaliter, I. 5. 4.
castigatorium, V. 16. 10.
indignatiuncula, VI. 17. 1.
praecursorius, IV. 13. 2.

b. Words which in earlier Latin are not used at all or used in a different sense:

adnotationes, VII. 20. 1.
cenatio, II. 17. 10.
comperendinationes, VI. 2. 6.
insalubris, IV. 2. 6.
supervivere, II. 1. 1.

Careful lists have been made, e.g., by Lagergren (*De Vita et Elocutione C. Plinii*), of words, arranged in different classes, which were, so far as we know, either newly formed by Pliny; or were used by him and contemporary writers (not earlier); or were used by earlier poets or prose writers, but in a different sense.

c. In the habit of inserting Greek sentences and single Greek words Pliny resembles Cicero in his letters. All educated persons knew Greek, and Greek was to Pliny what French was to Thackeray.

d. Greek words with Latin spelling are used especially to designate certain parts of a villa and in reference to provincial matters:

agon, IV. 22. 1.
cryptoporticus, II. 17. 16.
hypocauston, II. 17. 11.

The classical Latin was rich in verbs, but poor in nouns, especially abstracts. The tendency was constantly to enlarge the vocabulary in the department where it was deficient. We ought to praise rather than censure the post-Augustan writers for their contributions in this direction.

§ 2. Substantives

a. Plurals of abstract nouns; there are said to be eighty cases:

amores, II. 17. 20.
infirmitates, VIII. 16. 1.
secessibus, II. 1. 8.

b. Concrete singulars in a collective sense:

fraxino, populo, VIII. 8. 4.

c. Substantival use in both numbers and all genders of adjectives, adjective pronouns, and participles, the latter in past, present, or future time:

adeptos, II. 15. 1.
adversus incidentia, VI. 16. 16.
audituros, VI. 2. 3.

In the case of neuters this is not confined to the nominative and accusative cases:

his, IV. 12. 7.

§ 3. Case constructions

a. The use of the genitive with adjectives is extended far beyond its earlier limits:

omnis secreti capacissima, I. 12. 7.
certus fugae, VI. 16. 12.
arborum ferax, II. 17. 5.
pietatis totus, V. 16. 8.

b. The subjective genitive sometimes denotes that for which something is intended:

(triclinia) paucorum, I. 3. 1.
(cubiculum) noctis et somni, II. 17. 22.

c. The genitive of quality is sometimes attached directly to a noun designating an individual, without a common noun in apposition:

uxorem (i.e., Cottia, wife of Spurinna) (sc. *mulierem*) *singularis exempli*, III. 1. 5.

d. The use of the simple dative with verbs is much developed:

attendere (*his*), VII. 33. 9.
inerrare (*montibus*), I. 6. 3; (*oculis*), VII. 27. 6.
innutrire (*mari*), IX. 33. 6.

e. Dative of agent for ablative of agent; and this not confined to the compounded tenses of the passive:

finitimis oppidis . . . petantur, IV. 13. 9.
inhabitantibus, VII. 27. 6.

f. The dative is regularly used with *similis*, even of persons, except pronouns.

g. The dative is used very often to denote separation, this use not being confined, as it was earlier, to persons.

eripi oculis, VII. 19. 4.
litori abrepta, VIII. 20. 8.

h. Accusative instead of ablative with *de* after such verbs as *audire, cogitare, legere, narrare:*

quae facta, quos viros audias, III. 1. 6.
audita simulacra . . . narratam . . . effigiem, VII. 27. 7, 8.

i. Unusual or bold construction as simple direct object with certain verbs:

evadere (*Caesares*), II. 1. 3; (*valetudinem*), I. 12. 11.
excusari (*dies*), I. 18. 1.
egredi (*tecta*), VI. 20. 8.
excedere (*annum*), III. 7. 9.

Double accusative:

cogere (*istud . . . morituram*), II. 20. 11.

j. Accusative omitted with verbs normally transitive:

admittere, VI. 16. 17.
discere, IV. 13. 4.

k. Similarly *studere* (sc. *litteris*) is constantly used absolutely.

l. Ablative instead of accusative to express duration of time:

horis septem, IV. 16. 2.
pauculis diebus, IV. 13. 1.

m. Local ablative without a preposition:

circumitu, II. 17. 15.
officinis, IV. 7. 1.
spatiis, II. 10. 2.

n. Persons in the instrumental ablative. This cannot always be distinguished from the dative of agent:

cultoribus (a doubtful instance), III. 19. 6.
comoedis (a clear case), III. 1. 9.

o. Bold extended use of the modal ablative, thoroughly characteristic of the Silver Age:

solacio, VI. 20. 17.
somno, VI. 16. 13.
vetere testamento, V. 5. 2.

p. This shades off into the temporal ablative in such expressions as

hoc certamine, IX. 33. 4.
dolore recenti, I. 12. 12.
tempestatibus foedissimis, III. 18. 4.

§ 4. Prepositions

a. *Citra* = *sine*, as in Tacitus, etc.:

citra dolorem, II. 1. 4.

b. *Ab* in such phrases as

a pedibus, *a tergo*, II. 17. 21.
a petitore, *a possessore*, VI. 2. 2.

c. *Sub* with the ablative expressing effect or influence:

sub condicione, IV. 13. 10.
sub exemplo, III. 18. 2 *et passim*.
sub invidia, VI. 2. 3.

§ 5. ADVERBS

a. *Mox*, as usual in Silver Latin, has the sense, not of 'soon,' but of 'afterward'; e.g., in

VI. 20. 2.

b. *Utcumque*, not relative but indefinite; e.g., in

I. 12. 2; V. 5. 2; VI. 20. 19.

c. Adverbs and adverbial phrases used attributively:

latissime victor, III. 5. 4.
undique silvae, I. 6. 2.
sine honore nomen, I. 23. 1.
in mensa luxuria, II. 6. 6.
ex Hispania amicus, VI. 20. 10.
illud e ligno, IX. 39. 4.

d. Negatives and interrogatives:

haud does not occur.
non occurs with an imperative subjunctive, III. 19. 9.
nec non, not separated, IX. 33. 7.

e. In direct questions *ecquid* is frequent; e.g., in

III. 20. 11; VI. 2. 10.

f. Direct questions without any interrogative word:

vides hunc? IX. 23. 4.

g. In double questions the first interrogative particle is usually omitted:

Italicus es an provincialis? IX. 23. 2.

h. *An* implying an impossible alternative is used as in the Latin of the Golden Age:

An non videtur, III. 7. 11.
An ego . . . dubitem, IV. 17. 2.

i. *Nescio an* sometimes amounts to a mild negative; e.g.,

III. 1. 1; IV. 2. 1,

which is far from the strictly classical usage. But it also occurs in the sense of a mild affirmative, or inclining in that direction; e.g.,

I. 15. 3.

j. *Quamquam* as an adverb occurs frequently with adjectives, participles, and adverbs.

The coördinate *quamquam* (*correctivum*, 'and yet') is said to occur twenty-one times; it is followed by the indicative and in *oratio obliqua* by the infinitive.

§ 6. Conjunctions

a. *Etiam* is relatively frequent. It is often combined with asyndeton of three or more members; e.g.,

I. 9. 12 (3 members).
I. 22. 7 (4 members).
V. 14. 8 (7 members).

This is so frequent as to constitute a marked mannerism.

b. *Etiam* in the sense of 'yes,' 'to be sure'; e.g.,

IV. 13. 3; VI. 2. 8.

c. The author is extremely fond of *verum etiam* (for *sed etiam*), but *etiam* is often missing after *non tantum sed, non modo sed*.

§ 7. Tenses

a. The epistolary tenses are seldom used. This is because the letters are such rather in form than in essence. The epistolary use is most frequent in the letters to Trajan. There is an extensive use of the historical present, and some instances of the present indicative for the future in protasis.

Upon the whole, Pliny's use of the tenses cannot be considered as far from normal.

§ 8. Moods

a. The subjunctive of iteration or generalization in relative sentences:

quocumque me contulissem, vi. 10. 2.
quotiens . . . intraret, iii. 16. 4.

b. The subjunctive often follows *quamquam*. Kraut, § 39, says there are ten such cases.

c. Si modo regularly takes the indicative unless *oratio obliqua* requires the subjunctive.

d. Quamvis with the subjunctive is used of facts, not merely of argumentative concessions.

e. Substantive clauses, the objects of verbs of *asking*, *admonishing*, *bidding*, and the like, are often used without *ut;* e.g., after *rogare, orare, petere, postulare, hortari, monere, censere, optare, curare.* Of the thirty instances after *rogare,* twenty are without *ut.*

Iubere takes this construction, instead of the infinitive.

In ix. 33. 11 occurs the unique instance of the subjunctive without *ut* after *opus est.*

§ 9. Infinitive, Gerund, Voices

a. Infinitive.

1. As subject:

with *datur*, III. 1. 1; VIII. 20. 1.
negatur, II. 8. 10.
contingit, IV. 1. 17.

2. As object:

with *dissuadere*, II. 17. 26.

b. Gerund. Limiting genitive used in somewhat unusual connections:

constantiam . . . pronuntiandi, V. 1. 4.
pulchritudo iungendi, III. 19. 2.
tacendi modestia, sedendi dignitas, III. 20. 3.

c. Reflexive use of the passive voice:

continetur, III. 1. 4.
movetur, III. 1. 8.
remittor, I. 16. 7.

§ 10. Figures of Speech

a. Syllepsis. The commonest form is where one verb is used in different connections and has to be supplied in another (coördinate or subordinate) member of the sentence than that in which it occurs, either in the same or in a different form.

1. Completion from a preceding clause, in a different form:

fecisset from *fecit*, and
mortuus esset from *mortuus est*, VI. 2. 4.
te vidisse from *vidistine*, VIII. 8. 1.

2. From a following clause, in the same form:

debebatur, VI. 34. 1.

b. Parenthesis: forty-one cases have been counted in the first four books.

c. Asyndeton both of words and sentences is frequent.

Of sentences: in rapid narrative with much detail; e.g.,

I. 5; II. 10 (seven sentences); II. 18. 2.

Of words: the three-membered asyndeton is developed into a decided mannerism, about one hundred instances being counted in the letters and about thirty in the Panegyric; e.g.,

VII. 33. 10.

It often leads to an excessive multiplication of words. There are about forty cases of asyndeton of two members, and about twenty with more than three members.

d. Polysyndeton is comparatively infrequent; about thirty instances are counted.

e. Anaphora is very characteristic of such a rhetorical style as Pliny's, and was in general strongly developed in the Silver Age. Pliny uses it even in simple passages of quiet description, but in the Panegyric there are said to be thirty-six cases in the first fifteen chapters, and seven in the thirty-fourth chapter alone.

f. Hendiadys; perhaps but one instance:

novitatem odoremque, IX. 33. 9.

A sort of verbal hendiadys is illustrated in

componere et transigere, V. 1. 7.

g. Aposiopesis:

Interim Miseni ego et mater . . ., VI. 16. 21.

h. Ellipsis. In the extent of his use of this figure Pliny hardly exceeds Cicero (in his letters) and Tacitus.

1. The most common form is the omission of forms of the verb 'to be.' Pliny is peculiar in not confining ellipsis to *est, sunt,* and *esse,* but in extending it to other moods, other tenses, and other persons.
2. His omission of *verba dicendi, movendi, agendi,* etc., is not peculiar. It tends to brevity, and they are easily supplied.
3. Sometimes there is a continuous effort to secure brevity. An example of this is the whole of Ep. I. 5.

i. Similes are frequent.

j. Concinnity is elaborate, antithesis is constantly aimed at.

k. Oxymoron:

> *morti . . . immortalem gloriam,* VI. 16. 1.
> *semper victurus occiderit,* VI. 16. 2.
> *peregrinatio inter sua,* III. 19. 4.

l. Assonance:

> *facere scribenda aut scribere legenda,* VI. 16. 3.

m. Repetition of a word with change of form:

> *ratio rationem . . . timorem timor,* VI. 16. 16.
> *in exsilium exsilii causam,* VII. 19. 6.

n. Repetition of a word in the same form:

> *de vita eius . . . de vita pueri,* IV. 7. 2.
> *in praefectura . . . fuit, fuit et in consulata,* V. 14. 5.

But there is evident care not to repeat a word too often in quick succession. Note, for instance, in Ep. II. 17. 5 and 6, the variety of words for 'prospect.'

o. Fondness for pairs of nearly synonymous words:

gloria famaque . . . adsensio et laus, iv. 12. 6.
vetus et anticum, iii. 6. 3.

Sometimes three such words are grouped:

orare, hortari, iubere, vi. 20. 12.

p. Informal personification, by the use, in reference to inanimate objects, of words which properly apply to living beings, is characteristic of the age.

The poetic coloring of the prose of the Silver Age was not altogether the result of a conscious process. The language of the great classic poets had become a part of universal expression, and was used, in great part, unconsciously by all writers.

q. There are rather too many proverbs, *loci communes*, sententious phrases, which tend sometimes to produce the impression of banality.

gratia malorum tam infida est quam ipsi, i. 5. 16.
ratio quae sapientibus pro necessitate est, i. 12. 3.
perit gratia si reposcatur, i. 13. 6.

§ 11. Allusions to Pliny in Ancient Writers

Martial, x. 19.

Nec doctum satis et parum severum,
Sed non rusticulum nimis libellum
Facundo mea Plinio Thalia
I perfer: brevis et labor peractae
Altum vincere tramitem Suburae.
Illic Orphea protinus videbis
Udi vertice lubricum theatri
Mirantesque feras avemque regis,
Raptum quae Phryga pertulit Tonanti;

— the rest of the epigram is quoted in Ep. iii. 21.

MACROBIUS, *Sat.* v. 1.

Quattuor sunt genera dicendi; copiosum, in quo Cicero dominatur; breve, in quo Sallustius regnat; siccum, quod Frontoni adscribitur; pingue et floridum, in quo Plinius Secundus quondam et nunc nullo veterum minor Symmachus luxuriatur.

SIDONIUS APOLLINARIS, I. 1.

Epistolas omnes, retractatis exemplaribus enucleatisque, uno volumine includam, Q. Symmachi rotunditatem, C. Plinii disciplinam maturitatemque, vestigiis praesumptuosis insecuturis.

ID. IV. 3.

Si reare quemquam mortalium (cui tamen sermocinari Latialiter cordi est) non pavere, quum in examen aurium tuarum, quippe scriptus, adducitur; tuarum, inquam, aurium, quarum peritiae, si me decursorum ad hoc aevi temporum praerogativa non obruat, nec Frontinianae gravitatis aut ponderis Apuleiani fulmen aequiparem, cui Varrones vel Atacinus vel Terentius, Plinii vel avunculus vel Secundus, compositi impraesentiarum rusticabuntur.

ID. IV. 22.

Ego Plinio, ut discipulus, adsurgo.

ID. VIII. 10.

C. Plinius pro Accia Variola plus gloriae de centumvirali suggestu domum retulit, quam quum Marco Ulpio, incomparabili principi, comparabilem panegyricum dixit.

CASSIODORUS. *Chron. sub Traiano.*

Celsus et Crispinus: His consulibus Plinius Secundus Novocomensis orator et historicus insignis habetur, cuius ingenii plurima opera exstant.

III.

MANUSCRIPTS AND EDITIONS OF PLINY'S LETTERS

A. Manuscripts

M. — *Codex Mediceus,* of the tenth century, in the Laurentian Library at Florence, containing Books i.–viii. and twenty-six letters of Book ix.

V. — *Codex Vaticanus,* of the ninth or tenth century, in the Vatican Library at Rome, containing Books i.–iv. From the same original as M.

F. — *Codex Florentinus,* of the tenth century, in the Laurentian Library, containing Books i.–v. 16, but omitting iv. 26.

Riccard. — *Codex Riccardianus,* of the tenth or eleventh century, in the Laurentian Library, containing the same letters and copied from the same original as F.

D. — *Codex Dresdensis,* at Dresden, valuable as containing all the letters of Book ix., except the sixteenth. It contains all the letters of Books i.–vii., but omits Book viii. Book ix. is numbered viii. This is the best representative of a large number of fifteenth century manuscripts copied from one corrupt original. One of these is in the University Library at Princeton.

The complete correspondence between Pliny and Trajan was edited at the beginning of the sixteenth century from a manuscript no longer extant. Aldus, Venice, 1508.

B. Editions

The editions of the letters, complete or partial, have been very numerous ever since the fifteenth century. Platner's Bibliography contains a list of two hundred, from 1471 to 1894.

Among the earliest may be mentioned those upon which Keil's text is partly based.

p. — Editio Princeps, 1471, Venice, Books I.–VII., IX.

r. — Editio Romana I. of Schurener, Books I.–IX., 1474, Rome.

a. — Editio Aldina, Venice, 1st edition in 1502, various reprints later. Ten books.

ϛ. — By this symbol Keil designates three editions earlier than that of Aldus of 1508, viz.:

Editio Pomponii Laeti, Rome, 1490.
Editio Philippi Beroaldi, Bologna, 1498.
Editio I. M. Catanei, Milan, 1506.

In this century important ones are those of

G. E. Gierig, 2 vols. 8vo, Leipzig, 1st ed. 1800.
M. Döring, 2 vols. 8vo, Freiberg, 1843.

The standard critical edition at present is that of H. Keil, 1 vol., Leipzig, 1870, containing Mommsen's *index nominum*.

The smaller edition of Keil's text, Leipzig, 1853, reprinted 1873 and 1892, is in the Teubner Series.

Among recent English editions of selected letters may be mentioned those of

Church and Brodribb, London, 1871.
Prichard and Bernard, Oxford, 1872.
Mayor, Book III., London, 1880.
Prichard, 2 vols., Oxford, 1887.
Cowan, Books I. and II., London, 1889.
Hardy, Correspondence with Trajan, London, 1889.
Merrill, London and New York, 1903.

An exhaustive *Bibliography of the Younger Pliny* was published by Professor S. B. Platner, in the Western Reserve University Bulletin, April, 1895; 2d edition, May, 1901.

SELECTED LETTERS OF PLINY

C. PLINI CAECILI SECUNDI
EPISTULARUM

LIBER PRIMUS.

1. (I.)

C. PLINIUS SEPTICIO SUO S.

Dedicatory Epistle.

1 Frequenter hortatus es ut epistulas, siquas paulo curatius scripsissem, colligerem publicaremque. Collegi non servato temporis ordine (neque enim historiam com-
2 ponebam), sed ut quaeque in manus venerat. Superest ut nec te consilii nec me paeniteat obsequii. Ita enim 5 fiet ut eas quae adhuc neglectae iacent requiram, et siquas addidero, non supprimam. Vale.

2. (III.)

C. PLINIUS CANINIO RUFO SUO S.

Caninius is urged to employ his delightful leisure at Comum in authorship.

1 Quid agit Comum, tuae meaeque deliciae? quid suburbanum amoenissimum? quid illa porticus verna semper? quid platanon opacissimus? quid euripus viridis et 10 gemmeus? quid subiectus et serviens lacus? quid illa mollis et tamen solida gestatio? quid balineum illud, quod plurimus sol implet et circumit? quid triclinia illa popularia, illa paucorum? quid cubicula diurna, nocturna?

Possident te et per vices partiuntur? an, ut solebas, 2
intentione rei familiaris obeundae crebris excursionibus
avocaris? Si te possident, felix beatusque es; si minus,
unus ex multis. Quin tu (tempus est enim) humiles 3
5 et sordidas curas aliis mandas et ipse te in alto isto
pinguique secessu studiis adseris? Hoc sit negotium
tuum, hoc otium, hic labor, haec quies: in his vigilia, in
his etiam somnus reponatur. Effinge aliquid et exclude 4
quod sit perpetuo tuum. Nam reliqua rerum tuarum post
10 te alium atque alium dominum sortientur, hoc numquam
tuum desinet esse, si semel coeperit. Scio quem ani- 5
mum, quod horter ingenium. Tu modo enitere ut tibi
ipse sis tanti quanti videberis aliis si tibi fueris. Vale.

3. (IV.)

C. PLINIUS POMPEIAE CELERINAE SOCRUI S.

Pliny compliments his mother-in-law upon the comforts of her villas.

Quantum copiarum in Ocriculano, in Narniensi, in 1
15 Carsulano, in Perusino tuo! in Narniensi vero etiam
balineum. Ex epistulis meis (nam iam tuis opus non est)
una illa brevis et vetus sufficit. Non mehercule tam 2
mea sunt quae mea sunt quam quae tua: hoc tamen
differunt, quod sollicitius et intentius tui me quam mei
20 excipiunt. Idem fortasse eveniet tibi, si quando in 3
nostra deverteris. Quod velim facias, primum, ut perinde
nostris rebus ac nos tuis perfruaris, deinde, ut mei
expergiscantur aliquando, qui me secure ac prope neg-
legenter expectant. Nam mitium dominorum apud 4
25 servos ipsa consuetudine metus exolescit, novitatibus
excitantur probarique dominis per alios magis quam per
ipsos laborant. Vale.

4. (V.)

C. PLINIUS VOCONIO ROMANO SUO S.

How conscience made a coward of Regulus, the informer.

1 Vidistine quemquam M. Regulo timidiorem humiliorem post Domitiani mortem? sub quo non minora flagitia commiserat quam sub Nerone, sed tectiora. Coepit vereri ne sibi irascerer; nec fallebatur, irascebar.
2 Rustici Aruleni periculum foverat, exultaverat morte, 5 adeo ut librum recitaret publicaretque, in quo Rusticum insectatur atque etiam Stoicorum simiam appellat; adicit
3 Vitelliana cicatrice stigmosum. Agnoscis eloquentiam Reguli. Lacerat Herennium Senecionem, tam intemperanter quidem ut dixerit ei Metius Carus 'quid tibi cum 10 meis mortuis? numquid ego Crasso aut Camerino moles-
4 tus sum?' quos ille sub Nerone accusaverat. Haec me Regulus dolenter tulisse credebat, ideoque etiam cum recitaret librum, non adhibuerat. Praeterea reminiscebatur quam capitaliter ipsum me apud centumviros 15
5 lacessisset. Aderam Arrionillae, Timonis uxori, rogatu Aruleni Rustici; Regulus contra. Nitebamur nos in parte causae sententia Meti Modesti, optimi viri: is tunc in exilio erat, a Domitiano relegatus. Ecce tibi Regulus 'quaero' inquit, 'Secunde, quid de Modesto sentias.' 20 Vides quod periculum, si respondissem 'bene,' quod flagitium, si 'male.' Non possum dicere aliud tunc mihi quam deos adfuisse. 'Respondebo' inquam 'si de hoc centumviri iudicaturi sunt.' Rursus ille 'quaero quid
6 de Modesto sentias.' Iterum ego 'solebant testes in 25 reos, non in damnatos interrogari.' Tertio ille 'non iam quid de Modesto, sed quid de pietate Modesti sentias.'

'Quaeris' inquam 'quid sentiam: at ego ne interrogare 7
quidem fas puto de quo pronuntiatum est.' Conticuit:
me laus et gratulatio secuta est, quod nec famam meam
aliquo responso, utili fortasse, inhonesto tamen, laeseram
5 nec me laqueis tam insidiosae interrogationis involveram.
Nunc ergo conscientia exterritus adprehendit Caecili- 8
um Celerem, mox Fabium Iustum, rogat ut me sibi
reconcilient. Nec contentus, pervenit ad Spurinnam:
huic suppliciter, ut est cum timet abiectissimus, 'rogo'
10 inquit 'mane videas Plinium domi, sed plane mane (neque
enim diutius ferre sollicitudinem possum), et quoquo
modo efficias ne mihi irascatur.' Evigilaveram: nuntius 9
a Spurinna: 'venio ad te.' 'Immo ego ad te.' Coimus
in porticu Liviae, cum alter ad alterum tenderemus.
15 Exponit Reguli mandata, addit preces suas, ut decebat
optimum virum pro dissimillimo, parce. Cui ego 'di- 10
spicies ipse quid renuntiandum Regulo putes: te decipi a
me non oportet. Expecto Mauricum' (nondum ab exilio
venerat): 'ideo nihil alterutram in partem respondere tibi
20 possum, facturus quidquid ille decreverit; illum enim
esse huius consilii ducem, me comitem decet.' Paucos 11
post dies ipse me Regulus convenit in praetoris officio:
illuc persecutus secretum petit: ait timere se ne animo
meo penitus haereret quod in centumvirali iudicio ali-
25 quando dixisset, cum responderet mihi et Satrio Rufo,
'Satrius Rufus, cui non est cum Cicerone aemulatio, et
qui contentus est eloquentia saeculi nostri.' Respondi 12
nunc me intellegere maligne dictum, quia ipse confitere-
tur; ceterum potuisse honorificum existimari. 'Est
30 enim' inquam 'mihi cum Cicerone aemulatio, nec sum
contentus eloquentia saeculi nostri. Nam stultissimum 13
credo ad imitandum non optima quaeque proponere. Sed

tu, qui huius iudicii meministi, cur illius oblitus es in quo
me interrogasti quid de Meti Modesti pietate sentirem?'
Expalluit notabiliter, quamvis palleat semper, et haesitabundus 'interrogavi, non ut tibi nocerem, sed ut Modesto.'
Vide hominis crudelitatem, qui se non dissimulet exuli 5
14 nocere voluisse. Subiunxit egregiam causam: 'scripsit'
inquit 'in epistula quadam, quae apud Domitianum recitata est, "Regulus, omnium bipedum nequissimus;"' quod
15 quidem Modestus verissime scripserat. Hic fere nobis
sermonis terminus. Neque enim volui progredi longius, 10
ut mihi omnia libera servarem, dum Mauricus venit.
Nec me praeterit esse Regulum δυσκαθαίρετον: est enim
locuples factiosus, curatur a multis, timetur a pluribus,
quod plerumque fortius amore est. Potest tamen fieri
16 ut haec concussa labantur. Nam gratia malorum tam 15
infida est quam ipsi. Verum, ut idem saepius dicam,
expecto Mauricum. Vir est gravis, prudens, multis
experimentis eruditus, et qui futura possit ex praeteritis
providere. Mihi et temptandi aliquid et quiescendi illo
17 auctore ratio constabit. Haec tibi scripsi, quia aecum 20
erat te pro amore mutuo non solum omnia mea facta
dictaque verum etiam consilia cognoscere. Vale.

5. (VI.)

C. PLINIUS CORNELIO TACITO SUO S.

How Pliny took his note-book when he went a-hunting.

1 Ridebis, et licet rideas. Ego ille quem nosti apros
tres et quidem pulcherrimos cepi. 'Ipse?' inquis. Ipse;
non tamen ut omnino ab inertia mea et quiete discederem. Ad retia sedebam: erat in proximo non venabulum aut lancea, sed stilus et pugillares: meditabar 25

aliquid enotabamque, ut, si manus vacuas, plenas tamen ceras reportarem. Non est quod contemnas hoc studendi genus. Mirum est ut animus agitatione motuque corporis excitetur. Iam undique silvae et solitudo ipsumque
5 illud silentium quod venationi datur magna cogitationis incitamenta sunt. Proinde cum venabere, licebit auctore me ut panarium et laguncula sic etiam pugillares feras. Experieris non Dianam magis montibus quam Minervam inerrare. Vale.

6. (IX.)

C. PLINIUS MINUTIO FUNDANO SUO S.

Contrast between city-life and country-life; busy idleness vs. *industrious leisure.*

10 Mirum est quam singulis diebus in urbe ratio aut 1 constet aut constare videatur, pluribus iunctisque non constet. Nam si quem interroges 'hodie quid egisti?', 2 respondeat 'officio togae virilis interfui, sponsalia aut nuptias frequentavi, ille me ad signandum testamentum,
15 ille in advocationem, ille in consilium rogavit.' Haec 3 quo die feceris necessaria, eadem, si cotidie fecisse te reputes, inania videntur, multo magis cum secesseris. Tunc enim subit recordatio 'quot dies quam frigidis rebus absumpsi!' Quod evenit mihi, postquam in Lau- 4
20 rentino meo aut lego aliquid aut scribo aut etiam corpori vaco, cuius fulturis animus sustinetur. Nihil audio quod 5 audisse, nihil dico quod dixisse paeniteat: nemo apud me quemquam sinistris sermonibus carpit, neminem ipse reprehendo, nisi tamen me, cum parum commode scribo;
25 nulla spe, nullo timore sollicitor, nullis rumoribus inquietor: mecum tantum et cum libellis loquor. O rec- 6 tam sinceramque vitam, o dulce otium honestumque ac

paene omni negotio pulchrius! O mare, o litus, verum secretumque μουσεῖον, quam multa invenitis, quam multa
7 dictatis! Proinde tu quoque strepitum istum inanemque discursum et multum ineptos labores, ut primum fuerit
8 occasio, relinque teque studiis vel otio trade. Satius est 5 enim, ut Atilius noster eruditissime simul et facetissime dixit, otiosum esse quam nihil agere. Vale.

7. (XI.)

C. PLINIUS FABIO IUSTO SUO S.

Pliny chides his friend for not writing.

1 Olim mihi nullas epistulas mittis. Nihil est, inquis, quod scribam. At hoc ipsum scribe nihil esse quod scribas, vel solum illud unde incipere priores solebant 10 'si vales, bene est; ego valeo.' Hoc mihi sufficit; est
2 enim maximum. Ludere me putas? serio peto. Fac sciam quid agas, quod sine sollicitudine summa nescire non possum. Vale.

8. (XII.)

C. PLINIUS CALESTRIO TIRONI SUO S.

The suicide of Corellius Rufus.

1 Iacturam gravissimam feci, si iactura dicenda est tanti 15 viri amissio. Decessit Corellius Rufus, et quidem sponte, quod dolorem meum exulcerat. Est enim luctuosissimum genus mortis quae non ex natura nec fatalis videtur.
2 Nam utcumque in illis qui morbo finiuntur magnum ex ipsa necessitate solacium est, in eis vero quos arcessita 20 mors aufert hic insanabilis dolor est, quod creduntur
3 potuisse diu vivere. Corellium quidem summa ratio,

quae sapientibus pro necessitate est, ad hoc consilium
compulit, quamquam plurimas vivendi causas habentem,
optimam conscientiam, optimam famam, maximam auctoritatem, praeterea filiam uxorem nepotem sorores, inter-
5 que tot pignora veros amicos. Sed tam longa, tam iniqua 4
valetudine conflictabatur ut haec tanta pretia vivendi
mortis rationibus vincerentur. Tertio et tricesimo
anno, ut ipsum audiebam, pedum dolore correptus est.
Patrius hic illi: nam plerumque morbi quoque per suc-
10 cessiones quasdam, ut alia, traduntur. Hunc abstinentia 5
sanctitate, quoad viridis aetas, vicit et fregit; novissime
cum senectute ingravescentem viribus animi sustinebat,
cum quidem incredibilis cruciatus et indignissima tor- 6
menta pateretur. Iam enim dolor non pedibus solis, ut
15 prius, insidebat sed omnia membra pervagabatur. Veni ad
eum Domitiani temporibus in suburbano iacentem. Servi 7
e cubiculo recesserunt: habebat hoc moris, quotiens intrasset fidelior amicus; quin etiam uxor, quamquam omnis
secreti capacissima, digrediebatur. Circumtulit oculos et 8
20 'cur' inquit 'me putas hos tantos dolores tam diu susti-
nere? ut scilicet isti latroni vel uno die supersim.' Dedisses huic animo par corpus, fecisset quod optabat.
Adfuit tamen deus voto, cuius ille compos, ut iam securus
liberque moriturus, multa illa vitae sed minora retina-
25 cula abrupit. Increverat valetudo, quam temperantia 9
mitigare temptavit, perseverantem constantia fugit. Iam
dies alter tertius quartus: abstinebat cibo. Misit ad me
uxor eius Hispulla communem amicum C. Geminium
cum tristissimo nuntio, destinasse Corellium mori nec
30 aut suis aut filiae precibus flecti, solum superesse me a
quo revocari posset ad vitam. Cucurri: perveneram in 10
proximum, cum mihi ab eadem Hispulla Iulius Atticus

nuntiat nihil iam ne me quidem inpetraturum: tam obstinate magis ac magis induruisse. Dixerat sane medico admoventi cibum 'κέκρικα,' quae vox quantum admirationis in animo meo tantum desiderii reliquit. Cogito
11 quo amico, quo viro caream. Implevit quidem annum 5 septimum et sexagesimum, quae aetas etiam robustissimis satis longa est: scio. Evasit perpetuam valetudinem: scio. Decessit superstitibus suis, florente re publica, quae illi omnibus suis carior erat: et hoc scio.
12 Tamen tamquam et iuvenis et firmissimi mortem doleo, 10 doleo autem, licet me inbecillum putes, meo nomine. Amisi enim, amisi vitae meae testem rectorem magistrum. In summa, dicam quod recenti dolore contubernali meo Calvisio dixi, 'vereor ne neglegentius vivam.'
13 Proinde adhibe solacia mihi, non haec 'senex erat, in- 15 firmus erat' (haec enim novi), sed nova aliqua, sed magna, quae audierim numquam, legerim numquam. Nam quae audivi, quae legi, sponte succurrunt, sed tanto dolore superantur. Vale.

9. (XIII.)

C. PLINIUS SOSIO SENECIONI SUO S.

The unpopularity of public readings.

1 Magnum proventum poëtarum annus hic attulit. Toto 20 mense Aprili nullus fere dies quo non recitaret aliquis. Iuvat me quod vigent studia, proferunt se ingenia hominum et ostentant, tametsi ad audiendum pigre coitur.
2 Plerique in stationibus sedent tempusque audiendi fabulis conterunt ac subinde sibi nuntiari iubent an iam reci- 25 tator intraverit, an dixerit praefationem, an ex magna parte evolverit librum: tunc demum, ac tunc quoque

lente cunctanterque veniunt; nec tamen permanent, sea ante finem recedunt, alii dissimulanter et furtim, alii simpliciter et libere. At hercule memoria parentum 3 Claudium Caesarem ferunt, cum in palatio spatiaretur 5 audissetque clamorem, causam requisisse, cumque dictum esset recitare Nonianum, subitum recitanti inopinatumque venisse. Nunc otiosissimus quisque multo ante rogatus 4 et identidem admonitus aut non venit aut, si venit, queritur se diem, quia non perdiderit, perdidisse. Sed tanto 5 10 magis laudandi probandique sunt quos a scribendi recitandique studio haec auditorum vel desidia vel superbia non retardat. Equidem prope nemini defui. Erant sane plerique amici: neque enim est fere quisquam qui studia, ut non simul et nos amet. His ex causis longius quam 6 15 destinaveram tempus in urbe consumpsi. Possum iam repetere secessum et scribere aliquid quod non recitem, ne videar, quorum recitationibus adfui, non auditor fuisse sed creditor. Nam ut in ceteris rebus ita in audiendi officio perit gratia, si reposcatur. Vale.

10. (XIV.)

C. PLINIUS IUNIO MAURICO SUO S.

Choice of a husband for the daughter of Arulenus Rusticus.

20 Petis ut fratris tui filiae prospiciam maritum; quod 1 merito mihi potissimum iniungis. Scis enim quanto opere summum illum virum suspexerim dilexerimque, quibus ille adulescentiam meam exhortationibus foverit, quibus etiam laudibus ut laudandus viderer effecerit. 25 Nihil est quod a te mandari mihi aut maius aut gratius, 2 nihil quod honestius a me suscipi possit quam ut eligam

iuvenem ex quo nasci nepotes Aruleno Rustico deceat.
3 Qui quidem diu quaerendus fuisset, nisi paratus et quasi provisus esset Minicius Acilianus, qui me ut iuvenis iuvenem (est enim minor pauculis annis) familiarissime diligit, reveretur ut senem. Nam ita formari a me et in- 5
4 stitui cupit ut ego a vobis solebam. Patria est ei Brixia ex illa nostra Italia, quae multum adhuc verecundiae, frugalitatis atque etiam rusticitatis antiquae retinet ac
5 servat. Pater Minicius Macrinus, equestris ordinis princeps, quia nihil altius voluit: adlectus enim a divo Ves- 10 pasiano inter praetorios honestam quietem huic nostrae ambitioni dicam an dignitati constantissime praetulit.
6 Habet aviam maternam Serranam Proculam e municipio Patavino. Nosti loci mores: Serrana tamen Patavinis quoque severitatis exemplum est. Contigit et avunculus 15 ei P. Acilius, gravitate prudentia fide prope singulari. In summa, nihil erit in domo tota quod non tibi tamquam
7 in tua placeat. Aciliano vero ipsi plurimum vigoris industriae, quamquam in maxima verecundia. Quaesturam tribunatum praeturam honestissime percucurrit ac iam 20
8 pro se tibi necessitatem ambiendi remisit. Est illi facies liberalis, multo sanguine, multo rubore suffusa, est ingenua totius corporis pulchritudo et quidam senatorius decor. Quae ego nequaquam arbitror neglegenda: debet
9 enim hoc castitati puellarum quasi praemium dari. Ne- 25 scio an adiciam esse patri eius amplas facultates. Nam cum imaginor vos quibus quaerimus generum, silendum de facultatibus puto: cum publicos mores atque etiam leges civitatis intueor, quae vel in primis census hominum spectandos arbitrantur, ne id quidem praetereundum 30 videtur. Et sane de posteris et his pluribus cogitanti hic quoque in condicionibus deligendis ponendus est calculus.

Tu fortasse me putes indulsisse amori meo supraque ista 10
quam res patitur sustulisse. At ego fide mea spondeo
futurum ut omnia longe ampliora quam a me praedicantur
invenias. Diligo quidem adulescentem ardentissime,
5 sicut meretur; sed hoc ipsum amantis est, non onerare
eum laudibus. Vale.

11. (XV.)

C. PLINIUS SEPTICIO CLARO SUO S.

Septicius is scolded for breaking a dinner engagement.

Heus tu promittis ad cenam nec venis! Dicitur ius: ad 1
assem inpendium reddes, nec id modicum. Paratae erant 2
lactucae singulae, cochleae ternae, ova bina, alica cum
10 mulso et nive (nam hanc quoque computabis, immo hanc
in primis, quae periit in ferculo), olivae, betacei, cucurbitae,
bulbi, alia mille non minus lauta. Audisses comoedos
vel lectorem vel lyristen vel, quae mea liberalitas,
omnes. At tu apud nescio quem ostrea, vulvas, echinos, 3
15 Gaditanas maluisti. Dabis poenas, non dico quas. Dure
fecisti: invidisti, nescio an tibi, certe mihi, sed tamen et
tibi. Quantum nos lusissemus, risissemus, studuissemus!
Potes apparatius cenare apud multos, nusquam hilarius 4
simplicius incautius. In summa, experire, et nisi postea
20 te aliis potius excusaveris, mihi semper excusa. Vale.

12. (XVI.)

C. PLINIUS ERUCIO SUO S.

Saturninus's many talents.

1 Amabam Pompeium Saturninum, hunc dico nostrum, laudabamque eius ingenium, etiam antequam scirem quam varium, quam flexibile, quam multiplex esset: 2 nunc vero totum me tenet, habet, possidet. Audii causas agentem acriter et ardenter nec minus polite et ornate, 5 sive meditata sive subita proferret. Adsunt aptae crebraeque sententiae, gravis et decora constructio, sonantia verba et antiqua. Omnia haec mire placent, cum impetu quodam et flumine pervehuntur, placent, si retractentur. 3 Senties quod ego, cum orationes eius in manus sumpseris, 10 quas facile cuilibet veterum, quorum est aemulus, com- 4 parabis. Idem tamen in historia magis satisfaciet vel brevitate vel luce vel suavitate vel splendore etiam et sublimitate narrandi. Nam in contionibus idem qui in orationibus est, pressior tamen et circumscriptior 15 5 et adductior. Praeterea facit versus, quales Catullus aut Calvus. Quantum illis leporis, dulcedinis, amaritudinis, amoris! inserit sane, sed data opera, mollibus levibusque duriusculos quosdam, et hoc quasi Catullus aut 6 Calvus. Legit mihi nuper epistulas; uxoris esse dicebat: 20 Plautum vel Terentium metro solutum legi credidi. Quae sive uxoris sunt, ut adfirmat, sive ipsius, ut negat, pari gloria dignus qui aut illa componat aut uxorem, quam virginem accepit, tam doctam politamque reddiderit. 7 Est ergo mecum per diem totum: eundem antequam scri- 25 bam, eundem cum scripsi, eundem etiam cum remittor, non tamquam eundem lego. Quod te quoque ut facias et

hortor et moneo. Neque enim debet operibus eius obesse 8
quod vivit. An si inter eos quos numquam vidimus
floruisset, non solum libros eius verum etiam imagines
requireremus; eiusdem nunc honor praesentis et gratia
5 quasi satietate languescit? At hoc pravum malignumque 9
est, non admirari hominem admiratione dignissimum,
quia videre, adloqui, audire, complecti, nec laudare tantum verum etiam amare contigit. Vale.

13. (XVIII.)

C. PLINIUS SUETONIO TRANQUILLO SUO S.

Suetonius is alarmed by a dream. Pliny reassures him from his own experience.

Scribis te perterritum somnio vereri ne quid adversi in 1
10 actione patiaris, rogas ut dilationem petam et pauculos
dies, certe proximum, excusem. Difficile est, sed experiar: καὶ γάρ τ' ὄναρ ἐκ Διός ἐστιν. Refert tamen eventura 2
soleas an contraria somniare. Mihi reputanti somnium
meum istud quod times tu egregiam actionem portendere
15 videtur. Susceperam causam Iuni Pastoris, cum mihi 3
quiescenti visa est socrus mea advoluta genibus ne agerem obsecrare. Et eram acturus adulescentulus adhuc,
eram in quadruplici iudicio, eram contra potentissimos
civitatis atque etiam Caesaris amicos; quae singula
20 excutere mentem mihi post tam triste somnium pote-
rant. Egi tamen λογισάμενος illud 4

εἷς οἰωνὸς ἄριστος ἀμύνασθαι περὶ πάτρης.

Nam mihi patria et si quid carius fides videbatur. Pro-
spere cessit, atque adeo illa actio mihi aures hominum,
25 illa ianuam famae patefecit. Proinde dispice an tu quo- 5

que sub hoc exemplo somnium istud in bonum vertas, aut si tutius putas illud cautissimi cuiusque praeceptum 6 'quod dubites ne feceris,' id ipsum rescribe. Ego aliquam stropham inveniam agamque causam tuam, ut ipsam agere tu, cum voles, possis. Est enim sane alia 5 ratio tua, alia mea fuit. Nam iudicium centumvirale differri nullo modo, istud aegre quidem sed tamen potest. Vale.

14. (XIX.)

C. PLINIUS ROMATIO FIRMO SUO S.

Pliny offers his friend a fortune to enable him to enter the equestrian order.

1 Municeps tu meus et condiscipulus et ab ineunte aetate contubernalis, pater tuus et matri et avunculo meo, mihi 10 etiam, quantum aetatis diversitas passa est, familiaris; magnae et graves causae cur suscipere augere dignitatem 2 tuam debeam. Esse autem tibi centum milium censum satis indicat quod apud nos decurio es. Igitur ut te non decurione solum verum etiam equite Romano perfruamur, 15 offero tibi ad inplendas equestres facultates tre-3 centa milia nummum. Te memorem huius muneris amicitiae nostrae diuturnitas spondet: ego ne illud quidem admoneo, quod admonere deberem, nisi scirem sponte facturum, ut dignitate a me data quam modestis- 20 4 sime, ut a me data, utare. Nam sollicitius custodiendus est honor, in quo etiam beneficium amici tuendum est. Vale.

15. (XXII.)

C. PLINIUS CATILIO SEVERO SUO S.

The fortitude of Aristo in serious illness.

Diu iam in urbe haereo, et quidem attonitus. Pertur- 1
bat me longa et pertinax valetudo Titi Aristonis, quem
singulariter et miror et diligo. Nihil est enim illo gravius, sanctius, doctius, ut mihi non unus homo sed litterae
5 ipsae omnesque bonae artes in uno homine summum periculum adire videantur. Quam peritus ille et privati iuris 2
et publici! quantum rerum, quantum exemplorum, quantum antiquitatis tenet! Nihil est quod discere velis,
quod ille docere non possit: mihi certe, quotiens aliquid
10 abditum quaero, ille thesaurus est. Iam quanta sermoni- 3
bus eius fides, quanta auctoritas, quam pressa et decora
cunctatio! quid est quod non statim sciat? Et tamen
plerumque haesitat, dubitat diversitate rationum, quas
acri magnoque iudicio ab origine causisque primis re-
15 petit, discernit, expendit. Ad hoc quam parcus in victu, 4
quam modicus in cultu! Soleo ipsum cubiculum eius ipsumque lectum ut imaginem quandam priscae frugalitatis aspicere. Ornat haec magnitudo animi, quae nihil 5
ad ostentationem, omnia ad conscientiam refert recteque
20 facti non ex populi sermone mercedem sed ex facto petit.
In summa non facile quemquam ex istis qui sapientiae 6
studium habitu corporis praeferunt huic viro comparabis.
Non quidem gymnasia sectatur aut porticus nec disputa-
tionibus longis aliorum otium suumque delectat, sed in
25 toga negotiisque versatur, multos advocatione, plures consilio iuvat. Nemini tamen istorum castitate, pietate, ius- 7
titia, fortitudine etiam primo loco cesserit. Mirareris,

si interesses, qua patientia hanc ipsam valetudinem tole-
ret, ut dolori resistat, ut sitim differat, ut incredibilem
8 febrium ardorem inmotus opertusque transmittat. Nuper me paucosque mecum quos maxime diligit advocavit
rogavitque ut medicos consuleremus de summa valetudi- 5
nis, ut, si esset insuperabilis, sponte exiret e vita, si tan-
9 tum difficilis et longa, resisteret maneretque: dandum
enim precibus uxoris, dandum filiae lacrimis, dandum
etiam nobis amicis ne spes nostras, si modo non essent
10 inanes, voluntaria morte desereret. Id ego arduum in 10
primis et praecipua laude dignum puto. Nam impetu
quodam et instinctu procurrere ad mortem commune cum
multis, deliberare vero et causas eius expendere, utque
suaserit ratio, vitae mortisque consilium vel suscipere vel
11 ponere ingentis est animi. Et medici quidem secunda 15
nobis pollicentur: superest ut promissis deus adnuat
tandemque me hac sollicitudine exsolvat; qua liberatus
Laurentinum meum, hoc est libellos et pugillares studio-
sumque otium repetam. Nunc enim nihil legere, nihil
12 scribere aut adsidenti vacat aut anxio libet. Habes quid 20
timeam, quid optem, quid etiam in posterum destinem:
tu quid egeris, quid agas, quid velis agere, invicem nobis,
sed laetioribus epistulis scribe. Erit confusioni meae
non mediocre solacium, si tu nihil quereris. Vale.

16. (XXIII.)

C. PLINIUS POMPEIO FALCONI SUO S.

Should a tribune plead causes?

1 Consulis an existimem te in tribunatu causas agere 25
debere. Plurimum refert quid esse tribunatum putes,

inanem umbram et sine honore nomen an potestatem
sacrosanctam et quam in ordinem cogi ut a nullo ita ne
a se quidem deceat. Ipse cum tribunus essem, erraverim 2
fortasse qui me aliquid putavi, sed tamquam essem, ab-
5 stinui causis agendis: primum, quod deforme arbitrabar,
cui adsurgere, cui loco cedere omnis oporteret, hunc omnibus sedentibus stare; et qui iubere posset tacere quemcumque, huic silentium clepsydra indici; et quem interfari
nefas esset, hunc etiam convicia audire, et si inulta pate-
10 retur, inertem, si ulcisceretur, insolentem videri. Erat 3
hic quoque aestus ante oculos, si forte me appellasset vel
ille cui adessem vel ille quem contra, intercederem et
auxilium ferrem, an quiescerem sileremque et quasi eiurato magistratu privatum ipse me facerem. His rationi- 4
15 bus motus, malui me tribunum omnibus exhibere quam
paucis advocatum. Sed tu, iterum dicam, plurimum in- 5
terest quid esse tribunatum putes, quam personam tibi
inponas, quae sapienti viro ita aptanda est ut perferatur.
Vale.

17. (XXIV.)

C. PLINIUS BAEBIO HISPANO SUO S.

Suetonius wishes to buy a little farm.

20 Tranquillus, contubernalis meus, vult emere agellum 1
quem venditare amicus tuus dicitur. Rogo cures quanti 2
aecum est emat: ita enim delectabit emisse. Nam
mala emptio semper ingrata, eo maxime, quod expro-
brare stultitiam domino videtur. In hoc autem agello, 3
25 si modo adriserit pretium, Tranquilli mei stomachum
multa sollicitant, vicinitas urbis, opportunitas viae, mediocritas villae, modus ruris, qui avocet magis quam

4 distringat. Scholasticis porro dominis, ut hic est, sufficit abunde tantum soli ut relevare caput, reficere oculos, reptare per limitem unamque semitam terere omnisque viticulas suas nosse et numerare arbusculas possint. Haec tibi exposui, quo magis scires quantum esset ille 5 mihi, ego tibi debiturus, si praediolum istud, quod commendatur his dotibus, tam salubriter emerit ut paenitentiae locum non relinquat. Vale.

LIBER SECUNDUS.

18. (I.)

C. PLINIUS ROMANO SUO S.

Death of Verginius Rufus.

Post aliquot annos insigne atque etiam memorabile 1
populi Romani oculis spectaculum exhibuit publicum
funus Vergini Rufi, maximi et clarissimi civis, perinde
felicis. Triginta annis gloriae suae supervixit. Legit 2
5 scripta de se carmina, legit historias et posteritati suae
interfuit. Perfunctus est tertio consulatu, ut summum
fastigium privati hominis impleret, cum principis noluisset. Caesares quibus suspectus atque etiam invisus 3
virtutibus fuerat evasit, reliquit incolumem optimum
10 atque amicissimum, tamquam ad hunc ipsum honorem
publici funeris reservatus. Annum tertium et octoge- 4
simum excessit in altissima tranquillitate, pari veneratione. Usus est firma valetudine, nisi quod solebant ei
manus tremere, citra dolorem tamen. Aditus tantum
15 mortis durior longiorque, sed hic ipse laudabilis. Nam 5
cum vocem praepararet acturus in consulatu principi
gratias, liber quem forte acceperat grandiorem et seni
et stanti ipso pondere elapsus est. Hunc dum sequitur
colligitque, per leve et lubricum pavimentum fallente
20 vestigio cecidit coxamque fregit, quae parum apte collocata reluctante aetate male coiit. Huius viri exequiae 6
magnum ornamentum principi, magnum saeculo, magnum

etiam foro et rostris attulerunt. Laudatus est a consule
Cornelio Tacito: nam hic supremus felicitati eius cumu-
7 lus accessit, laudator eloquentissimus. Et ille quidem
plenus annis abiit, plenus honoribus, illis etiam quos
recusavit: nobis tamen quaerendus ac desiderandus est 5
ut exemplar aevi prioris, mihi vero praecipue, qui illum
non solum publice quantum admirabar tantum diligebam;
8 primum quod utrique eadem regio, municipia finitima,
agri etiam possessionesque coniunctae, praeterea quod
ille mihi tutor relictus adfectum parentis exhibuit. Sic 10
candidatum me suffragio ornavit, sic ad omnes honores
meos ex secessibus accucurrit, cum iam pridem eiusmodi
officiis renuntiasset, sic illo die quo sacerdotes solent
nominare quos dignissimos sacerdotio iudicant me sem-
9 per nominabat. Quin etiam in hac novissima valetudine 15
veritus ne forte inter quinqueviros crearetur, qui minuendis publicis sumptibus iudicio senatus constituebantur,
cum illi tot amici senes consularesque superessent, me
huius aetatis per quem excusaretur elegit, his quidem
10 verbis 'etiam si filium haberem, tibi mandarem.' Quibus 20
ex causis necesse est tamquam immaturam mortem eius
in sinu tuo defleam; si tamen fas est aut flere aut omnino
mortem vocare, qua tanti viri mortalitas magis finita
11 quam vita est. Vivit enim vivetque semper atque etiam
latius in memoria hominum et sermone versabitur, post- 25
12 quam ab oculis recessit. Volui tibi multa alia scribere,
sed totus animus in hac una contemplatione defixus est.
Verginium cogito, Verginium video, Verginium iam vanis
imaginibus, recentibus tamen, audio, adloquor, teneo;
cui fortasse cives aliquos virtutibus pares et habemus et 30
habebimus, gloria neminem. Vale.

19. (IV.)

C. PLINIUS CALVINAE SUAE S.

Pliny renounces his claims against the estate of Calvina's father.

Si pluribus pater tuus vel uni cuilibet alii quam mihi 1 debuisset, fuisset fortasse dubitandum an adires hereditatem etiam viro gravem. Cum vero ego ductus adfinita- 2 tis officio, dimissis omnibus qui, non dico molestiores, sed 5 diligentiores erant, creditor solus exstiterim, cumque ego nubenti tibi in dotem centum milia contulerim praeter eam summam quam pater tuus quasi de meo dixit (erat enim solvenda de meo), magnum habes facilitatis meae pignus, cuius fiducia debes famam defuncti pudoremque 10 suscipere; ad quod ne te verbis magis quam rebus horter, quidquid mihi pater tuus debuit, acceptum tibi fieri iubebo. Nec est quod verearis ne sit mihi onerosa ista 3 donatio. Sunt quidem omnino nobis modicae facultates, dignitas sumptuosa, reditus propter condicionem agello- 15 rum nescio minor an incertior: sed quod cessat ex reditu frugalitate suppletur, ex qua velut fonte liberalitas nostra decurrit; quae tamen ita temperanda est ne nimia profu- 4 sione inarescat, sed temperanda in aliis, in te vero facile ratio constabit, etiamsi modum excesserit. Vale.

20. (VI.)

C. PLINIUS AVITO SUO S.

A shabby entertainer.

20 Longum est altius repetere, nec refert quemadmodum 1 acciderit ut homo minime familiaris cenarem apud quendam, ut sibi videbatur, lautum et diligentem, ut mihi, sordidum simul et sumptuosum. Nam sibi et paucis 2

opima quaedam, ceteris vilia et minuta ponebat. Vinum etiam parvolis lagunculis in tria genera discripserat, non ut potestas eligendi, sed ne ius esset recusandi, aliud sibi et nobis, aliud minoribus amicis (nam gradatim amicos 3 habet), aliud suis nostrisque libertis. Animadvertit qui 5 mihi proximus recumbebat et an probarem interrogavit. Negavi. 'Tu ergo' inquit 'quam consuetudinem sequeris?' 'Eadem omnibus pono: ad cenam enim, non ad notam invito cunctisque rebus exaequo quos mensa et 4 toro aequavi.' 'Etiamne libertos?' 'Etiam: convictores enim tunc, non libertos puto.' 10 Et ille 'magno tibi constat?' 'Minime.' 'Qui fieri potest?' 'Quia scilicet liberti mei non idem quod ego bibunt, sed idem ego quod 5 liberti.' Et hercule si gulae temperes, non est onerosum quo utaris ipse communicare cum pluribus. Illa ergo 15 reprimenda, illa quasi in ordinem redigenda est, si sumptibus parcas, quibus aliquanto rectius tua continentia 6 quam aliena contumelia consulas. Quorsus haec? ne tibi, optimae indolis iuveni, quorundam in mensa luxuria specie frugalitatis inponat. Convenit autem amori in te 20 meo, quotiens tale aliquid inciderit, sub exemplo praemo-7 nere quid debeas fugere. Igitur memento nihil magis esse vitandum quam istam luxuriae et sordium novam societatem; quae cum sint turpissima discreta ac separata, turpius iunguntur. Vale. 25

21. (VIII.)

C. PLINIUS CANINIO SUO S.

Unable to leave town, Pliny envies his friend in the country.

1 Studes an piscaris an venaris an simul omnia? Possunt enim omnia simul fieri ad Larium nostrum. Nam lacus

piscem, feras silvae quibus lacus cingitur, studia altissimus iste secessus adfatim suggerunt. 2 Sed sive omnia simul sive aliquid facis, non possum dicere 'invideo': angor tamen non et mihi licere quae sic concupisco ut 5 aegri vinum, balinea, fontes. Numquamne hos artissimos laqueos, si solvere negatur, abrumpam? 3 Numquam, puto. Nam veteribus negotiis nova adcrescunt, nec tamen priora peraguntur: tot nexibus, tot quasi catenis maius in dies occupationum agmen extenditur. Vale.

22. (IX.)

C. PLINIUS APOLLINARI SUO S.

The candidacy of Erucius for the tribuneship.

10 1 Anxium me et inquietum habet petitio Sexti Eruci mei. Adficior cura et quam pro me sollicitudinem non adii quasi pro me altero patior; et alioqui meus pudor, mea existimatio, mea dignitas in discrimen adducitur. 2 Ego Sexto latum clavum a Caesare nostro, ego quaesturam inpetravi, 15 meo suffragio pervenit ad ius tribunatum petendi, quem nisi obtinet in senatu, vereor ne decepisse Caesarem videar. 3 Proinde adnitendum est mihi ut talem eum iudicent omnes, qualem esse princeps mihi credidit. Quae causa si studium meum non incitaret, adiutum 20 tamen cuperem iuvenem probissimum, gravissimum, eruditissimum, omni denique laude dignissimum, et quidem cum tota domo. 4 Nam pater ei Erucius Clarus, vir sanctus, anticus, disertus, atque in agendis causis exercitatus, quas summa fide, pari constantia, nec verecundia minore 25 defendit. Habet avunculum C. Septicium, quo nihil verius, nihil simplicius, nihil candidius, nihil fidelius novi. 5 Omnes me certatim et tamen aequaliter amant,

omnibus nunc ego in uno referre gratiam possum. Itaque prenso amicos, supplico, ambio, domos stationesque circumeo, quantumque vel auctoritate vel gratia valeam
6 precibus experior. Teque obsecro ut aliquam oneris mei partem suscipere tanti putes. Reddam vicem, si reposces, 5
reddam et si non reposces. Diligeris, coleris, frequentaris: ostende modo velle te, nec deerunt qui quod tu velis cupiant. Vale.

23. (X.)

C. PLINIUS OCTAVIO SUO S.

Exhortation to publish.

1 Hominem te patientem vel potius durum ac paene
2 crudelem, qui tam insignes libros tam diu teneas! Quousque 10
et tibi et nobis invidebis, tibi maxima laude, nobis voluptate? Sine per ora hominum ferantur isdemque quibus lingua Romana spatiis pervagentur. Magna et iam longa expectatio est, quam frustrari adhuc et differre
3 non debes. Enotuerunt quidam tui versus et invito te 15
claustra sua refregerunt. Hos nisi retrahis in corpus, quandoque ut errones aliquem cuius dicantur invenient.
4 Habe ante oculos mortalitatem, a qua adserere te hoc uno monimento potes: nam cetera fragilia et caduca non minus quam ipsi homines occidunt desinuntque. Dices, 20
5 ut soles, 'amici mei viderint.' Opto equidem amicos tibi tam fideles, tam eruditos, tam laboriosos, ut tantum curae intentionisque suscipere et possint et velint, sed dispice ne sit parum providum sperare ex aliis quod tibi
6 ipse non praestes. Et de editione quidem interim ut 25
voles: recita saltem, quo magis libeat emittere, utque tandem percipias gaudium, quod ego olim pro te non
7 temere praesumo. Imaginor enim qui concursus, quae

admiratio te, qui clamor, quod etiam silentium maneat, quo ego, cum dico vel recito, non minus quam clamore delector, sit modo silentium acre et intentum et cupidum ulteriora audiendi. Hoc fructu tanto, tam parato desine 8
5 studia tua infinita ista cunctatione fraudare; quae cum modum excedit, verendum est ne inertiae et desidiae vel etiam timiditatis nomen accipiat. Vale.

24. (XIII.)

C. PLINIUS PRISCO SUO S.

Pliny begs the interest of Priscus for Voconius Romanus.

Et tu occasiones obligandi me avidissime amplecteris, 1 et ego nemini libentius debeo. Duabus ergo de causis a 2
10 te potissimum petere constitui quod inpetratum maxime cupio. Regis exercitum amplissimum: hinc tibi beneficiorum larga materia, longum praeterea tempus quo amicos tuos exornare potuisti. Convertere ad nostros, 3 nec hos multos. Malles tu quidem multos, sed meae
15 verecundiae sufficit unus aut alter, ac potius unus. Is erit Voconius Romanus. Pater ei in equestri gradu 4 clarus, clarior vitricus, immo pater alius: nam huic quoque nomini pietate successit. Mater e primis citerioris Hispaniae: scis quod iudicium provinciae illius, quanta
20 sit gravitas. Flamen proxime fuit. Hunc ego, cum 5 simul studeremus, arte familiariterque dilexi: ille meus in urbe, ille in secessu contubernalis, cum hoc seria, cum hoc iocos miscui. Quid enim illo aut fidelius amico aut 6 sodale iucundius? Mira in sermone, mira etiam in ore
25 ipso vultuque suavitas. Ad hoc ingenium excelsum, sub- 7 tile, dulce, facile, eruditum in causis agendis: epistulas quidem scribit, ut Musas ipsas Latine loqui credas. Ama- 8

tur a me plurimum nec tamen vincitur. Equidem iuvenis statim iuveni quantum potui per aetatem avidissime contuli et nuper ab optimo principe trium liberorum ius impetravi. Quod quamquam parce et cum delectu daret,
9 mihi tamen, tamquam eligeret, indulsit. Haec beneficia 5
mea tueri nullo modo melius quam ut augeam possum, praesertim cum ipse illa tam grate interpretetur ut, dum
10 priora accipit, posteriora mereatur. Habes qualis, quam probatus carusque sit nobis, quem rogo pro ingenio, pro fortuna tua exornes. In primis ama hominem: nam licet 10
tribuas ei quantum amplissimum potes, nihil tamen amplius potes amicitia tua; cuius esse eum usque ad intimam familiaritatem capacem quo magis scires, breviter tibi
11 studia, mores, omnem denique vitam eius expressi. Extenderem preces, nisi et tu rogari diu nolles, et ego tota 15
hoc epistula fecissem: rogat enim, et quidem efficacissime, qui reddit causas rogandi. Vale.

25. (XIV.)

C. PLINIUS MAXIMO SUO S.

Degeneracy of legal eloquence.

1 Verum opinaris: distringor centumviralibus causis, quae me exercent magis quam delectant. Sunt enim pleraeque parvae et exiles: raro incidit vel personarum 20
2 claritate vel negotii magnitudine insignis. Ad hoc pauci cum quibus iuvet dicere: ceteri audaces atque etiam magna ex parte adulescentuli obscuri ad declamandum huc transierunt, tam inreverenter et temere ut mihi Atilius noster expresse dixisse videatur sic in foro pueros a 25
centumviralibus causis auspicari ut ab Homero in scholis.
3 Nam hic quoque ut illic primum coepit esse quod maxi-

mum est. At hercule ante memoriam meam (ita maiores natu solent dicere) ne nobilissimis quidem adulescentibus locus erat nisi aliquo consulari producente: tanta veneratione pulcherrimum opus colebatur. Nunc refractis 4
5 pudoris et reverentiae claustris omnia patent omnibus, nec inducuntur sed inrumpunt. Secuntur auditores actoribus similes, conducti et redempti: manceps convenitur: in media basilica tam palam sportulae quam in triclinio dantur: ex iudicio in iudicium pari mercede
10 transitur. Inde iam non inurbane Σοφοκλεῖς vocantur 5 [ἀπὸ τοῦ σοφῶς καὶ καλεῖσθαι]: isdem Latinum nomen inpositum est Laudiceni. Et tamen crescit in dies foeditas 6 utraque lingua notata. Here duo nomenclatores mei (habent sane aetatem eorum qui nuper togas sumpserint)
15 ternis denariis ad laudandum trahebantur. Tanti constat ut sis disertissimus. Hoc pretio quamlibet numerosa subsellia inplentur, hoc ingens corona colligitur, hoc infiniti clamores commoventur, cum mesochorus dedit sig- 7 num: opus est enim signo apud non intellegentes, ne
20 audientes quidem; nam plerique non audiunt, nec ulli 8 magis laudant. Si quando transibis per basilicam et voles scire quo modo quisque dicat, nihil est quod tribunal ascendas, nihil quod praebeas aurem; facilis divinatio: scito eum pessime dicere qui laudabitur maxime.
25 Primus hunc audiendi morem induxit Largius Licinus, 9 hactenus tamen ut auditores corrogaret: ita certe ex 10 Quintiliano, praeceptore meo, audisse memini. Narrabat ille 'adsectabar Domitium Afrum: cum apud centumviros diceret graviter et lente (hoc enim illi actionis genus
30 erat), audit ex proximo inmodicum insolitumque clamorem. Admiratus reticuit. Ubi silentium factum est, repetiit quod abruperat. Iterum clamor, iterum reticuit, 11

et post silentium coepit idem tertio. Novissime quis diceret quaesivit: responsum est 'Licinus.' Tum intermissa causa 'centumviri' inquit, 'hoc artificium perit.'' 12 Quod alioqui perire incipiebat, cum perisse Afro videretur, nunc vero prope funditus extinctum et eversum est. 5 Pudet referre quae quam fracta pronuntiatione dicantur, 13 quibus quam teneris clamoribus excipiantur. Plausus tantum ac potius sola cymbala et tympana illis canticis desunt: ululatus quidem (neque enim alio vocabulo potest exprimi theatris quoque indecora laudatio) large super- 10 14 sunt. Nos tamen adhuc et utilitas amicorum et ratio aetatis moratur ac retinet: veremur enim ne forte non has indignitates reliquisse sed laborem fugisse videamur. Sumus tamen solito rariores, quod initium est gradatim desinendi. Vale. 15

26. (XV.)

C. PLINIUS VALERIANO SUO S.

How does Valerianus like his new farm?

1 Quo modo te veteres Marsi tui? quo modo emptio nova? Placent agri, postquam tui facti sunt? Rarum id quidem: 2 nihil enim aeque gratum est adeptis quam concupiscentibus. Me praedia materna parum commode tractant, delectant tamen ut materna, et alioqui longa patientia 20 occallui. Habent hunc finem adsiduae querellae quod queri pudet. Vale.

27. (XVII.)

C. PLINIUS GALLO SUO S.

Description of Pliny's Laurentine villa.

1 Miraris cur me Laurentinum vel, si ita mavis, Laurens meum tanto opere delectet: desines mirari, cum cogno-

veris gratiam villae, opportunitatem loci, litoris spatium.
Decem et septem milibus passuum ab urbe secessit, ut 2
peractis quae agenda fuerint salvo iam et composito die
possis ibi manere. Aditur non una via; nam et Lauren-
5 tina et Ostiensis eodem ferunt, sed Laurentina a quarto
decimo lapide, Ostiensis ab undecimo relinquenda est.
Utrimque excipit iter aliqua ex parte harenosum, iunctis
paulo gravius et longius, equo breve et molle. Varia 3
hinc atque inde facies: nam modo occurrentibus silvis
10 via coartatur, modo latissimis pratis diffunditur et patescit; multi greges ovium, multa ibi equorum boum
armenta, quae montibus hieme depulsa herbis et tepore
verno nitescunt. Villa usibus capax, non sumptuosa
tutela. Cuius in prima parte atrium frugi nec tamen 4
15 sordidum, deinde porticus in D litterae similitudinem
circumactae, quibus parvola sed festiva area includitur.
Egregium hae adversus tempestates receptaculum: nam
specularibus ac multo magis imminentibus tectis muniuntur. Est contra medias cavaedium hilare, mox triclinium 5
20 satis pulchrum, quod in litus excurrit, ac si quando Africo
mare inpulsum est, fractis iam et novissimis fluctibus leviter adluitur. Undique valvas aut fenestras non minores
valvis habet, atque ita a lateribus a fronte quasi tria maria
prospectat; a tergo cavaedium, porticum, aream, porticum
25 rursus, mox atrium, silvas et longinquos respicit montes.
Huius a laeva retractius paulo cubiculum est amplum, 6
deinde aliud minus, quod altera fenestra admittit orientem, occidentem altera retinet, hac et subiacens mare
longius quidem sed securius intuetur. Huius cubiculi et 7
30 triclinii illius obiectu includitur angulus, qui purissimum
solem continet et accendit. Hoc hibernaculum, hoc etiam
gymnasium meorum est: ibi omnes silent venti exceptis

qui nubilum inducunt et serenum ante quam usum loci
8 eripiunt. Adnectitur angulo cubiculum in hapsida curvatum, quod ambitum solis fenestris omnibus sequitur.
Parieti eius in bibliothecae speciem armarium insertum
9 est, quod non legendos libros sed lectitandos capit. Ad- 5
haeret dormitorium membrum transitu interiacente, qui
suspensus et tubulatus conceptum vaporem salubri temperamento huc illuc digerit et ministrat. Reliqua pars
lateris huius servorum libertorumque usibus detinetur,
10 plerisque tam mundis ut accipere hospites possint. Ex 10
alio latere cubiculum est politissimum; deinde vel cubiculum grande vel modica cenatio, quae plurimo sole, plurimo mari lucet; post hanc cubiculum cum procoetone,
altitudine aestivum, munimentis hibernum: est enim
subductum omnibus ventis. Huic cubiculo aliud et pro- 15
11 coeton communi pariete iunguntur. Inde balinei cella
frigidaria spatiosa et effusa, cuius in contrariis parietibus duo baptisteria velut eiecta sinuantur, abunde capacia, si mare in proximo cogites. Adiacet unctorium,
hypocauston, adiacet propnigeon balinei, mox duae cel- 20
lae magis elegantes quam sumptuosae: cohaeret calida
12 piscina mirifica, ex qua natantes mare aspiciunt, nec
procul sphaeristerium, quod calidissimo soli inclinato
iam die occurrit. Hic turris erigitur, sub qua diaetae
duae, totidem in ipsa, praeterea cenatio, quae latissimum 25
mare, longissimum litus, villas amoenissimas prospicit.
13 Est et alia turris: in hac cubiculum, in quo sol nascitur
conditurque: lata post apotheca et horreum: sub hoc
triclinium, quod turbati maris non nisi fragorem et sonum patitur, eumque iam languidum et desinentem; 30
hortum et gestationem videt, qua hortus includitur.
14 Gestatio buxo aut rore marino, ubi deficit buxus, ambi-

tur: nam buxus, qua parte defenditur tectis, abunde viret; aperto caelo apertoque vento et quamquam longinqua aspergine maris inarescit. Adiacet gestationi 15 interiore circumitu vinea tenera et umbrosa nudisque
5 etiam pedibus mollis et cedens. Hortum morus et ficus frequens vestit, quarum arborum illa vel maxime ferax terra est, malignior ceteris. Hac non deteriore quam maris facie cenatio remota a mari fruitur: cingitur diaetis duabus a tergo, quarum fenestris subiacet vesti-
10 bulum villae et hortus alius pinguis et rusticus. Hinc 16 cryptoporticus prope publici operis extenditur. Utrimque fenestrae, a mari plures, ab horto singulae, sed alternis pauciores. Hae, cum serenus dies et inmotus, omnes; cum hinc vel inde ventis inquietus, qua venti
15 quiescunt, sine iniuria patent. Ante cryptoporticum 17 xystus violis odoratus: teporem solis infusi repercussu cryptoporticus auget, quae ut tenet solem sic aquilonem inhibet summovetque, quantumque caloris ante tantum retro frigoris. Similiter Africum sistit, atque ita diver-
20 sissimos ventos alium alio latere frangit et finit. Haec 18 iucunditas eius hieme, maior aestate. Nam ante meridiem xystum, post meridiem gestationis hortique proximam partem umbra sua temperat, quae, ut dies crevit decrevitve, modo brevior modo longior hac vel illa cadit.
25 Ipsa vero cryptoporticus tum maxime caret sole, cum 19 ardentissimus culmini eius insistit. Ad hoc patentibus fenestris favonios accipit transmittitque nec umquam aëre pigro et manente ingravescit. In capite xysti deinceps 20 cryptoporticus horti diaeta est, amores mei; re vera
30 amores: ipse posui. In hac heliocaminus quidem alia xystum alia mare utraque solem, cubiculum autem valvis cryptoporticum, fenestra prospicit mare. Contra parie- 21

tem medium zotheca perquam eleganter recedit, quae specularibus et velis obductis reductisve modo adicitur cubiculo modo aufertur. Lectum et duas cathedras capit: a pedibus mare, a tergo villae, a capite silvae: tot facies
22 locorum totidem fenestris et distinguit et miscet. Iunc- 5
tum est cubiculum noctis et somni. Non illud voces servulorum, non maris murmur, non tempestatum motus, non fulgurum lumen ac ne diem quidem sentit, nisi fenestris apertis. Tam alti abditique secreti illa ratio,
quod interiacens andron parietem cubiculi hortique 10
distinguit atque ita omnem sonum media inanitate
23 consumit. Adplicitum est cubiculo hypocauston perexiguum, quod angusta fenestra suppositum calorem, ut ratio exigit, aut effundit aut retinet. Procoeton inde
et cubiculum porrigitur in solem, quem orientem statim 15
exceptum ultra meridiem oblicum quidem sed tamen ser-
24 vat. In hanc ego diaetam cum me recepi, abesse mihi etiam a villa mea videor, magnamque eius voluptatem praecipue Saturnalibus capio, cum reliqua pars tecti
licentia dierum festisque clamoribus personat: nam nec 20
ipse meorum lusibus nec illi studiis meis obstrepunt.
25 Haec utilitas, haec amoenitas deficitur aqua salienti, sed puteos ac potius fontes habet: sunt enim in summo. Et omnino litoris illius mira natura: quocumque loco
moveris humum, obvius et paratus umor occurrit, isque 25
sincerus ac ne leviter quidem tanta maris vicinitate cor-
26 ruptus. Suggerunt adfatim ligna proximae silvae: ceteras copias Ostiensis colonia ministrat. Frugi quidem homini sufficit etiam vicus quem una villa discernit: in
hoc balinea meritoria tria, magna commoditas, si forte 30
balineum domi vel subitus adventus vel brevior mora
27 calfacere dissuadeat. Litus ornant varietate gratissima

nunc continua nunc intermissa tecta villarum, quae praestant multarum urbium faciem, sive mari sive ipso litore utare; quod non numquam longa tranquillitas mollit, saepius frequens et contrarius fluctus indurat. Mare 28
5 non sane pretiosis piscibus abundat, soleas tamen et squillas optimas egerit. Villa vero nostra etiam mediterraneas copias praestat, lac in primis: nam illuc e pascuis pecora conveniunt, si quando aquam umbramve sectantur. Iustisne de causis iam tibi videor incolere, 29
10 inhabitare, diligere secessum, quem tu nimis urbanus es nisi concupiscis? Atque utinam concupiscas! ut tot tantisque dotibus villulae nostrae maxima commendatio ex tuo contubernio accedat. Vale.

28. (XVIII.)

C. PLINIUS MAURICO SUO S.

Selection of a teacher for the sons of Arulenus Rusticus.

Quid a te mihi iucundius potuit iniungi, quam ut prae- 1
15 ceptorem fratris tui liberis quaererem? Nam beneficio tuo in scholam redeo et illam dulcissimam aetatem quasi resumo: sedeo inter iuvenes, ut solebam, atque etiam experior quantum apud illos auctoritatis ex studiis habeam. Nam proxime frequenti auditorio inter se coram 2
20 multis ordinis nostri clare loquebantur: intravi, conticuerunt; quod non referrem, nisi ad illorum magis laudem quam ad meam pertineret, ac nisi sperare te vellem posse fratris tui filios probe discere. Quod superest, cum 3 omnes qui profitentur audiero, quid de quoque sentiam
25 scribam efficiamque, quantum tamen epistula consequi potero, ut ipse omnes audisse videaris. Debeo enim tibi, 4 debeo memoriae fratris tui hanc fidem, hoc studium,

praesertim super tanta re. Nam quid magis interest vestra quam ut liberi (dicerem tui, nisi nunc illos magis amares) digni illo patre, te patruo reperiantur? quam curam mihi, etiam si non mandasses, vindicassem. Nec ignoro suscipiendas offensas in eligendo praeceptore, sed oportet me non modo offensas verum etiam simultates pro fratris tui filiis tam aequo animo subire quam parentes pro suis. Vale.

29. (XX.)

C. PLINIUS CALVISIO SUO S.

Regulus as a legacy-hunter.

1 Assem para et accipe auream fabulam, fabulas immo: nam me priorum nova admonuit, nec refert a qua potissimum incipiam. 2 Verania Pisonis graviter iacebat, huius dico Pisonis quem Galba adoptavit. Ad hanc Regulus venit. Primum inpudentiam hominis qui venerit ad aegram, cuius marito inimicissimus, ipsi invisissimus fuerat. 3 Esto, si venit tantum: at ille etiam proximus toro sedit, quo die, qua hora nata esset interrogavit. Ubi audiit, componit vultum, intendit oculos, movet labra, agitat digitos, computat; nihil: ut diu miseram expectatione suspendit, 'habes' inquit 'climactericum tempus, sed evades. 4 Quod ut tibi magis liqueat, haruspicem consulam quem sum frequenter expertus.' 5 Nec mora: sacrificium facit, adfirmat exta cum siderum significatione congruere. Illa, ut in periculo credula, poscit codicillos, legatum Regulo scribit: mox ingravescit: clamat moriens hominem nequam, perfidum ac plus etiam quam periurum, qui sibi per salutem filii peierasset. 6 Facit hoc Regulus non minus scelerate quam

frequenter, quod iram deorum, quos ipse cotidie fallit, in caput infelicis pueri detestatur. Velleius Blaesus, 7 ille locuples consularis, novissima valetudine conflictabatur: cupiebat mutare testamentum. Regulus, qui spe-
5 raret aliquid ex novis tabulis, quia nuper captare eum coeperat, medicos hortari, rogare quoquo modo spiritum homini prorogarent. Postquam signatum est testamen- 8 tum, mutat personam, vertit adlocutionem, isdemque medicis 'quousque miserum cruciatis? quid invidetis
10 bona morte cui dare vitam non potestis?' Moritur Blaesus, et tamquam omnia audisset, Regulo ne tantulum quidem. Sufficiunt duae fabulae, an scholastica 9 lege tertiam poscis? est unde fiat. Aurelia, ornata 10 femina, signatura testamentum sumpserat pulcherrimas
15 tunicas. Regulus cum venisset ad signandum, 'rogo' inquit 'has mihi leges.' Aurelia ludere hominem puta- 11 bat, ille serio instabat: ne multa, coëgit mulierem aperire tabulas ac sibi tunicas quas erat induta legare: observavit scribentem, inspexit an scripsisset. Et Aurelia qui-
20 dem vivit, ille tamen istud tamquam morituram coëgit. Et hic hereditates, hic legata, quasi mereatur, accipit. 'Αλλὰ τί διατείνομαι in ea civitate, in qua iam pridem non 12 minora praemia, immo maiora, nequitia et improbitas quam pudor et virtus habent? Aspice Regulum, qui 13
25 ex paupere et tenui ad tantas opes per flagitia processit ut ipse mihi dixerit, cum consuleret quam cito sestertium sescenties inpleturus esset, invenisse se exta duplicia, quibus portendi milies et ducenties habiturum. Et ha- 14 bebit, si modo, ut coepit, aliena testamenta, quod est
30 inprobissimum genus falsi, ipsis quorum sunt illa dictaverit. Vale.

LIBER TERTIUS.

30. (I.)

C. PLINIUS CALVISIO SUO S.

How Spurinna spent his days in his old age.

1 Nescio an ullum iucundius tempus exegerim quam quo nuper apud Spurinnam fui, adeo quidem ut neminem magis in senectute, si modo senescere datum est, aemulari 2 velim: nihil est enim illo vitae genere distinctius. Me autem ut certus siderum cursus ita vita hominum dispo- 5 sita delectat, senum praesertim. Nam iuvenes confusa adhuc quaedam et quasi turbata non indecent; senibus placida omnia et ordinata conveniunt, quibus industria 3 sera, turpis ambitio est. Hanc regulam Spurinna constantissime servat; quin etiam parva haec, parva, si non 10 cotidie fiant, ordine quodam et velut orbe circumagit. 4 Mane lectulo continetur, hora secunda calceos poscit, ambulat milia passuum tria nec minus animum quam corpus exercet. Si adsunt amici, honestissimi sermones explicantur: si non, liber legitur; interdum etiam prae- 15 5 sentibus amicis, si tamen illi non gravantur. Deinde considit, et liber rursus aut sermo libro potior: mox vehiculum ascendit, adsumit uxorem singularis exempli vel 6 aliquem amicorum, ut me proxime. Quam pulchrum illud, quam dulce secretum! quantum ibi antiquitatis! 20 quae facta, quos viros audias! quibus praeceptis imbuare! quamvis ille hoc temperamentum modestiae suae indix-

erit, ne praecipere videatur. Peractis septem milibus passuum iterum ambulat mille, iterum residit vel se cubiculo ac stilo reddit. Scribit enim, et quidem utraque lingua, lyrica doctissima: mira illis dulcedo, mira suavitas, mira hilaritas, cuius gratiam cumulat sanctitas scribentis. Ubi hora balinei nuntiata est (est autem hieme nona, aestate octava), in sole, si caret vento, ambulat nudus. Deinde movetur pila vehementer et diu: nam hoc quoque exercitationis genere pugnat cum senectute. Lotus accubat et paulisper cibum differt: interim audit legentem remissius aliquid et dulcius. Per hoc omne tempus liberum est amicis vel eadem facere vel alia, si malint. Adponitur cena non minus nitida quam frugi in argento puro et antiquo: sunt in usu et Corinthia, quibus delectatur nec adficitur. Frequenter comoedis cena distinguitur, ut voluptates quoque studiis condiantur. Sumit aliquid de nocte et aestate: nemini hoc longum est; tanta comitate convivium trahitur. Inde illi post septimum et septuagesimum annum aurium oculorum vigor integer, inde agile et vividum corpus solaque ex senectute prudentia. Hanc ego vitam voto et cogitatione praesumo, ingressurus avidissime, ut primum ratio aetatis receptui canere permiserit. Interim mille laboribus conteror, quorum mihi et solacium et exemplum est idem Spurinna: nam ille quoque, quoad honestum fuit, obiit officia, gessit magistratus, provincias rexit, multoque labore hoc otium meruit. Igitur eundem mihi cursum, eundem terminum statuo, idque iam nunc apud te subsigno, ut, si me longius evehi videris, in ius voces ad hanc epistulam meam et quiescere iubeas, cum inertiae crimen effugero. Vale.

31. (V.)

C. PLINIUS BAEBIO MACRO SUO S.

The works of the elder Pliny.

1 Pergratum est mihi quod tam diligenter libros avunculi mei lectitas ut habere omnes velis quaerasque qui sint
2 omnes. Fungar indicis partibus atque etiam quo sint ordine scripti notum tibi faciam: est enim haec quoque
3 studiosis non iniucunda cognitio. 'De iaculatione eques- 5 tri unus': hunc, cum praefectus alae militaret, pari ingenio curaque conposuit. 'De vita Pomponi Secundi duo'; a quo singulariter amatus hoc memoriae amici
4 quasi debitum munus exsolvit. 'Bellorum Germaniae viginti'; quibus omnia quae cum Germanis gessimus 10 bella collegit. Incohavit, cum in Germania militaret, somnio monitus: adstitit ei quiescenti Drusi Neronis effigies, qui Germaniae latissime victor ibi periit, commendabat memoriam suam orabatque ut se ab iniuria
5 oblivionis adsereret. 'Studiosi tres,' in sex volumina 15 propter amplitudinem divisi, quibus oratorem ab incunabulis instituit et perficit. 'Dubii sermonis octo': scripsit sub Nerone novissimis annis, cum omne studiorum genus paulo liberius et erectius periculosum servitus fe-
6 cisset. 'A fine Aufidi Bassi triginta unus.' 'Naturae 20 historiarum triginta septem,' opus diffusum, eruditum,
7 nec minus varium quam ipsa natura. Miraris quod tot volumina multaque in his tam scrupulosa homo occupatus absolverit? magis miraberis, si scieris illum aliquandiu causas actitasse, decessisse anno sexto et quinquagesimo, 25 medium tempus distentum impeditumque qua officiis max-
8 imis qua amicitia principum egisse. Sed erat acre inge-

nium, incredibile studium, summa vigilantia. Lucubrare
Vulcanalibus incipiebat, non auspicandi causa sed studendi,
statim a nocte multa, hieme vero ab hora septima,
vel cum tardissime, octava, saepe sexta. Erat sane somni
5 paratissimi, non numquam etiam inter ipsa studia instantis
et deserentis. Ante lucem ibat ad Vespasianum imperatorem 9
(nam ille quoque noctibus utebatur), inde ad
delegatum sibi officium. Reversus domum, quod relicum
temporis, studiis reddebat. Post cibum saepe, quem interdiu 10
10 levem et facilem veterum more sumebat, aestate,
si quid otii, iacebat in sole, liber legebatur, adnotabat
excerpebatque. Nihil enim legit quod non excerperet:
dicere etiam solebat nullum esse librum tam malum ut
non aliqua parte prodesset. Post solem plerumque frigida 11
15 lavabatur: deinde gustabat dormiebatque minimum:
mox quasi alio die studebat in cenae tempus. Super hanc
liber legebatur, adnotabatur, et quidem cursim. Memini 12
quendam ex amicis, cum lector quaedam perperam pronuntiasset,
revocasse et repeti coëgisse, huic avunculum
20 meum dixisse 'intellexeras nempe?' cum ille adnuisset,
'cur ergo revocabas? decem amplius versus hac tua interpellatione
perdidimus.' Tanta erat parsimonia temporis. 13
Surgebat aestate a cena luce, hieme intra primam noctis,
et tamquam aliqua lege cogente. Haec inter medios labores
25 urbisque fremitum. In secessu solum balinei tempus 14
studiis eximebatur: cum dico balinei, de interioribus
loquor; nam dum destringitur tergiturque, audiebat aliquid
aut dictabat. In itinere quasi solutus ceteris curis 15
huic uni vacabat: ad latus notarius cum libro et pugillaribus,
30 cuius manus hieme manicis muniebantur, ut ne
caeli quidem asperitas ullum studiis tempus eriperet;
qua ex causa Romae quoque sella vehebatur. Repeto 16

me correptum ab eo cur ambularem: 'poteras' inquit 'has horas non perdere'; nam perire omne tempus arbi-
17 trabatur quod studiis non impenderetur. Hac intentione tot ista volumina peregit electorumque commentarios centum sexaginta mihi reliquit, opisthographos quidem et 5
minutissime scriptos; qua ratione multiplicatur hic numerus. Referebat ipse potuisse se, cum procuraret in Hispania, vendere hos commentarios Largio Licino quadringentis milibus nummum, et tunc aliquanto pauciores
18 erant. Nonne videtur tibi recordanti quantum legerit, 10
quantum scripserit, nec in officiis ullis nec in amicitia principis fuisse, rursus, cum audis quid studiis laboris inpenderit, nec scripsisse satis nec legisse? Quid est enim quod non aut illae occupationes inpedire aut haec
19 instantia non possit efficere? Itaque soleo ridere, cum 15
me quidam studiosum vocant, qui, si comparer illi, sum desidiosissimus. Ego autem tantum, quem partim publica partim amicorum officia distringunt? quis ex istis qui tota vita litteris adsident collatus illi non quasi
20 somno et inertiae deditus erubescat? Extendi epistu- 20
lam, cum hoc solum quod requirebas scribere destinassem, quos libros reliquisset: confido tamen haec quoque tibi non minus grata quam ipsos libros futura, quae te non tantum ad legendos eos verum etiam ad simile aliquid elaborandum possunt aemulationis stimulis excitare. 25
Vale.

32. (VI.)

C. PLINIUS ANNIO SEVERO SUO S.

A bronze statuette.

1 Ex hereditate quae mihi obvenit emi proxime Corinthium signum, modicum quidem sed festivum et expres-

sum, quantum ego sapio, qui fortasse in omni re, in hac certe perquam exiguum sapio: hoc tamen signum ego quoque intellego. Est enim nudum nec aut vitia, si qua 2 sunt, celat aut laudes parum ostentat: effingit senem 5 stantem; ossa, musculi, nervi, venae, rugae etiam ut spirantis apparent, rari et cedentes capilli, lata frons, contracta facies, exile collum, pendent lacerti, papillae iacent, venter recessit. A tergo quoque eadem aetas ut 3 a tergo. Aes ipsum, quantum verus color indicat, vetus 10 et anticum. Talia denique omnia ut possint artificum oculos tenere, delectare imperitorum. Quod me quam- 4 quam tirunculum sollicitavit ad emendum. Emi autem, non ut haberem domi (neque enim ullum adhuc Corinthium domi habeo), verum ut in patria nostra celebri loco 15 ponerem, ac potissimum in Iovis templo: videtur enim 5 dignum templo, dignum deo donum. Tu ergo, ut soles omnia quae a me tibi iniunguntur, suscipe hanc curam et iam nunc iube basim fieri, ex quo voles marmore, quae nomen meum honoresque capiat, si hos quoque putabis 20 addendos. Ego signum ipsum, ut primum invenero ali- 6 quem qui non gravetur, mittam tibi, vel ipse, quod mavis, adferam mecum. Destino enim, si tamen officii ratio permiserit, excurrere isto. Gaudes quod me venturum esse 7 polliceor, sed contrahes frontem, cum adiecero ad paucos 25 dies: neque enim diutius abesse me eadem haec quae nondum exire patiuntur. Vale.

33. (VII.)

C. PLINIUS CANINIO RUFO SUO S.

Reflections upon the death of Silius Italicus.

Modo nuntiatus est Silius Italicus in Neapolitano suo 1 inedia finisse vitam. Causa mortis valetudo. Erat illi 2

natus insanabilis clavus, cuius taedio ad mortem inrevocabili constantia decucurrit, usque ad supremum diem beatus et felix, nisi quod minorem ex liberis duobus amisit, sed maiorem melioremque florentem atque etiam
3 consularem reliquit. Laeserat famam suam sub Nerone, 5
credebatur sponte accusasse; sed in Vitelli amicitia sapienter se et comiter gesserat, ex proconsulatu Asiae gloriam reportaverat, maculam veteris industriae lauda-
4 bili otio abluerat. Fuit inter principes civitatis sine potentia, sine invidia: salutabatur, colebatur, multumque 10
in lectulo iacens cubiculo semper non ex fortuna frequenti doctissimis sermonibus dies transigebat cum a
5 scribendo vacaret. Scribebat carmina maiore cura quam ingenio, non numquam iudicia hominum recitationibus
6 experiebatur. Novissime ita suadentibus annis ab urbe 15
secessit, seque in Campania tenuit, ac ne adventu quidem
7 novi principis inde commotus est. Magna Caesaris laus, sub quo hoc liberum fuit, magna illius, qui hac libertate ausus est uti. Erat φιλόκαλος usque ad emacitatis rep-
8 rehensionem. Plures isdem in locis villas possidebat 20
adamatisque novis priores neglegebat. Multum ubique librorum, multum statuarum, multum imaginum, quas non habebat modo verum etiam venerabatur, Vergili ante omnes, cuius natalem religiosius quam suum celebrabat, Neapoli maxime, ubi monimentum eius adire ut 25
9 templum solebat. In hac tranquillitate annum quintum et septuagesimum excessit, delicato magis corpore quam infirmo; utque novissimus a Nerone factus est consul, ita postremus ex omnibus quos Nero consules fecerat
10 decessit. Illud etiam notabile, ultimus ex Neronianis 30
consularibus obiit quo consule Nero periit. Quod me
11 recordantem fragilitatis humanae miseratio subit. Quid

enim tam circumcisum, tam breve quam hominis vita longissima? An non videtur tibi Nero modo modo fuisse? cum interim ex eis qui sub illo gesserant consulatum nemo iam superest. Quamquam quid hoc miror? 12
5 nuper L. Piso, pater Pisonis illius qui a Valerio Festo per summum facinus in Africa occisus est, dicere solebat neminem se videre in senatu quem consul ipse sententiam rogavisset. Tam angustis terminis tantae multitudinis 13 vivacitas ipsa concluditur, ut mihi non venia solum dignae
10 verum etiam laude videantur illae regiae lacrimae. Nam ferunt Xerxen, cum immensum exercitum oculis obisset, inlacrimasse, quod tot milibus tam brevis immineret occasus. Sed tanto magis hoc quidquid est temporis 14 futilis et caduci, si non datur factis (nam horum materia
15 in aliena manu), certe studiis proferamus, et quatenus nobis denegatur diu vivere, relinquamus aliquid quo nos vixisse testemur. Scio te stimulis non egere; me tamen 15 tui caritas evocat ut currentem quoque instigem, sicut tu soles me. Ἀγαθὴ δ' ἔρις, cum invicem se mutuis exhorta-
20 tionibus amici ad amorem immortalitatis exacuunt. Vale.

34. (XI.)

C. PLINIUS IULIO GENITORI SUO S.

Pliny's loyalty to Artemidorus.

Est omnino Artemidori nostri tam benigna natura ut 1 officia amicorum in maius extollat: inde etiam meum meritum ut vera ita supra meritum praedicatione circumfert. Equidem, cum essent philosophi ab urbe summoti, 2
25 fui apud illum in suburbano, et quo notabilius, hoc est periculosius esset, fui praetor. Pecuniam etiam, qua

tunc illi ampliore opus erat, ut aes alienum exsolveret
contractum ex pulcherrimis causis, mussantibus magnis
quibusdam et locupletibus amicis, mutuatus ipse gratui-
3 tam dedi. Atque haec feci, cum septem amicis meis aut
occisis aut relegatis, occisis Senecione Rustico Helvidio, 5
relegatis Maurico Gratilla Arria Fannia, tot circa me
iactis fulminibus quasi ambustus mihi quoque inpendere
4 idem exitium certis quibusdam notis augurarer. Non
ideo tamen eximiam gloriam meruisse me, ut ille prae-
5 dicat, credo sed tantum effugisse flagitium. Nam et 10
C. Musonium, socerum eius, quantum licitum est per aetatem, cum admiratione dilexi et Artemidorum ipsum iam
tum, cum in Syria tribunus militarem, arta familiaritate
complexus sum, idque primum non nullius indolis dedi
specimen, quod virum aut sapientem aut proximum simil- 15
6 limumque sapienti intellegere sum visus. Nam ex omnibus qui nunc se philosophos vocant vix unum aut alterum
invenies tanta sinceritate, tanta veritate. Mitto qua patientia corporis hiemes iuxta et aestates ferat, ut nullis
laboribus cedat, ut nihil in cibo, in potu voluptatibus tri- 20
7 buat, ut oculos animumque contineat. Sunt haec magna,
sed in alio; in hoc vero minima, si ceteris virtutibus com-
parentur, quibus meruit ut a C. Musonio ex omnibus om-
8 nium ordinum adsectatoribus gener adsumeretur. Quae
mihi recordanti est quidem iucundum quod me cum apud 25
alios tum apud te tantis laudibus cumulat, vereor tamen
ne modum excedat, quem benignitas eius (illuc enim unde
9 coepi revertor) non solet tenere. Nam in hoc uno interdum vir alioqui prudentissimus honesto quidem sed tamen errore versatur, quod pluris amicos suos quam sunt 30
arbitratur. Vale.

35. (XII.)

C. PLINIUS CATILIO SEVERO SUO S.

Pliny accepts an invitation to dinner.

Veniam ad cenam, sed iam nunc paciscor sit expedita, 1
sit parca, Socraticis tantum sermonibus abundet, in his
quoque teneat modum. Erunt officia antelucana, in quae 2
incidere inpune ne Catoni quidem licuit, quem tamen
5 C. Caesar ita reprehendit ut laudet. Describit enim eos 3
quibus obvius fuerit cum caput ebrii retexissent, erubuisse: deinde adicit 'putares non ab illis Catonem, sed
illos a Catone deprehensos.' Potuitne plus auctoritatis
tribui Catoni quam si ebrius quoque tam venerabilis erat?
10 Nostrae tamen cenae ut apparatus et inpendii sic tempo- 4
ris modus constet. Neque enim ei sumus quos vituperare
ne inimici quidem possint nisi ut simul laudent. Vale.

36. (XIII.)

C. PLINIUS VOCONIO ROMANO SUO S.

The Panegyric is sent to Voconius for criticism.

Librum quo nuper optimo principi consul gratias egi 1
misi exigenti tibi, missurus, etsi non exegisses. In hoc 2
15 consideres velim ut pulchritudinem materiae ita difficultatem. In ceteris enim lectorem novitas ipsa intentum
habet, in hac nota vulgata dicta sunt omnia; quo fit ut
quasi otiosus securusque lector tantum elocutioni vacet,
in qua satisfacere difficilius est, cum sola aestimatur.
20 Atque utinam ordo saltem et transitus et figurae simul 3
spectarentur! Nam invenire praeclare, enuntiare magnifice interdum etiam barbari solent, disponere apte, figu-

4 rare varie nisi eruditis negatum est. Nec vero adfectanda sunt semper elata et excelsa. Nam ut in pictura lumen non alia res magis quam umbra commendat, ita oratio-
5 nem tam summittere quam attollere decet. Sed quid ego haec doctissimo viro? quin potius illud, adnota quae 5 putaveris corrigenda. Ita enim magis credam cetera tibi placere, si quaedam displicuisse cognovero. Vale.

37. (XVI.)

C. PLINIUS NEPOTI SUO S.

Arria's life was as brave as her death.

1 Adnotasse videor facta dictaque virorum feminarumque
2 alia clariora esse alia maiora. Confirmata est opinio mea hesterno Fanniae sermone. Neptis haec Arriae illius 10 quae marito et solacium mortis et exemplum fuit. Multa referebat aviae suae non minora hoc sed obscuriora; quae tibi existimo tam mirabilia legenti fore, quam mihi au-
3 dienti fuerunt. Aegrotabat Caecina Paetus, maritus eius, aegrotabat et filius, uterque mortifere, ut videbatur: 15 filius decessit eximia pulchritudine, pari verecundia, et parentibus non minus ob alia carus, quam quod filius
4 erat. Huic illa ita funus paravit, ita duxit exequias ut ignoraret maritus: quin immo, quotiens cubiculum eius intraret, vivere filium atque etiam commodiorem esse 20 simulabat, ac persaepe interroganti quid ageret puer
5 respondebat 'bene quievit, libenter cibum sumpsit.' Deinde, cum diu cohibitae lacrimae vincerent prorumperentque, egrediebatur: tunc se dolori dabat: satiata siccis oculis composito vultu redibat, tamquam orbitatem 25
6 foris reliquisset. Praeclarum quidem illud eiusdem,

ferrum stringere, perfodere pectus, extrahere pugionem, porrigere marito, addere vocem immortalem ac paene divinam 'Paete, non dolet.' Sed tamen ista facienti, ista dicenti gloria et aeternitas ante oculos erant; quo
5 maius est sine praemio aeternitatis, sine praemio gloriae abdere lacrimas, operire luctum, amissoque filio matrem adhuc agere. Scribonianus arma in Illyrico contra Clau- 7 dium moverat: fuerat Paetus in partibus et occiso Scriboniano Romam trahebatur. Erat ascensurus navem. 8
10 Arria milites orabat ut simul inponeretur. 'Nempe enim' inquit 'daturi estis consulari viro servulos aliquos, quorum e manu cibum capiat, a quibus vestiatur, a quibus calcietur: omnia sola praestabo.' Non impetra- 9 vit: conduxit piscatoriam nauculam ingensque navigium
15 minimo secuta est. Eadem apud Claudium uxori Scriboniani, cum illa profiteretur indicium, 'ego' inquit 'te audiam, cuius in gremio Scribonianus occisus est, et vivis?' Ex quo manifestum est ei consilium pulcherrimae mortis non subitum fuisse. Quin etiam, cum Thra- 10
20 sea, gener eius, deprecaretur ne mori pergeret interque alia dixisset 'vis ergo filiam tuam, si mihi pereundum fuerit, mori mecum?' respondit 'si tam diu tantaque concordia vixerit tecum quam ego cum Paeto, volo.' Auxerat hoc responso curam suorum, attentius custodie- 11
25 batur: sensit et 'nihil agitis' inquit: 'potestis enim efficere ut male moriar, ut non moriar non potestis.' Dum haec dicit, exsiluit cathedra adversoque parieti 12 caput ingenti impetu impegit et corruit. Focilata 'dixeram' inquit 'vobis inventuram me quamlibet duram ad
30 mortem viam, si vos facilem negassetis.' Videnturne 13 haec tibi maiora illo 'Paete, non dolet,' ad quod per haec perventum est? cum interim illud quidem ingens

fama, haec nulla circumfert. Unde colligitur quod initio dixi, alia esse clariora alia maiora. Vale.

38. (XVIII.)

C. PLINIUS CURIO SEVERO SUO S.

About the Panegyric, and how Pliny's friends listened to it for three days.

1 Officium consulatus iniunxit mihi ut rei publicae nomine principi gratias agerem. Quod ego in senatu cum ad rationem et loci et temporis ex more fecissem, bono 5 civi convenientissimum credidi eadem illa spatiosius et 2 uberius volumine amplecti; primum, ut imperatori nostro virtutes suae veris laudibus commendarentur, deinde, ut futuri principes non quasi a magistro, sed tamen sub exemplo praemonerentur qua potissimum via possent ad 10 3 eandem gloriam niti. Nam praecipere qualis esse debeat princeps pulchrum quidem, sed onerosum ac prope superbum est, laudare vero optimum principem ac per hoc posteris velut e specula lumen quod sequantur ostendere 4 idem utilitatis habet, adrogantiae nihil. Cepi autem non 15 mediocrem voluptatem quod, hunc librum cum amicis recitare voluissem, non per codicillos, non per libellos, sed 'si commodum' et 'si valde vacaret' admoniti (numquam porro aut valde vacat Romae aut commodum est audire recitantem), foedissimis insuper tempestatibus, 20 per biduum convenerunt, cumque modestia mea finem recitationi facere voluisset, ut adicerem tertium diem 5 exegerunt. Mihi hunc honorem habitum putem an stu- 6 diis? studiis malo, quae prope extincta refoventur. At cui materiae hanc sedulitatem praestiterunt? nempe quam 25 in senatu quoque, ubi perpeti necesse erat, gravari tamen

vel puncto temporis solebamus, eandem nunc et qui recitare et qui audire triduo velint inveniuntur, non quia
eloquentius quam prius, sed quia liberius, ideoque etiam
libentius scribitur. Accedet ergo hoc quoque laudibus 7
5 principis nostri, quod res antea tam invisa quam falsa
nunc ut vera ita amabilis facta est. Sed ego cum studium 8
audientium tum iudicium mire probavi: animadverti
enim severissima quaeque vel maxime satisfacere. Me- 9
mini quidem me non multis recitasse quod omnibus
10 scripsi, nihilo minus tamen, tamquam sit eadem omnium
futura sententia, hac severitate aurium laetor, ac sicut
olim theatra male musicos canere docuerunt, ita nunc in
spem adducor posse fieri ut eadem theatra bene canere
musicos doceant. Omnes enim qui placendi causa scri- 10
15 bunt qualia placere viderint scribent. Ac mihi quidem
confido in hoc genere materiae laetioris stili constare rationem, cum ea potius quae pressius et adstrictius quam
illa quae hilarius et quasi exultantius scripsi possint
videri arcessita et inducta: non ideo tamen segnius pre-
20 cor ut quandoque veniat dies (utinamque iam venerit!)
quo austeris illis severisque dulcia haec blandaque vel
iusta possessione decedant. Habes acta mea tridui; 11
quibus cognitis volui tantum te voluptatis absentem et
studiorum nomine et meo capere, quantum praesens per-
25 cipere potuisses. Vale.

39. (XIX.)

C. PLINIUS CALVISIO RUFO SUO S.

Pliny asks advice about the purchase of another estate.

Adsumo te in consilium rei familiaris, ut soleo. Prae- 1
dia agris meis vicina atque etiam inserta venalia sunt.

In his me multa sollicitant, aliqua nec minora deterrent.
2 Sollicitat primum ipsa pulchritudo iungendi, deinde quod non minus utile quam voluptuosum posse utraque eadem opera, eodem viatico invisere, sub eodem procuratore ac paene isdem actoribus habere, unam villam colere et 5
3 ornare, alteram tantum tueri. Inest huic computationi sumptus supellectilis, sumptus atriensium, topiariorum, fabrorum atque etiam venatorii instrumenti; quae plurimum refert unum in locum conferas an in diversa dis-
4 pergas. Contra vereor ne sit incautum rem tam magnam 10 isdem tempestatibus, isdem casibus subdere: tutius videtur incerta fortunae possessionum varietatibus experiri. Habet etiam multum iucunditatis soli caelique mutatio
5 ipsaque illa peregrinatio inter sua. Iam, quod deliberationis nostrae caput est, agri sunt fertiles pingues aquosi, 15 constant campis vineis silvis, quae materiam et ex ea
6 reditum sicut modicum ita statum praestant. Sed haec felicitas terrae imbecillis cultoribus fatigatur. Nam possessor prior saepius vendidit pignora, et dum reliqua colonorum minuit ad tempus, vires in posterum exhausit, 20
7 quarum defectione rursus reliqua creverunt. Sunt ergo instruendi eo pluris, quod frugi mancipiis: nam nec ipse usquam vinctos habeo nec ibi quisquam. Superest ut scias quanti videantur posse emi; sestertio tricies, non quia non aliquando quinquagies fuerint, verum et hac 25 penuria colonorum et communi temporis iniquitate ut
8 reditus agrorum sic etiam pretium retro abiit. Quaeris an hoc ipsum tricies facile colligere possimus? sum quidem prope totus in praediis, aliquid tamen faenero, nec molestum erit mutuari; accipiam a socru, cuius arca non 30
9 secus ac mea utor. Proinde hoc te non moveat, si cetera non refragantur, quae velim quam diligentissime exa-

mines. Nam cum in omnibus rebus tum in disponendis facultatibus plurimum tibi et usus et providentiae superest. Vale.

40. (XX.)

C. PLINIUS MESSIO MAXIMO SUO S.

The ballot in the Senate.

Meministine te saepe legisse quantas contentiones exci- 1
5 tarit lex tabellaria quantumque ipsi latori vel gloriae vel reprehensionis attulerit? At nunc in senatu sine ulla 2 dissensione hoc idem ut optimum placuit: omnes comitiorum die tabellas postulaverunt. Excesseramus sane 3 manifestis illis apertisque suffragiis licentiam contio-
10 num. Non tempus loquendi, non tacendi modestia, non denique sedendi dignitas custodiebatur. Magni undique 4 dissonique clamores, procurrebant omnes cum suis candidatis, multa agmina in medio multique circuli et indecora confusio: adeo desciveramus a consuetudine parentum,
15 apud quos omnia disposita moderata tranquilla, maiestatem loci pudoremque retinebant. Supersunt senes, ex 5 quibus audire soleo hunc ordinem comitiorum: citato nomine candidati silentium summum; dicebat ipse pro se, explicabat vitam suam, testes et laudatores dabat,
20 vel eum sub quo militaverat vel eum cui quaestor fuerat vel utrumque, si poterat, addebat quosdam ex suffragatoribus: illi graviter et paucis loquebantur. Plus hoc 6 quam preces proderat. Non numquam candidatus aut natales competitoris aut annos aut etiam mores argue-
25 bat. Audiebat senatus gravitate censoria. Ita saepius digni quam gratiosi praevalebant. Quae nunc inmodico 7 favore corrupta, ad tacita suffragia quasi ad remedium

decucurrerunt; quod interim plane remedium fuit: erat
8 enim novum et subitum. Sed vereor ne procedente tempore ex ipso remedio vitia nascantur. Est enim periculum ne tacitis suffragiis inpudentia inrepat. Nam quoto
9 cuique eadem honestatis cura secreto quae palam? Multi 5
famam, conscientiam pauci verentur. Sed nimis cito de futuris: interim beneficio tabellarum habebimus magistratus qui maxime fieri debuerunt. Nam ut in reciperatoriis iudiciis sic nos in his comitiis quasi repente
10 adprehensi sinceri iudices fuimus. Haec tibi scripsi, 10
primum, ut aliquid novi scriberem, deinde, ut non numquam de re publica loquerer, cuius materiae nobis quanto rarior quam veteribus occasio tanto minus omittenda est.
11 Et hercule quousque illa vulgaria 'quid agis? ecquid commode vales?' Habeant nostrae quoque litterae ali- 15
quid non humile nec sordidum nec privatis rebus inclu-
12 sum. Sunt quidem cuncta sub unius arbitrio, qui pro utilitate communi solus omnium curas laboresque suscepit; quidam tamen salubri temperamento ad nos quoque velut rivi ex illo benignissimo fonte decurrunt, quos et 20
haurire ipsi et absentibus amicis quasi ministrare epistulis possumus. Vale.

41. (XXI)

C. PLINIUS CORNELIO PRISCO SUO S.

Martial's death; an epigram of his in Pliny's honor.

1 Audio Valerium Martialem decessisse et moleste fero. Erat homo ingeniosus acutus acer, et qui plurimum in scribendo et salis haberet et fellis nec candoris minus. 25
2 Prosecutus eram viatico secedentem: dederam hoc amicitiae, dederam etiam versiculis quos de me composuit.

Fuit moris antiqui eos qui vel singulorum laudes vel 3
urbium scripserant aut honoribus aut pecunia ornare;
nostris vero temporibus ut alia speciosa et egregia ita
hoc in primis exolevit. Nam postquam desiimus facere
5 laudanda, laudari quoque ineptum putamus. Quaeris 4
qui sint versiculi quibus gratiam rettuli? Remitterem
te ad ipsum volumen, nisi quosdam tenerem: tu, si placuerint
hi, ceteros in libro requires. Adloquitur Musam, 5
mandat ut domum meam Esquiliis quaerat, adeat reve-
10 renter:

Sed ne tempore non tuo disertam
pulses ebria ianuam videto:
totos dat tetricae dies Minervae,
dum centum studet auribus virorum
15 hoc quod saecula posterique possint
Arpinis quoque comparare chartis.
seras tutior ibis ad lucernas:
haec hora est tua, cum furit Lyaeus,
cum regnat rosa, cum madent capilli:
20 tunc me vel rigidi legant Catones.

Meritone eum qui haec de me scripsit et tunc dimisi ami- 6
cissime et nunc ut amicissimum defunctum esse doleo?
Dedit enim mihi quantum maximum potuit, daturus
amplius, si potuisset. Tametsi quid homini potest dari
25 maius quam gloria et laus et aeternitas? At non erunt
aeterna quae scripsit: non erunt fortasse, ille tamen
scripsit tamquam essent futura. Vale.

LIBER QUARTUS

42. (I.)

C. PLINIUS FABATO PROSOCERO SUO S.

A long deferred visit.

1 Cupis post longum tempus neptem tuam meque una videre. Gratum est utrique nostrum quod cupis; mutuo
2 mehercule. Nam invicem nos incredibili quodam desiderio vestri tenemur, quod non ultra differemus; atque adeo iam sarcinulas alligamus festinaturi, quantum iti- 5
3 neris ratio permiserit. Erit una sed brevis mora: deflectemus in Tuscos, non ut agros remque familiarem oculis subiciamus (id enim postponi potest), sed ut fungamur
4 necessario officio. Oppidum est praediis nostris vicinum, (nomen Tiferni Tiberini,) quod me paene adhuc puerum 10 patronum cooptavit, tanto maiore studio quanto minore iudicio. Adventus meos celebrat, profectionibus angitur,
5 honoribus gaudet. In hoc ego, ut referrem gratiam (nam vinci in amore turpissimum est), templum pecunia mea exstruxi, cuius dedicationem, cum sit paratum, differre 15
6 longius inreligiosum est. Erimus ergo ibi dedicationis die, quem epulo celebrare constitui. Subsistemus fortasse et sequenti, sed tanto magis viam ipsam corripie-
7 mus. Contingat modo te filiamque tuam fortes invenire! nam continget hilares, si nos incolumes receperitis. 20 Vale.

43. (II.)

C. PLINIUS ATTIO CLEMENTI SUO S.

Absurd mourning of Regulus for his son's death.

Regulus filium amisit, hoc uno malo indignus, quod 1
nescio an malum putet. Erat puer acris ingenii sed
ambigui, qui tamen posset recta sectari, si patrem non
referret. Hunc Regulus emancipavit, ut heres matris 2
5 existeret; mancipatum (ita vulgo ex moribus hominis
loquebantur) foeda et insolita parentibus indulgentiae
simulatione captabat. Incredibile, sed Regulum cogita.
Amissum tamen luget insane. Habebat puer mannulos 3
multos et iunctos et solutos, habebat canes maiores mi-
10 noresque, habebat luscinias, psittacos, merulas: omnes
Regulus circa rogum trucidavit. Nec dolor erat ille, 4
sed ostentatio doloris. Convenitur ad eum mira celebritate. Cuncti detestantur oderunt, et quasi probent,
quasi diligant, cursant frequentant, utque breviter quod
15 sentio enuntiem, in Regulo demerendo Regulum imitan-
tur. Tenet se trans Tiberim in hortis, in quibus latis- 5
simum solum porticibus inmensis, ripam statuis suis
occupavit, ut est in summa avaritia sumptuosus, in
summa infamia gloriosus. Vexat ergo civitatem insalu- 6
20 berrimo tempore, et quod vexat solacium putat. Dicit
se velle ducere uxorem: hoc quoque, sicut alia, perverse.
Audies brevi nuptias lugentis, nuptias senis; quorum 7
alterum immaturum alterum serum est. Unde hoc 8
augurer quaeris: non quia adfirmat ipse, quo mendacius
25 nihil est, sed quia certum est Regulum esse facturum
quidquid fieri non oportet. Vale.

44. (VII.)

C. PLINIUS CATIO LEPIDO SUO S.

Regulus an absurd mourner and a bad orator.

1 Saepe tibi dico inesse vim Regulo. Mirum est quam efficiat in quod incubuit. Placuit ei lugere filium; luget ut nemo; placuit statuas eius et imagines quam plurimas facere; hoc omnibus officinis agit, illum coloribus, illum cera, illum aere, illum argento, illum auro, ebore, mar- 5
2 more effingit. Ipse vero nuper adhibito ingenti auditorio librum de vita eius recitavit, de vita pueri: recitavit tamen; eundem in exemplaria mille transscriptum per totam Italiam provinciasque dimisit. Scripsit publice ut a decurionibus eligeretur vocalissimus aliquis ex ipsis 10
3 qui legeret eum populo: factum est. Hanc ille vim, seu quo alio nomine vocanda est intentio quidquid velis obtinendi, si ad potiora vertisset, quantum boni efficere potuisset! Quamquam minor vis bonis quam malis inest, ac sicut ἀμαθία μὲν θράσος λογισμὸς δὲ ὄκνον φέρει, ita recta 15 ingenia debilitat verecundia, perversa confirmat audacia.
4 Exemplo est Regulus. Imbecillum latus, os confusum, haesitans lingua, tardissima inventio, memoria nulla, nihil denique praeter ingenium insanum; et tamen eo inpudentia ipsoque illo furore pervenit ut orator habea- 20
5 tur. Itaque Herennius Senecio mirifice Catonis illud de oratore in hunc e contrario vertit 'orator est vir malus dicendi imperitus.' Non mehercule Cato ipse tam bene
6 verum oratorem quam hic Regulum expressit. Habesne quo tali epistulae parem gratiam referas? habes, si scrip- 25 seris num aliquis in municipio vestro ex sodalibus meis, num etiam ipse tu hunc luctuosum Reguli librum ut cir-

culator in foro legeris, ἐπάρας scilicet, ut ait Demosthenes, τὴν φωνὴν καὶ γεγηθὼς καὶ λαρυγγίζων. Est enim tam 7 ineptus ut risum magis possit exprimere quam gemitum: credas non de puero scriptum sed a puero. Vale.

45. (VIII.)

C. PLINIUS MATURO ARRIANO SUO S.

Pliny succeeds Frontinus in the College of Augurs.

5 Gratularis mihi quod acceperim auguratum. Iure 1 gratularis, primum, quod gravissimi principis iudicium in minoribus etiam rebus consequi pulchrum est, deinde, quod sacerdotium ipsum cum priscum et religiosum tum hoc quoque sacrum plane et insigne est quod non adimi-
10 tur viventi. Nam alia quamquam dignitate propemodum 2 paria ut tribuuntur sic auferuntur, in hoc fortunae hactenus licet ut dari possit. Mihi vero illud etiam gratu- 3 latione dignum videtur quod successi Iulio Frontino, principi viro, qui me nominationis die per hos continuos
15 annos inter sacerdotes nominabat, tamquam in locum suum cooptaret; quod nunc eventus ita conprobavit ut non fortuitum videretur. Te quidem, ut scribis, ob hoc 4 maxime delectat auguratus meus quod M. Tullius augur fuit. Laetaris enim quod honoribus eius insistam quem
20 aemulari studiis cupio. Sed utinam, ut sacerdotium 5 idem, ut consulatum multo etiam iuvenior quam ille sum consecutus, ita senex saltem ingenium eius aliqua ex parte adsequi possim! Sed nimirum, quae sunt in manu 6 hominum et mihi et multis contigerunt, illud vero ut
25 adipisci arduum sic etiam sperare nimium est quod dari non nisi a deis potest. Vale.

46. (X.)

C. PLINIUS STATIO SABINO SUO S.

The known wishes of a testatrix are to be fulfilled, even if not duly expressed.

1 Scribis mihi Sabinam, quae nos reliquit heredes, Modestum servum suum nusquam liberum esse iussisse, eidem tamen sic adscripsisse legatum 'Modesto quem liberum 2 esse iussi.' Quaeris quid sentiam. Contuli cum peritis iuris. Convenit inter omnes nec libertatem deberi, quia 5 non sit data, nec legatum, quia servo suo dederit. Sed mihi manifestus error videtur, ideoque puto nobis, quasi scripserit Sabina, faciendum quod ipsa scripsisse se 3 credidit. Confido accessurum te sententiae meae, cum religiosissime soleas custodire defunctorum voluntatem, 10 quam bonis heredibus intellexisse pro iure est. Neque enim minus apud nos honestas quam apud alios neces-4 sitas valet. Moretur ergo in libertate sinentibus nobis, fruatur legato, quasi omnia diligentissime caverit. Cavit enim quae heredes bene elegit. Vale. 15

47. (XII.)

C. PLINIUS MATURO ARRIANO SUO S.

A scrupulous quaestor.

1 Amas Egnatium Marcellinum atque etiam mihi saepe commendas: amabis magis commendabisque, si cogno-2 veris eius recens factum. Cum in provinciam quaestor exisset scribamque qui sorte obtigerat ante legitimum salarii tempus amisisset, quod acceperat scribae daturus 20 3 intellexit et statuit subsidere apud se non oportere. Ita-

que reversus Caesarem, deinde Caesare auctore senatum consuluit quid fieri de salario vellet. Parva quaestio, sed tamen quaestio. Heredes scribae sibi, praefecti aerarii populo vindicabant. Acta causa est: dixit here- 4
5 dum advocatus, deinde populi, uterque percommode. Caecilius Strabo aerario censuit inferendum, Baebius Macer heredibus dandum: obtinuit Strabo. Tu lauda 5 Marcellinum, ut ego statim feci. Quamvis enim abunde sufficiat illi quod est et a principe et a senatu probatus,
10 gaudebit tamen testimonio tuo. Omnes enim qui gloria 6 famaque ducuntur mirum in modum adsensio et laus a minoribus etiam profecta delectat. Te vero Marcellinus ita reveretur ut iudicio tuo plurimum tribuat. Accedit 7 his quod, si cognoverit factum suum isto usque pene-
15 trasse, necesse est laudis suae spatio et cursu et peregrinatione laetetur. Etenim, nescio quo pacto, vel magis homines iuvat gloria lata quam magna. Vale.

48. (XIII.)

C. PLINIUS TACITO SUO S.

Pliny helps to endow a school at Comum.

Salvum te in urbem venisse gaudeo; venisti autem, si 1 quando alias, nunc maxime mihi desideratus. Ipse pau-
20 culis adhuc diebus in Tusculano commorabor, ut opusculum quod est in manibus absolvam. Vereor enim ne, 2 si hanc intentionem iam in fine intermisero, aegre resumam. Interim ne quid festinationi meae pereat, quod sum praesens petiturus hac quasi praecursoria epistula
25 rogo. Sed prius accipe causas rogandi. Proxime cum 3 in patria mea fui, venit ad me salutandum municipis mei filius praetextatus. Huic ego 'studes?' inquam.

Respondit 'etiam.' 'Ubi?' 'Mediolani.' 'Cur non
hic?' Et pater eius (erat enim una atque etiam ipse
adduxerat puerum) 'quia nullos hic praeceptores habe-
4 mus.' 'Quare nullos? nam vehementer intererat vestra,
qui patres estis,' et opportune conplures patres audie- 5
bant, 'liberos vestros hic potissimum discere. Ubi enim
aut iucundius morarentur quam in patria aut pudicius
continerentur quam sub oculis parentum aut minore
5 sumptu quam domi? Quantulum est ergo collata pecunia conducere praeceptores, quodque nunc in habita- 10
tiones, in viatica, in ea quae peregre emuntur (omnia
autem peregre emuntur) inpenditis adicere mercedibus?
Atque adeo ego, qui nondum liberos habeo, paratus sum
pro re publica nostra, quasi pro filia vel parente, tertiam
6 partem eius quod conferre vobis placebit dare. Totum 15
etiam pollicerer, nisi timerem ne hoc munus meum
quandoque ambitu corrumperetur, ut accidere multis in
7 locis video, in quibus praeceptores publice conducuntur.
Huic vitio occurri uno remedio potest, si parentibus solis
ius conducendi relinquatur isdemque religio recte iudi- 20
8 candi necessitate collationis addatur. Nam qui fortasse
de alieno neglegentes, certe de suo diligentes erunt dabunt-
que operam ne a me pecuniam non nisi dignus accipiat,
9 si accepturus et ab ipsis erit. Proinde consentite, con-
spirate maioremque animum ex meo sumite, qui cupio 25
esse quam plurimum quod debeam conferre. Nihil honestius praestare liberis vestris, nihil gratius patriae
potestis. Educentur hic qui hic nascuntur statimque
ab infantia natale solum amare frequentare consuescant.
Atque utinam tam claros praeceptores inducatis ut fini- 30
timis oppidis studia hinc petantur, utque nunc liberi
vestri aliena in loca, ita mox alieni in hunc locum con-

fluant!' Haec putavi altius et quasi a fonte repetenda, 10
quo magis scires quam gratum mihi foret, si susciperes
quod iniungo. Iniungo autem et pro rei magnitudine
rogo ut ex copia studiosorum, quae ad te ex admiratione
5 ingenii tui convenit, circumspicias praeceptores quos
sollicitare possimus, sub ea tamen condicione ne cui
fidem meam obstringam. Omnia enim libera parentibus
servo. Illi iudicent, illi eligant: ego mihi curam tantum
et inpendium vindico. Proinde si quis fuerit repertus 11
10 qui ingenio suo fidat, eat illuc ea lege ut hinc nihil aliud
certum quam fiduciam suam ferat. Vale.

49. (XVI.)

C. PLINIUS VALERIO PAULINO SUO S.

Pliny's oratory wins approval.

Gaude meo, gaude tuo, gaude etiam publico nomine: 1
adhuc honor studiis durat. Proxime cum dicturus apud
centumviros essem, adeundi mihi locus nisi a tribunali,
15 nisi per ipsos iudices non fuit: tanta stipatione cetera
tenebantur. Ad hoc quidam ornatus adulescens scissis 2
tunicis, ut in frequentia solet fieri, sola velatus toga
perstitit, et quidem horis septem. Nam tam diu dixi
magno cum labore, maiore cum fructu. Studeamus ergo 3
20 nec desidiae nostrae praetendamus alienam. Sunt qui
audiant, sunt qui legant, nos modo dignum aliquid auribus, dignum chartis elaboremus. Vale.

50. (XVII.)

C. PLINIUS ASINIO GALLO SUO S.

Pliny undertakes the case of Corellius's daughter.

Et admones et rogas ut suscipiam causam Corelliae 1
absentis contra C. Caecilium, consulem designatum.

Quod admones gratias ago, quod rogas queror. Admoneri enim debeo, ut sciam, rogari non debeo ut faciam
2 quod mihi non facere turpissimum est. An ego tueri Corelli filiam dubitem? Est quidem mihi cum isto contra quem me advocas non plane familiaris sed tamen 5
3 amicitia. Accedit huc dignitas hominis atque hic ipse cui destinatus est honor; cuius nobis hoc maior habenda reverentia est quod iam illo functi sumus. Naturale est enim ut ea quae quis adeptus est ipse quam amplissima
4 existimari velit. Sed mihi cogitanti adfuturum me 10 Corelli filiae omnia ista frigida et inania videntur. Obversatur oculis ille vir, quo neminem aetas nostra graviorem sanctiorem subtiliorem tulit; quem ego cum ex admiratione diligere coepissem, quod evenire contra solet, magis admiratus sum, postquam penitus inspexi. 15
5 Inspexi enim penitus: nihil a me ille secretum, non
6 ioculare, non serium, non triste, non laetum. Adulescentulus eram, et iam mihi ab illo honor atque etiam, audebo dicere, reverentia ut aequali habebatur. Ille meus in petendis honoribus suffragator et testis, ille 20 in incohandis deductor et comes, ille in gerendis consiliator et rector, ille denique in omnibus officiis nostris, quamquam et inbecillus et senior, quasi iuvenis et vali-
7 dus conspiciebatur. Quantum ille famae meae domi, in
8 publico, quantum etiam apud principem adstruxit! Nam 25 cum forte de bonis iuvenibus apud Nervam imperatorem sermo incidisset et plerique me laudibus ferrent, paulisper se intra silentium tenuit, quod illi plurimum auctoritatis addebat; deinde gravitate quam noras 'necesse est' inquit 'parcius laudem Secundum, quia nihil nisi 30
9 ex consilio meo facit.' Qua voce tribuit mihi quantum petere voto inmodicum erat, nihil me facere non sapien-

tissime, cum omnia ex consilio sapientissimi viri facerem. Quin etiam moriens filiae suae, ut ipsa solet praedicare, 'multos quidem amicos tibi ut longiore vita paravi, praecipuos tamen Secundum et Cornutum.' Quod cum recor-
5 dor, intellego mihi laborandum ne qua parte videar hanc 10
de me fiduciam providentissimi viri destituisse. Quare 11
ego vero Corelliae adero promptissime nec subire offensas recusabo: quamquam non solum veniam me verum etiam laudem apud istum ipsum a quo, ut ais, nova lis fortasse
10 ut feminae intenditur arbitror consecuturum, si haec eadem in actione, latius scilicet et uberius quam epistularum angustiae sinunt, vel in excusationem vel etiam commendationem meam dixero. Vale.

51. (XIX.)

C. PLINIUS CALPURNIAE HISPULLAE SUAE S.

Pliny praises his wife to her aunt.

Cum sis pietatis exemplum fratremque optimum et 1
15 amantissimum tui pari caritate dilexeris filiamque eius ut tuam diligas nec tantum amitae ei adfectum verum etiam patris amissi repraesentes, non dubito maximo tibi gaudio fore, cum cognoveris dignam patre, dignam te, dignam avo evadere. Summum est acumen, summa fru- 2
20 galitas: amat me, quod castitatis indicium est. Accedit his studium litterarum, quod ex mei caritate concepit. Meos libellos habet, lectitat, ediscit etiam. Qua illa 3
sollicitudine, cum videor acturus, quanto, cum egi, gaudio adficitur! Disponit qui nuntient sibi quem adsensum,
25 quos clamores excitarim, quem eventum iudicii tulerim. Eadem, si quando recito, in proximo discreta velo sedet laudesque nostras avidissimis auribus excipit. Versus 4

quidem meos cantat etiam formatque cithara, non artifice aliquo docente sed amore, qui magister est optimus.
5 His ex causis in spem certissimam adducor perpetuam nobis maioremque in dies futuram esse concordiam. Non enim aetatem meam aut corpus, quae paulatim 5
6 occidunt ac senescunt, sed gloriam diligit. Nec aliud decet tuis manibus educatam, tuis praeceptis institutam, quae nihil in contubernio tuo viderit nisi sanctum honestumque, quae denique amare me ex tua praedicatione
7 consueverit. Nam cum matrem meam parentis vice 10 verereris, me a pueritia statim formare, laudare talem-
8 que qualis nunc uxori meae videor ominari solebas. Certatim ergo tibi gratias agimus, ego quod illam mihi, illa quod me sibi dederis, quasi invicem elegeris. Vale.

52. (XXII.)

C. PLINIUS SEMPRONIO RUFO SUO S.

How boldly Junius Mauricus spoke his mind.

1 Interfui principis optimi cognitioni, in consilium ad- 15 sumptus. Gymnicus agon apud Viennenses ex cuiusdam testamento celebrabatur. Hunc Trebonius Rufinus, vir egregius nobisque amicus, in duumviratu tollendum abolendumque curavit. Negabatur ex auctoritate publica
2 fecisse. Egit ipse causam non minus feliciter quam 20 diserte. Conmendabat actionem quod tamquam homo Romanus et bonus civis in negotio suo mature et graviter
3 loquebatur. Cum sententiae perrogarentur, dixit Iunius Mauricus, quo viro nihil firmius, nihil verius, non esse restituendum Viennensibus agona: adiecit 'vellem etiam 25
4 Romae tolli posset.' 'Constanter,' inquis, 'et fortiter.' Quidni? sed hoc a Maurico novum non est. Idem apud

imperatorem Nervam non minus fortiter. Cenabat Nerva cum paucis: Veiento proximus atque etiam in sinu recumbebat: dixi omnia, cum hominem nominavi. Incidit sermo de Catullo Messalino, qui luminibus orba- 5
5 tus ingenio saevo mala caecitatis addiderat: non verebatur, non erubescebat, non miserebatur; quo saepius a Domitiano non secus ac tela, quae et ipsa caeca et inprovida feruntur, in optimum quemque contorquebatur. De huius nequitia sanguinariisque sententiis in commune 6
10 omnes super cenam loquebantur, cum ipse imperator 'quid putamus passurum fuisse, si viveret?' et Mauricus 'nobiscum cenaret.' Longius abii, libens tamen. 7 Placuit agona tolli, qui mores Viennensium infecerat, ut noster hic omnium. Nam Viennensium vitia intra ipsos
15 residunt, nostra late vagantur, utque in corporibus sic in imperio gravissimus est morbus qui a capite diffunditur. Vale.

53. (XXIV.)

C. PLINIUS FABIO VALENTI SUO S.

Great changes since Pliny began to practise at the bar.

Proxime cum apud centumviros in quadruplici iudicio 1 dixissem, subiit recordatio egisse me iuvenem aeque in
20 quadruplici. Processit animus, ut solet, longius: coepi 2 reputare quos in hoc iudicio, quos in illo socios laboris habuissem. Solus eram qui in utroque dixissem: tantas conversiones aut fragilitas mortalitatis aut fortunae mobilitas facit. Quidam ex eis qui tunc egerant decesserunt, 3
25 exsulant alii, huic aetas et valetudo silentium suasit, hic sponte beatissimo otio fruitur, alius exercitum regit, illum civilibus officiis principis amicitia exemit. Circa 4 nos ipsos quam multa mutata sunt! Studiis processi-

mus, studiis periclitati sumus, rursusque processimus.
5 Profuerunt nobis bonorum amicitiae, bonorum obfuerunt iterumque prosunt. Si conputes annos, exiguum tempus,
6 si vices rerum, aevum putes. Quod potest esse documento nihil desperare, nulli rei fidere, cum videamus tot 5
7 varietates tam volubili orbe circumagi. Mihi autem familiare est omnes cogitationes meas tecum communicare isdemque te vel praeceptis vel exemplis monere quibus ipse me moneo; quae ratio huius epistulae fuit. Vale. 10

54. (XXV.)

C. PLINIUS MESSIO MAXIMO SUO S.

Abuse of the ballot in the Senate.

1 Scripseram tibi verendum esse ne ex tacitis suffragiis vitium aliquod existeret. Factum est. Proximis comitiis in quibusdam tabellis multa iocularia atque etiam foeda dictu, in una vero pro candidatorum nominibus
2 suffragatorum nomina inventa sunt. Excanduit senatus 15 magnoque clamore ei qui scripsisset iratum principem est comprecatus. Ille tamen fefellit et latuit, fortasse
3 etiam inter indignantes fuit. Quid hunc putamus domi facere, qui in tanta re tam serio tempore tam scurriliter ludat, qui denique omnino in senatu dicax et urbanus et 20
4 bellus est? Tantum licentiae pravis ingeniis adicit illa fiducia 'quis enim sciet?' Poposcit tabellam, stilum accepit, demisit caput, neminem veretur, se contemnit. Inde ista ludibria scaena et pulpito digna. Quo te vertas? quae remedia conquiras? ubique vitia remediis 25 fortiora. Ἀλλὰ ταῦτα τῷ ὑπὲρ ἡμᾶς μελήσει, cui multum cotidie vigiliarum, multum laboris adicit haec nostra
5 iners et tamen effrenata petulantia. Vale.

LIBER QUINTUS.

55. (I.)

C. PLINIUS ANNIO SEVERO SUO S.

Why Pliny was proud of his legacy.

Legatum mihi obvenit modicum sed amplissimo gratius. 1
Cur amplissimo gratius? Pomponia Galla exheredato filio
Asudio Curiano heredem reliquerat me, dederat coheredes
Sertorium Severum, praetorium virum, aliosque splendi-
5 dos equites Romanos. Curianus orabat ut sibi donarem 2
portionem meam seque praeiudicio iuvarem; eandem
tacita conventione salvam mihi pollicebatur. Responde- 3
bam non convenire moribus meis aliud palam aliud agere
secreto, praeterea non esse satis honestum donare et locu-
10 pleti et orbo, in summa, non profuturum ei, si donassem,
profuturum, si cessissem, esse autem me paratum cedere,
si inique exheredatum mihi liqueret. Ad hoc ille 'rogo 4
cognoscas.' Cunctatus paulum 'faciam' inquam: 'neque
enim video cur ipse me minorem putem quam tibi videor.
15 Sed iam nunc memento non defuturam mihi constantiam,
si ita fides duxerit, secundum matrem tuam pronuntiandi.'
'Ut voles' ait: 'voles enim quod aequissimum.' Adhi- 5
bui in consilium duos quos tunc civitas nostra spectatissimos habuit, Corellium et Frontinum. His circumdatus
20 in cubiculo meo sedi. Dixit Curianus quae pro se puta- 6
bat. Respondi paucis ego; neque enim aderat alius qui
defunctae pudorem tueretur: deinde secessi et ex consilii

sententia 'videtur' inquam, 'Curiane, mater tua iustas habuisse causas irascendi tibi.' Post hoc ille cum ceteris subscripsit centumvirale iudicium, non subscripsit mecum.
7 Adpetebat iudicii dies: coheredes mei conponere et transigere cupiebant, non diffidentia causae sed metu tem- 5 porum. Verebantur quod videbant multis accidisse, ne
8 ex centumvirali iudicio capitis rei exirent. Et erant quidam in illis quibus obici et Gratillae amicitia et Rustici posset. Rogant me ut cum Curiano loquar.
9 Convenimus in aedem Concordiae. Ibi ego 'si mater' 10 inquam 'te ex parte quarta scripsisset heredem, num queri posses? Quid si heredem quidem instituisset ex asse, sed legatis ita exhausisset ut non amplius apud te quam quarta remaneret? Igitur sufficere tibi debet, si exheredatus a matre quartam partem ab heredibus eius 15
10 accipias, quam tamen ego augebo. Scis te non subscripsisse mecum et iam biennium transisse omniaque me usu cepisse. Sed ut te coheredes mei tractabiliorem experiantur utque tibi nihil abstulerit reverentia mei, offero
11 pro mea parte tantundem.' Tuli fructum non conscien- 20 tiae modo verum etiam famae. Ille ergo Curianus legatum mihi reliquit et factum meum, nisi forte blandior
12 mihi, anticum notabili honore signavit. Haec tibi scripsi, quia de omnibus quae me vel delectant vel angunt non aliter tecum quam mecum loqui soleo; deinde, 25 quod durum existimabam te amantissimum mei fraudare
13 voluptate quam ipse capiebam. Neque enim sum tam sapiens ut nihil mea intersit an eis quae honeste fecisse me credo testificatio quaedam et quasi praemium accedat. Vale.

56. (II.)

C. PLINIUS CALPURNIO FLACCO SUO S.

Thanks for a gift of thrushes.

Accepi pulcherrimos turdos, cum quibus parem calcu- 1
lum ponere nec urbis copiis ex Laurentino nec maris
tam turbidis tempestatibus possum. Recipies ergo epis- 2
tulas steriles et simpliciter ingratas ac ne illam quidem
5 sollertiam Diomedis in permutando munere imitantes.
Sed, quae facilitas tua, hoc magis dabis veniam quod
se non mereri fatentur. Vale.

57. (V.)

C. PLINIUS NONIO MAXIMO SUO S.

The death of Fannius and how he had been forewarned in a dream.

Nuntiatum mihi est C. Fannium decessisse, qui nuntius 1
me gravi dolore confudit, primum, quod amavi hominem
10 elegantem disertum, deinde, quod iudicio eius uti solebam. Erat enim acutus natura, usu exercitatus, veritate
promptissimus. Angit me super ista casus ipsius : deces- 2
sit vetere testamento, omisit quos maxime diligebat, prosecutus est quibus offensior erat. Sed hoc utcumque
15 tolerabile, gravius illud, quod pulcherrimum opus imper-
fectum reliquit. Quamvis enim agendis causis distrin- 3
geretur, scribebat tamen exitus occisorum aut relega-
torum a Nerone, et iam tres libros absolverat, subtiles
et diligentes et Latinos atque inter sermonem historiam-
20 que medios, ac tanto magis reliquos perficere cupiebat
quanto frequentius hi lectitabantur. Mihi autem videtur 4

acerba semper et inmatura mors eorum qui immortale aliquid parant. Nam qui voluptatibus dediti quasi in diem vivunt vivendi causas cotidie finiunt; qui vero posteros cogitant et memoriam sui operibus extendunt, his nulla mors non repentina est, ut quae semper incoha- 5
5 tum aliquid abrumpat. Gaius quidem Fannius, quod accidit, multo ante praesensit. Visus est sibi per nocturnam quietem iacere in lectulo suo compositus in habitu studentis, habere ante se scrinium (ita solebat): mox imaginatus est venisse Neronem, in toro resedisse, prompsisse 10 primum librum quem de sceleribus eius ediderat eumque ad extremum revolvisse, idem in secundo ac tertio fecisse,
6 tunc abisse. Expavit et sic interpretatus est, tamquam idem sibi futurus esset scribendi finis qui fuisset illi
7 legendi, et fuit idem. Quod me recordantem miseratio 15 subit quantum vigiliarum, quantum laboris exhauserit frustra. Occursant animo mea mortalitas, mea scripta. Nec dubito te quoque eadem cogitatione terreri pro istis
8 quae inter manus habes. Proinde, dum suppetit vita, enitamur ut mors quam paucissima quae abolere possit 20 inveniat. Vale.

58. (X.)

C. PLINIUS SUETONIO TRANQUILLO SUO S.

Suetonius is begged not to delay longer the publication of his work.

1 Libera tandem hendecasyllaborum meorum fidem, qui scripta tua communibus amicis spoponderunt. Appellantur cotidie et flagitantur, ac iam periculum est ne
2 cogantur ad exhibendum formulam accipere. Sum et 25 ipse in edendo haesitator, tu tamen meam quoque cunctationem tarditatemque vicisti. Proinde aut rumpe iam

moras aut cave ne eosdem istos libellos, quos tibi hendecasyllabi nostri blanditiis elicere non possunt, convicio scazontes extorqueant. Perfectum opus absolutumque 3 est, nec iam splendescit lima sed atteritur. Patere me 5 videre titulum tuum, patere audire describi legi venire volumina Tranquilli mei. Aecum est nos in amore tam mutuo eandem percipere ex te voluptatem, qua tu perfrueris ex nobis. Vale.

59. (XIV.)

C. PLINIUS PONTIO SUO S.

Pliny's friend and colleague, Cornutus Tertullus.

Secesseram in municipium, cum mihi nuntiatum est 1 10 Cornutum Tertullum accepisse Aemiliae viae curam. Exprimere non possum quanto sim gaudio adfectus et 2 ipsius et meo nomine; ipsius, quod, sit licet, sicut est, ab omni ambitione longe remotus, debet tamen ei iucundus honor esse ultro datus; meo, quod aliquanto magis 15 me delectat mandatum mihi officium, postquam par Cornuto datum video. Neque enim augeri dignitate quam 3 aequari bonis gratius. Cornuto autem quid melius? quid sanctius? quid in omni genere laudis ad exemplar antiquitatis expressius? quod mihi cognitum est non fama, 20 qua alioqui optima et meritissima fruitur, sed longis magnisque experimentis. Una diligimus, una dileximus 4 omnes fere quos aetas nostra in utroque sexu aemulandos tulit; quae societas amicitiarum artissima nos familiaritate coniunxit. Accessit vinculum necessitudinis publi- 5 25 cae. Idem enim mihi, ut scis, collega quasi voto petitus in praefectura aerarii fuit, fuit et in consulatu. Tum

ego qui vir et quantus esset altissime inspexi, cum sequerer ut magistrum, ut parentem vererer, quod non tam
6 aetatis maturitate quam vitae merebatur. His ex causis ut illi sic mihi gratulor, nec privatim magis quam publice, quod tandem homines non ad pericula, ut prius, verum 5
7 ad honores virtute perveniunt. In infinitum epistulam extendam, si gaudio meo indulgeam. Praevertor ad ea
8 quae me agentem hic nuntius deprehendit. Eram cum prosocero meo, eram cum amita uxoris, eram cum amicis diu desideratis, circumibam agellos, audiebam multum 10 rusticarum querellarum, rationes legebam invitus et cursim (aliis enim chartis, aliis sum litteris initiatus), coepe-
9 ram etiam itineri me praeparare. Nam includor angustiis commeatus, eoque ipso quod delegatum Cornuto audio officium mei admoneor. Cupio te quoque sub idem tempus 15 Campania tua remittat, ne quis, cum in urbem rediero, contubernio nostro dies pereat. Vale.

60. (XVI.)

C. PLINIUS MARCELLINO SUO S.

Sad death of Fundanus's young daughter.

1 Tristissimus haec tibi scribo, Fundani nostri filia minore defuncta, qua puella nihil umquam festivius, amabilius, nec modo longiore vita sed prope immortalitate 20
2 dignius vidi. Nondum annos quattuordecim impleverat, et iam illi anilis prudentia, matronalis gravitas erat, et
3 tamen suavitas puellaris cum virginali verecundia. Ut illa patris cervicibus inhaerebat! ut nos amicos paternos et amanter et modeste complectebatur! ut nutrices, ut 25 paedagogos, ut praeceptores pro suo quemque officio dili-

gebat! quam studiose, quam intellegenter lectitabat! ut parce custoditeque ludebat! Qua illa temperantia, qua patientia, qua etiam constantia novissimam valetudinem tulit! Medicis obsequebatur, sororem, patrem adhorta- 4
5 batur, ipsamque se destitutam corporis viribus vigore animi sustinebat. Duravit hic illi usque ad extremum 5 nec aut spatio valetudinis aut metu mortis infractus est, quo plures gravioresque nobis causas relinqueret et desiderii et doloris. O triste plane acerbumque funus! o 6
10 morte ipsa mortis tempus indignius! iam destinata erat egregio iuveni, iam electus nuptiarum dies, iam nos vocati. Quod gaudium quo maerore mutatum est! Non 7 possum exprimere verbis quantum animo vulnus acceperim, cum audivi Fundanum ipsum, ut multa luctuosa
15 dolor invenit, praecipientem, quod in vestes margarita gemmas fuerat erogaturus, hoc in tus et unguenta et odores inpenderetur. Est quidem ille eruditus et sa- 8 piens, ut qui se ab ineunte aetate altioribus studiis artibusque dediderit, sed nunc omnia quae audiit saepe, quae
20 dixit aspernatur expulsisque virtutibus aliis pietatis est totus. Ignosces, laudabis etiam, si cogitaveris quid ami- 9 serit. Amisit enim filiam quae non minus mores eius quam os vultumque referebat totumque patrem mira similitudine exscripserat. Proinde si quas ad eum de 10
25 dolore tam iusto litteras mittes, memento adhibere solacium, non quasi castigatorium et nimis forte, sed molle et humanum. Quod ut facilius admittat multum faciet medii temporis spatium. Ut enim crudum adhuc vulnus 11 medentium manus reformidat, deinde patitur atque ultro
30 requirit, sic recens animi dolor consolationes reicit ac refugit, mox desiderat et clementer admotis adquiescit. Vale.

61. (XVIII.)

C. PLINIUS CALPURNIO MACRO SUO S.

Country joys.

1 Bene est mihi, quia tibi bene est. Habes uxorem tecum, habes filium; frueris mari, fontibus, viridibus, agro, villa amoenissima. Neque enim dubito esse amoenissimam, in qua se conposuerat homo felicior ante quam 2 felicissimus fieret. Ego in Tuscis et venor et studeo, 5 quae interdum alternis interdum simul facio, nec tamen adhuc possum pronuntiare utrum sit difficilius capere aliquid an scribere. Vale.

62. (XXI.)

C. PLINIUS SATURNINO SUO S.

Illness of Julius Valens and death of Julius Avitus.

1 Varie me adfecerunt litterae tuae: nam partim laeta partim tristia continebant: laeta, quod te in urbe teneri 10 nuntiabant; 'nollem' inquis, sed ego volo: praeterea, quod recitaturum statim ut venissem pollicebantur; ago 2 gratias quod expector. Triste illud quod Iulius Valens graviter iacet; quamquam ne hoc quidem triste, si illius utilitatibus aestimetur, cuius interest quam maturissime 15 3 inexplicabili morbo liberari. Illud plane non triste solum verum etiam luctuosum quod Iulius Avitus decessit, dum ex quaestura redit, decessit in navi, procul a fratre 4 amantissimo, procul a matre, a sororibus. Nihil ista ad mortuum pertinent, sed pertinuerunt, cum moreretur, 20 pertinent ad hos qui supersunt. Iam quod in flore primo tantae indolis iuvenis extinctus est, summa conse-

cuturus, si virtutes eius maturuissent. Quo ille studio- 5
rum amore flagrabat! quantum legit, quantum etiam
scripsit! quae nunc omnia cum ipso sine fructu posteri-
tatis abierunt. Sed quid ego indulgeo dolori? cui si 6
5 frenos remittas, nulla materia non maxima est. Finem
epistulae faciam, ut facere possim etiam lacrimis quas
epistula expressit. Vale.

LIBER SEXTUS.

63. (II.)

C. PLINIUS ARRIANO SUO S.

The death of Regulus a loss to the bar.

1 Soleo non numquam in iudiciis quaerere M. Regulum, 2 nolo enim dicere, desiderare. Cur ergo quaero? Habebat studiis honorem, timebat, pallebat, scribebat, quamvis non posset ediscere. Illud ipsum, quod oculum modo dextrum modo sinistrum circumlinebat, dextrum, si a 5 petitore, alterum, si a possessore esset acturus, quod candidum splenium in hoc aut in illud supercilium transferebat, quod semper haruspices consulebat de actionis eventu, a nimia superstitione, sed tamen et a magno 3 studiorum honore veniebat. Iam illa perquam iucunda 10 una dicentibus, quod libera tempora petebat, quod audituros corrogabat. Quid enim iucundius quam sub alterius invidia quam diu velis et in alieno auditorio quasi 4 deprehensum commode dicere? Sed utcumque se habent ista, bene fecit Regulus quod est mortuus; melius, si 15 ante. Nunc enim sane poterat sine malo publico vivere sub eo principe sub quo nocere non poterat. Ideo fas 5 est non numquam eum quaerere. Nam postquam obiit ille, increbruit passim et invaluit consuetudo binas vel singulas clepsydras, interdum etiam dimidias et dandi et 20 petendi. Nam et qui dicunt egisse malunt quam agere et qui audiunt finire quam iudicare. Tanta neglegentia, tanta desidia, tanta denique inreverentia studiorum peri-

culorumque est. An nos sapientiores maioribus nostris, 6
nos legibus ipsis iustiores, quae tot horas, tot dies, tot
comperendinationes largiuntur? hebetes illi et supra
modum tardi, nos apertius dicimus, celerius intellegimus,
5 religiosius iudicamus, quia paucioribus clepsydris prae-
cipitamus causas quam diebus explicari solebant? O 7
Regule, qui ambitione ab omnibus obtinebas quod fidei
paucissimi praestant! Equidem quotiens iudico, quod
vel saepius facio quam dico, quantum quis plurimum
10 postulat aquae do. Etenim temerarium existimo divi- 8
nare quam spatiosa sit causa inaudita tempusque negotio
finire cuius modum ignores, praesertim cum primam
religioni suae iudex patientiam debeat, quae pars magna
iustitiae est. At quaedam supervacua dicuntur. Etiam:
15 sed satius est et haec dici quam non dici necessaria.
Praeterea an sint supervacua, nisi cum audieris, scire 9
non possis. Sed de his melius coram, ut de pluribus
vitiis civitatis. Nam tu quoque amore communium
soles emendari cupere quae iam corrigere difficile est.
20 Nunc respiciamus domos nostras. Ecquid omnia in tua 10
recte? in mea novi nihil. Mihi autem et gratiora sunt
bona, quod perseverant, et leviora incommoda, quod
adsuevi. Vale.

64. (III.)

C. PLINIUS VERO SUO S.

The little farm given by Pliny to his old nurse.

Gratias ago quod agellum quem nutrici meae donave- 1
25 ram colendum suscepisti. Erat, cum donarem, centum
milium nummum: postea decrescente reditu etiam pretium minuit, quod nunc te curante reparabit. Tu modo 2

memineris commendari tibi a me non arbores et terram, quamquam haec quoque, sed munusculum meum; quod esse quam fructuosissimum non illius magis interest quae accepit quam mea qui dedi. Vale.

65. (IV.)

C. PLINIUS CALPURNIAE SUAE S.

Letter to his absent wife.

1 Numquam sum magis de occupationibus meis questus, 5 quae me non sunt passae aut proficiscentem te valetudinis causa in Campaniam prosequi aut profectam e vestigio 2 subsequi. Nunc enim praecipue simul esse cupiebam, ut oculis meis crederem quid viribus, quid corpusculo adpa-rares, ecquid denique secessus voluptates regionisque 10 3 abundantiam inoffensa transmitteres. Equidem etiam fortem te non sine cura desiderarem; est enim suspensum et anxium de eo quem ardentissime diligas interdum 4 nihil scire: nunc vero me cum absentiae tum infirmitatis tuae ratio incerta et varia sollicitudine exterret. Vereor 15 omnia, imaginor omnia, quaeque natura metuentum est, 5 ea maxime mihi quae maxime abominor fingo. Quo in-pensius rogo ut timori meo cotidie singulis vel etiam binis epistulis consulas. Ero enim securior, dum lego, statim-que timebo, cum legero. Vale. 20

66. (VI.)

C. PLINIUS FUNDANO SUO S.

Fundanus is asked to favor the candidacy of Julius Naso.

1 Si quando, nunc praecipue cuperem esse te Romae, et sis rogo. Opus est mihi voti laboris sollicitudinis socio.

Petit honores Iulius Naso, petit cum multis, cum bonis, quos ut gloriosum sic est difficile superare. Pendeo ergo 2 et exerceor spe, adficior metu, et me consularem esse non sentio: nam rursus mihi videor omnium quae decucurri
5 candidatus. Meretur hanc curam longa mei caritate. 3 Est mihi cum illo non sane paterna amicitia; neque enim esse potuit per meam aetatem: solebat tamen vixdum adulescentulo mihi pater eius cum magna laude monstrari. Erat non studiorum tantum verum etiam studio-
10 sorum amantissimus, ac prope cotidie ad audiendos, quos tunc ego frequentabam, Quintilianum, Niceten Sacerdotem ventitabat, vir alioqui clarus et gravis et qui prodesse filio memoria sui debeat. Sed multi nunc in senatu qui- 4 bus ignotus ille, multi quibus notus, sed non nisi viventes
15 reverentur: quo magis huic omissa gloria patris, in qua magnum ornamentum, gratia infirma, ipsi enitendum, ipsi elaborandum est. Quod quidem semper, quasi pro- 5 videret hoc tempus, sedulo fecit: paravit amicos, quos paraverat coluit, me certe, ut primum sibi iudicare per-
20 misit, ad amorem imitationemque delegit. Dicenti mihi 6 sollicitus adsistit, adsidet recitanti: primis etiam et cum maxime nascentibus opusculis meis interest, nunc solus, ante cum fratre, cuius nuper amissi ego suscipere partes, ego vicem debeo inplere. Doleo enim et illum inmatura 7
25 morte indignissime raptum et hunc optimi fratris adiumento destitutum solisque amicis relictum. Quibus ex 8 causis exigo ut venias et suffragio meo tuum iungas. Permultum interest mea te ostentare, tecum circumire. Ea est auctoritas tua ut putem me efficacius tecum etiam
30 meos amicos rogaturum. Abrumpe, si qua te retinent: 9 hoc tempus meum, hoc fides, hoc etiam dignitas postulat. Suscepi candidatum, et suscepisse me notum est: ego

ambio, ego periclitor: in summa, si datur Nasoni quod petit, illius honor; si negatur, mea repulsa est. Vale.

67. (IX.)

C. PLINIUS TACITO SUO S.

Tacitus has begged Pliny to support Julius Naso.

1 Commendas mihi Iulium Nasonem candidatum. Nasonem mihi? quid si me ipsum? Fero tamen et ignosco. Eundem enim commendassem tibi, si te Romae morante 5 ipse afuissem. Habet hoc sollicitudo, quod omnia necessaria putat. 2 Tu tamen, censeo, alios roges; ego precum tuarum minister adiutor particeps ero. Vale.

68. (X.)

C. PLINIUS ALBINO SUO S.

Pliny's mother-in-law owns a villa which once belonged to Verginius Rufus.

1 Cum venissem in socrus meae villam Alsiensem, quae aliquando Rufi Vergini fuit, ipse mihi locus optimi illius 10 et maximi viri desiderium non sine dolore renovavit. Hunc enim colere secessum atque etiam senectutis suae nidulum vocare consueverat. 2 Quocumque me contulissem, illum animus, illum oculi requirebant. Libuit etiam 3 monimentum eius videre, et vidisse paenituit. Est enim 15 adhuc inperfectum, nec difficultas operis in causa, modici ac potius exigui, sed inertia eius cui cura mandata est. Subit indignatio cum miseratione, post decimum mortis annum reliquias neglectumque cinerem sine titulo, sine nomine iacere. cuius memoria orbem terrarum gloria per- 20

vagetur. At ille mandaverat caveratque ut divinum illud 4
et immortale factum versibus inscriberetur:

Hic situs est Rufus, pulso qui Vindice quondam
imperium adseruit non sibi sed patriae.

5 Tam rara in amicitiis fides, tam parata oblivio mortuorum 5
ut ipsi nobis debeamus etiam conditoria exstruere omniaque heredum officia praesumere. Nam cui non est ve- 6
rendum quod videmus accidisse Verginio? cuius iniuriam
ut indigniorem sic etiam notiorem ipsius claritas facit.
10 Vale.

69. (XV.)

C. PLINIUS ROMANO SUO S.

Rude witticism of a famous jurist.

Mirificae rei non interfuisti: ne ego quidem; sed me 1
recens fabula excepit. Passennus Paullus, splendidus
eques Romanus et in primis eruditus, scribit elegos.
Gentilicium hoc illi: est enim municeps Properti atque
15 etiam inter maiores suos Propertium numerat. Is cum 2
recitaret, ita coepit dicere 'Prisce, iubes.' Ad hoc Iavolenus Priscus (aderat enim, ut Paullo amicissimus) 'ego
vero non iubeo.' Cogita qui risus hominum, qui ioci.
Est omnino Priscus dubiae sanitatis, interest tamen offi- 3
20 ciis, adhibetur consiliis atque etiam ius civile publice
respondet: quo magis quod tunc fecit et ridiculum et
notabile fuit. Interim Paullo aliena deliratio aliquantum 4
frigoris attulit. Tam sollicite recitaturis providendum
est non solum ut sint ipsi sani verum etiam ut sanos
25 adhibeant. Vale.

70. (XVI.)

C. PLINIUS TACITO SUO S.

How Pliny the Elder perished in the eruption of Vesuvius

1 Petis ut tibi avunculi mei exitum scribam, quo verius
tradere posteris possis. Gratias ago: nam video morti
eius, si celebretur a te, immortalem gloriam esse proposi-
2 tam. Quamvis enim pulcherrimarum clade terrarum, ut
populi, ut urbes, memorabili casu quasi semper victurus 5
occiderit, quamvis ipse plurima opera et mansura condi-
derit; multum tamen perpetuitati eius scriptorum tuorum
3 aeternitas addet. Equidem beatos puto quibus deorum
munere datum est aut facere scribenda aut scribere
legenda, beatissimos vero quibus utrumque. Horum in 10
numero avunculus meus et suis libris et tuis erit. Quo
4 libentius suscipio, deposco etiam quod iniungis. Erat
Miseni classemque imperio praesens regebat. Nonum
Kal. Septembres, hora fere septima, mater mea indicat
ei apparere nubem inusitata et magnitudine et specie. 15
5 Usus ille sole, mox frigida, gustaverat iacens studebat-
que: poscit soleas, ascendit locum ex quo maxime miraculum illud conspici poterat. Nubes, incertum procul
intuentibus ex quo monte (Vesuvium fuisse postea cognitum est), oriebatur, cuius similitudinem et formam non 20
6 alia magis arbor quam pinus expresserit. Nam longis-
simo velut trunco elata in altum quibusdam ramis diffun-
debatur, credo, quia recenti spiritu evecta, dein senescente
eo destituta aut etiam pondere suo victa in latitudinem
vanescebat; candida interdum, interdum sordida et macu- 25
7 losa, prout terram cineremve sustulerat. Magnum pro-
piusque noscendum, ut eruditissimo viro, visum. Iubet

Liburnicam aptari: mihi, si venire una vellem, facit
copiam: respondi studere me malle, et forte ipse quod
scriberem dederat. Egrediebatur domo: accipit codicil- 8
los Rectinae Tasci inminenti periculo exterritae (nam
5 villa eius subiacebat, nec ulla nisi navibus fuga): ut se
tanto discrimini eriperet orabat. Vertit ille consilium et 9
quod studioso animo incohaverat obit maximo. Deducit
quadriremes, ascendit ipse, non Rectinae modo sed multis
(erat enim frequens amoenitas orae) laturus auxilium.
10 Properat illuc unde alii fugiunt, rectumque cursum, recta 10
gubernacula in periculum tenet, adeo solutus metu ut
omnis illius mali motus, omnis figuras, ut deprenderat
oculis, dictaret enotaretque. Iam navibus cinis incide- 11
bat, quo propius accederent, calidior et densior, iam
15 pumices etiam nigrique et ambusti et fracti igne lapides,
iam vadum subitum ruinaque montis litora obstantia.
Cunctatus paulum an retro flecteret, mox gubernatori ut
ita faceret monenti 'fortes' inquit 'fortuna iuvat: Pomponianum pete.' Stabiis erat, diremptus sinu medio; 12
20 nam sensim circumactis curvatisque litoribus mare infun-
ditur. Ibi, quamquam nondum periculo adpropinquante,
conspicuo tamen, et cum cresceret, proximo, sarcinas contulerat in naves, certus fugae, si contrarius ventus rese-
disset; quo tunc avunculus meus secundissimo invectus
25 conplectitur trepidantem, consolatur, hortatur, utque timorem eius sua securitate leniret, deferri in balineum iubet:
lotus accubat, cenat aut hilaris aut, quod aeque magnum,
similis hilari. Interim e Vesuvio monte pluribus in locis 13
latissimae flammae altaque incendia relucebant, quorum
30 fulgor et claritas tenebris noctis excitabatur. Ille agres-
tium trepidatione ignes relictos desertasque villas per
solitudinem ardere in remedium formidinis dictitabat.

Tum se quieti dedit, et quievit verissimo quidem somno. Nam meatus animae, qui illi propter amplitudinem corporis gravior et sonantior erat, ab eis qui limini obversa-
14 bantur audiebatur. Sed area ex qua diaeta adibatur ita iam cinere mixtisque pumicibus oppleta surrexerat ut, si 5 longior in cubiculo mora, exitus negaretur. Excitatus procedit seque Pomponiano ceterisque qui pervigilave-
15 rant reddit. In commune consultant, intra tecta subsistant an in aperto vagentur. Nam crebris vastisque tremoribus tecta nutabant et quasi emota sedibus suis 10
16 nunc huc nunc illuc abire aut referri videbantur. Sub dio rursus quamquam levium exesorumque pumicum casus metuebatur; quod tamen periculorum collatio elegit. Et apud illum quidem ratio rationem, apud alios timorem timor vicit. Cervicalia capitibus inposita lin- 15 teis constringunt: id munimentum adversus incidentia
17 fuit. Iam dies alibi, illic nox omnibus noctibus nigrior densiorque; quam tamen faces multae variaque lumina solabantur. Placuit egredi in litus et ex proximo aspicere ecquid iam mare admitteret; quod adhuc vastum et 20
18 adversum permanebat. Ibi super abiectum linteum recubans semel atque iterum frigidam aquam poposcit hausitque. Deinde flammae flammarumque praenuntius odor
19 sulpuris alios in fugam vertunt, excitant illum. Innitens servulis duobus adsurrexit, et statim concidit, ut ego 25 colligo, crassiore caligine spiritu obstructo clausoque stomacho, qui illi natura invalidus et angustus et fre-
20 quenter aestuans erat. Ubi dies redditus (is ab eo quem novissime viderat tertius), corpus inventum integrum, inlaesum opertumque ut fuerat indutus: habitus corporis 30
21 quiescenti quam defuncto similior. Interim Miseni ego et mater — sed nihil ad historiam, nec tu aliud quam de

exitu eius scire voluisti. Finem ergo faciam. Unum 22
adiciam omnia me quibus interfueram quaeque statim,
cum maxime vera memorantur, audieram persecutum.
Tu potissima excerpes. Aliud est enim epistulam aliud
5 historiam, aliud amico aliud omnibus scribere. Vale.

71. (XX.)

C. PLINIUS TACITO SUO S.

Experience of Pliny and his mother during the eruption of Vesuvius.

Ais te adductum litteris quas exigenti tibi de morte 1
avunculi mei scripsi cupere cognoscere quos ego Miseni
relictus (id enim ingressus abruperam) non solum metus
verum etiam casus pertulerim. 'Quamquam animus me-
10 minisse horret, incipiam.' Profecto avunculo ipse reli- 2
quum tempus studiis (ideo enim remanseram) inpendi:
mox balineum, cena, somnus inquietus et brevis. Prae- 3
cesserat per multos dies tremor terrae minus formi-
dolosus quia Campaniae solitus. Illa vero nocte ita
15 invaluit ut non moveri omnia sed verti crederentur. In- 4
rumpit cubiculum meum mater: surgebam, invicem, si
quiesceret, excitaturus. Residimus in area domus, quae
mare a tectis modico spatio dividebat. Dubito constan- 5
tiam vocare an inprudentiam debeam; agebam enim duo-
20 devicesimum annum: posco librum Titi Livi et quasi
per otium lego atque etiam, ut coeperam, excerpo. Ecce,
amicus avunculi, qui nuper ad eum ex Hispania venerat,
ut me et matrem sedentes, me vero etiam legentem videt,
illius patientiam, securitatem meam corripit: nihilo seg-
25 nius ego intentus in librum. Iam hora diei prima, et 6
adhuc dubius et quasi languidus dies. Iam quassatis

circumiacentibus tectis, quamquam in aperto loco, an-
7 gusto tamen, magnus et certus ruinae metus. Tum demum excedere oppido visum: sequitur vulgus attonitum,
quodque in pavore simile prudentiae, alienum consilium
suo praefert ingentique agmine abeuntis premit et in- 5
8 pellit. Egressi tecta consistimus. Multa ibi miranda,
multas formidines patimur. Nam vehicula quae produci
iusseramus, quamquam in planissimo campo, in contra-
rias partes agebantur ac ne lapidibus quidem fulta in
9 eodem vestigio quiescebant. Praeterea mare in se resor- 10
beri et tremore terrae quasi repelli videbamus. Certe
processerat litus multaque animalia maris siccis harenis
detinebat. Ab altero latere nubes atra et horrenda ignei
spiritus tortis vibratisque discursibus rupta in longas
flammarum figuras dehiscebat: fulguribus illae et similes 15
10 et maiores erant. Tum vero idem ille ex Hispania amicus acrius et instantius 'si frater' inquit 'tuus, tuus
avunculus vivit, vult esse vos salvos: si periit, super-
stites voluit: proinde quid cessatis evadere?' Respon-
dimus non commissuros nos ut de salute illius incerti 20
11 nostrae consuleremus. Non moratus ultra proripit se
effusoque cursu periculo aufertur. Nec multo post illa
nubes descendere in terras, operire maria: cinxerat Capreas et absconderat: Miseni quod procurrit abstulerat.
12 Tum mater orare, hortari, iubere quoquo modo fugerem; 25
posse enim iuvenem, se et annis et corpore gravem bene
morituram, si mihi causa mortis non fuisset. Ego contra salvum me nisi una non futurum: dein manum eius
amplexus, addere gradum cogo. Paret aegre incusatque
13 se quod me moretur. Iam cinis, adhuc tamen rarus: 30
respicio; densa caligo tergis imminebat, quae nos tor-
rentis modo infusa terrae sequebatur. 'Deflectamus'

inquam, 'dum videmus ne in via strati comitantium turba in tenebris obteramur.' Vix consideramus, et nox, non qualis inlunis aut nubila, sed qualis in locis clausis lumine extincto. Audires ululatus feminarum, infantum quiritatus, clamores virorum: alii parentes, alii liberos, alii coniuges vocibus requirebant, vocibus noscitabant: hi suum casum, illi suorum miserabantur: erant qui metu mortis mortem precarentur: multi ad deos manus tollere, plures nusquam iam deos ullos, aeternamque illam et novissimam noctem mundo interpretabantur. Nec defuerunt qui fictis mentitisque terroribus vera pericula augerent. Aderant qui Miseni illud ruisse, illud ardere, falso sed credentibus, nuntiabant. Paulum reluxit; quod non dies nobis sed adventantis ignis indicium videbatur. Et ignis quidem longius substitit, tenebrae rursus, cinis rursus multus et gravis. Hunc identidem adsurgentes excutiebamus: operti alioqui atque etiam oblisi pondere essemus. Possem gloriari non gemitum mihi, non vocem parum fortem in tantis periculis excidisse, nisi me cum omnibus, omnia mecum perire misero, magno tamen mortalitatis solacio credidissem. Tandem illa caligo tenuata quasi in fumum nebulamve discessit: mox dies verus, sol etiam effulsit, luridus tamen, qualis esse, cum deficit, solet. Occursabant trepidantibus adhuc oculis mutata omnia altoque cinere, tamquam nive, obducta. Regressi Misenum, curatis utcumque corporibus suspensam dubiamque noctem spe ac metu exegimus. Metus praevalebat: nam et tremor terrae perseverabat et plerique lymphati terrificis vaticinationibus et sua et aliena mala ludificabantur. Nobis tamen ne tunc quidem, quamquam et expertis periculum et exspectantibus, abeundi consilium, donec de avunculo nuntius. Haec nequaquam historia digna non scripturus leges et tibi, scilicet qui requisisti, inputabis, si digna ne epistula quidem videbuntur. Vale.

72. (XXX.)

C. PLINIUS FABATO PROSOCERO SUO S.

About a country estate of Fabatus.

1 Debemus mehercule natales tuos perinde ac nostros celebrare, cum laetitia nostrorum ex tuis pendeat, cuius 5
2 diligentia et cura hic hilares, istic securi sumus. Villa Camilliana, quam in Campania possides, est quidem vetustate vexata; ea tamen quae sunt pretiosiora aut integra
3 manent aut levissime laesa sunt. Attendimus ergo ut quam saluberrime reficiantur. Ego videor habere multos 10 amicos, sed huius generis cuius et tu quaeris et res exigit
4 prope neminem. Sunt enim omnes togati et urbani: rusticorum autem praediorum administratio poscit durum aliquem et agrestem, cui nec labor ille gravis nec cura
5 sordida nec tristis solitudo videatur. Tu de Rufo hones- 15 tissime cogitas: fuit enim filio tuo familiaris. Quid tamen nobis ibi praestare possit ignoro, velle plurimum credo. Vale.

73. (XXXIII.)

C. PLINIUS ROMANO SUO S.

A contested will case in the Centumviral Court.

1 'Tollite cuncta' inquit 'coeptosque auferte labores.'
Seu scribis aliquid seu legis, tolli auferri iube et accipe 20 orationem meam, ut illa arma, divinam (num superbius potui?), re vera, ut inter meas, pulchram; nam mihi satis

est certare mecum. Est haec pro Attia Viriola, et digni- 2
tate personae et exempli raritate et iudicii magnitudine
insignis. Nam femina splendide nata, nupta praetorio
viro, exheredata ab octogenario patre intra undecim dies
5 quam illi novercam amore captus induxerat, quadruplici
iudicio bona paterna repetebat. Sedebant centum et octo- 3
ginta iudices; tot enim quattuor consiliis colliguntur: ingens utrimque advocatio et numerosa subsellia, praeterea
densa circumstantium corona latissimum iudicium multi-
10 plici circulo ambibat. Ad hoc stipatum tribunal, atque 4
etiam ex superiore basilicae parte qua feminae qua viri
et audiendi, quod difficile, et quod facile, visendi studio
imminebant. Magna exspectatio patrum, magna filiarum,
magna etiam novercarum. Secutus est varius eventus.
15 Nam duobus consiliis vicimus, totidem victi sumus. No- 5
tabilis prorsus et mira eadem in causa, isdem iudicibus,
isdem advocatis, eodem tempore tanta diversitas accidit,
casu, non quod casus videretur. Victa est noverca, ipsa 6
heres ex parte sexta, victus Suberinus, qui exheredatus
20 a patre singulari inpudentia alieni patris bona vindicabat,
non ausus sui petere. Haec tibi exposui, primum, ut ex 7
epistula scires quae ex oratione non poteras: deinde (nam
detegam artes), ut orationem libentius legeres, si non legere tibi sed interesse iudicio videreris; quam, sit licet
25 magna, non despero gratiam brevissimae impetraturam.
Nam et copia rerum et arguta divisione et narratiunculis 8
pluribus et eloquendi varietate renovatur. Sunt multa
(non auderem nisi tibi dicere) elata, multa pugnacia, multa
subtilia. Intervenit enim acribus illis et erectis frequens 9
30 necessitas conputandi ac paene calculos tabulamque pos-
cendi, ut repente in privati iudicii formam centumvirale
vertatur. Dedimus vela indignationi, dedimus irae, dedi- 10

mus dolori, et in amplissima causa, quasi magno mari,
11 pluribus ventis sumus vecti. In summa, solent quidam
ex contubernalibus nostris existimare hanc orationem,
iterum dicam, ut inter meas, ὑπὲρ Κτησιφῶντος esse: an
vere, tu facillime iudicabis, qui tam memoriter tenes om- 5
nes ut conferre cum hac, dum hanc solam legis, possis.
Vale.

74. (XXXIV.)

C. PLINIUS MAXIMO SUO S.

A gladiatorial exhibition at Verona.

1 Recte fecisti quod gladiatorum munus Veronensibus nostris promisisti, a quibus olim amaris, suspiceris, ornaris.
Inde etiam uxorem carissimam tibi et probatissimam 10
habuisti, cuius memoriae aut opus aliquod aut spectaculum, atque hoc potissimum quod maxime funeri, debebatur.
2 Praeterea tanto consensu rogabaris ut negare non
constans sed durum videretur. Illud quoque egregie
3 quod tam facilis, tam liberalis in edendo fuisti. Nam 15
per haec etiam magnus animus ostenditur. Vellem Africanae quas coëmeras plurimas ad praefinitum diem occurrissent: sed licet cessaverint illae tempestate detentae,
tu tamen meruisti ut acceptum tibi fieret quod quo minus
exhiberes non per te stetit. Vale. 20

LIBER SEPTIMUS.

75. (V.)

C. PLINIUS CALPURNIAE SUAE S.

A love letter.

Incredibile est quanto desiderio tui tenear. In causa 1
amor primum, deinde quod non consuevimus abesse.
Inde est quod magnam noctium partem in imagine tua
vigil exigo, inde quod interdiu quibus horis te visere sole-
5 bam ad diaetam tuam ipsi me, ut verissime dicitur, pedes
ducunt, quod denique aeger et maestus ac similis excluso
a vacuo limine recedo. Unum tempus his tormentis
caret, quo in foro amicorum litibus conteror. Aestima 2
tu quae vita mea sit, cui requies in labore, in miseria
10 curisque solacium. Vale.

76. (XI.)

C. PLINIUS FABATO PROSOCERO SUO S.

Pliny's generous bargain with Corellia.

Miraris quod Hermes, libertus meus, hereditarios agros 1
quos ego iusseram proscribi non exspectata auctione pro
meo quincunce ex septingentis milibus Corelliae addixerit. Adicis hos nongentis milibus posse venire ac tanto
15 magis quaeris an quod gessit ratum servem. Ego vero 2
servo: quibus ex causis, accipe. Cupio enim et tibi pro-
batum et coheredibus meis excusatum esse quod me ab
illis maiore officio iubente secerno. Corelliam cum summa 3

reverentia diligo, primum ut sororem Corelli Rufi, cuius mihi memoria sacrosancta est, deinde ut matri meae
4 familiarissimam. Sunt mihi et cum marito eius, Minicio Iusto, optimo viro, vetera iura; fuerunt et cum filio maxima, adeo quidem ut praetore me ludis meis praese- 5
5 derit. Haec, cum proxime istic fui, indicavit mihi cupere se aliquid circa Larium nostrum possidere. Ego illi ex praediis meis quod vellet et quanti vellet obtuli, exceptis maternis paternisque: his enim cedere ne Corelliae quidem
6 possum. Igitur cum obvenisset mihi hereditas in qua 10 praedia ista, scripsi ei venalia futura. Has epistulas Hermes tulit exigentique ut statim portionem meam sibi addiceret paruit. Vides quam ratum debeam habere
7 quod libertus meus meis moribus gessit? Superest ut coheredes aequo animo ferant separatim me vendidisse 15 quod mihi licuit omnino non vendere. Nec vero cogun-
8 tur imitari meum exemplum. Non enim illis eadem cum Corellia iura. Possunt ergo intueri utilitatem suam, pro qua mihi fuit amicitia. Vale.

77. (XIV.)

C. PLINIUS CORELLIAE SUAE S.

Corellia is reluctant to accept the favor.

1 Tu quidem honestissime, quod tam inpense et rogas et 20 exigis ut accipi iubeam a te pretium agrorum non ex septingentis milibus, quanti illos a liberto meo, sed ex nongentis, quanti a publicanis partem vicesimam emisti.
2 Invicem ego et rogo et exigo ut non solum quid te, verum etiam quid me deceat aspicias patiarisque me in hoc 25 uno tibi eodem animo repugnare quo in omnibus obsequi soleo. Vale.

78. (XVIII.)

C. PLINIUS CANINIO SUO S.

How to make an endowment perpetual.

Deliberas mecum quemadmodum pecunia quam municipibus nostris in epulum obtulisti post te quoque salva sit. Honesta consultatio, non expedita sententia. Numeres rei publicae summam? verendum est ne dilabatur. Des agros? ut publici neglegentur. Equidem nihil commodius invenio quam quod ipse feci. Nam pro quingentis milibus nummum, quae in alimenta ingenuorum ingenuarumque promiseram, agrum ex meis longe pluris actori publico mancipavi: eundem vectigali inposito recepi, tricena milia annua daturus. Per hoc enim et rei publicae sors in tuto nec reditus incertus, et ager ipse propter id quod vectigal large supercurrit semper dominum, a quo exerceatur, inveniet. Nec ignoro me plus aliquanto quam donasse videor erogavisse, cum pulcherrimi agri pretium necessitas vectigalis infregerit. Sed oportet privatis utilitatibus publicas, mortalibus aeternas anteferre, multoque diligentius muneri suo consulere quam facultatibus. Vale.

79. (XIX.)

C. PLINIUS PRISCO SUO S.

Illness of Fannia; her noble character.

Angit me Fanniae valetudo. Contraxit hanc, dum adsidet Iuniae virgini, sponte primum (est enim adfinis), deinde etiam ex auctoritate pontificum. Nam virgines, cum vi morbi atrio Vestae coguntur excedere, matrona-

rum curae custodiaeque mandantur. Quo munere Fannia
3 dum sedulo fungitur, hoc discrimine inplicita est. Insident febres, tussis increscit, summa macies, summa defectio: animus tantum et spiritus viget Helvidio marito,
Thrasea patre dignissimus; reliqua labuntur meque non 5
4 metu tantum verum etiam dolore conficiunt. Doleo enim feminam maximam eripi oculis civitatis, nescio an aliquid simile visuris. Quae castitas illi! quae sanctitas! quanta gravitas! quanta constantia! Bis maritum secuta in ex-
5 silium est, tertio ipsa propter maritum relegata. Nam 10
cum Senecio reus esset, quod de vita Helvidi libros composuisset, rogatumque se a Fannia in defensione dixisset, quaerente minaciter Metio Caro an rogasset respondit 'rogavi,' an commentarios scripturo dedisset, 'dedi,' an sciente matre, 'nesciente'; postremo nullam vocem ce- 15
6 dentem periculo emisit. Quin etiam illos ipsos libros, quamquam ex necessitate et metu temporum abolitos senatus consulto, publicatis bonis servavit habuit, tulit-
7 que in exsilium exsilii causam. Eadem quam iucunda, quam comis, quam denique, quod paucis datum est, non 20
minus amabilis quam veneranda! Eritne quam postea uxoribus nostris ostentare possimus? erit a qua viri quoque fortitudinis exempla sumamus? quam sic cernentes audientesque miremur ut illas quae leguntur?
8 Ac mihi domus ipsa nutare convulsaque sedibus suis rui- 25
tura supra videtur, licet adhuc posteros habeat. Quantis enim virtutibus quantisque factis adsequentur ut haec
9 non novissima occiderit? Me quidem illud etiam adfligit et torquet quod matrem eius, illam (nihil possum inlustrius dicere) tantae feminae matrem, rursus videor 30
amittere, quam haec, ut reddit ac refert nobis, sic auferet secum meque et novo pariter et rescisso vulnere adficiet.

Utramque colui, utramque dilexi; utram magis nescio, nec 10
discerni volebant. Habuerunt officia mea in secundis,
habuerunt in adversis. Ego solacium relegatarum, ego
ultor reversarum; non feci tamen paria, atque eo magis
5 hanc cupio servari, ut mihi solvendi tempora supersint.
In his eram curis, cum scriberem ad te; quas si deus 11
aliquis in gaudium verterit, de metu non querar. Vale.

80. (XX.)

C. PLINIUS TACITO SUO S.

Interest of Pliny and Tacitus in each other's works.

Librum tuum legi et quam diligentissime potui adno- 1
tavi quae commutanda, quae eximenda arbitrarer. Nam
10 et ego verum dicere adsuevi et tu libenter audire. Neque
enim ulli patientius reprehenduntur quam qui maxime
laudari merentur. Nunc a te librum meum cum adnotationibus tuis exspecto. O iucundas, o pulchras vices! 2
Quam me delectat quod, si qua posteris cura nostri, us-
15 quequaque narrabitur qua concordia simplicitate fide
vixerimus! Erit rarum et insigne duos homines aetate 3
dignitate propemodum aequales, non nullius in litteris
nominis (cogor enim de te quoque parcius dicere, quia
de me simul dico), alterum alterius studia fovisse. Equi- 4
20 dem adulescentulus, cum iam tu fama gloriaque floreres,
te sequi, tibi longo sed proximus intervallo et esse et
haberi concupiscebam. Et erant multa clarissima ingenia: sed tu mihi (ita similitudo naturae ferebat) maxime
imitabilis, maxime imitandus videbaris. Quo magis 5
25 gaudeo quod, si quis de studiis sermo, una nominamur,
quod de te loquentibus statim occurro. Nec desunt qui
utrique nostrum praeferantur. Sed nos, nihil interest 6

mea quo loco, iungimur: nam mihi primus qui a te proximus. Quin etiam in testamentis debes adnotasse: nisi quis forte alterutri nostrum amicissimus, eadem 7 legata et quidem pariter accipimus. Quae omnia huc spectant ut invicem ardentius diligamus, cum tot vin- 5 culis nos studia, mores, fama, suprema denique hominum iudicia constringant. Vale.

81. (XXVII.)

C. PLINIUS SURAE SUO S.

Two ghost stories.

1 Et mihi discendi et tibi docendi facultatem otium praebet. Igitur perquam velim scire, esse phantasmata et habere propriam figuram numenque aliquod putes an 10 2 inania et vana ex metu nostro imaginem accipere. Ego ut esse credam in primis eo ducor quod audio accidisse Curtio Rufo. Tenuis adhuc et obscurus obtinenti Africam comes haeserat: inclinato die spatiabatur in porticu: offertur ei mulieris figura humana grandior pulchriorque: 15 perterrito Africam se, futurorum praenuntiam, dixit; iturum enim Romam honoresque gesturum atque etiam cum summo imperio in eandem provinciam reversurum 3 ibique moriturum. Facta sunt omnia. Praeterea accedenti Carthaginem egredientique nave eadem figura in 20 litore occurrisse narratur. Ipse certe inplicitus morbo, futura praeteritis, adversa secundis auguratus, spem 4 salutis nullo suorum desperante proiecit. Iam illud nonne et magis terribile et non minus mirum est, quod 5 exponam ut accepi? Erat Athenis spatiosa et capax 25 domus, sed infamis et pestilens. Per silentium noctis sonus ferri, et si attenderes acrius, strepitus vinculorum

longius primo, deinde e proximo reddebatur : mox apparebat idolon, senex macie et squalore confectus, promissa barba, horrenti capillo: cruribus compedes, manibus catenas gerebat quatiebatque. Inde inhabitantibus tristes diraeque noctes per metum vigilabantur: vigiliam morbus et crescente formidine mors sequebatur. Nam interdiu quoque, quamquam abscesserat imago, memoria imaginis oculis inerrabat, longiorque causis timoris timor erat. Deserta inde et damnata solitudine domus totaque illi monstro relicta; proscribebatur tamen, seu quis emere, seu quis conducere ignarus tanti mali vellet. Venit Athenas philosophus Athenodorus, legit titulum, auditoque pretio, quia suspecta vilitas, percunctatus, omnia docetur ac nihilo minus, immo tanto magis conducit. Ubi coepit advesperascere, iubet sterni sibi prima domus parte, poscit pugillares stilum lumen: suos omnes in interiora dimittit, ipse ad scribendum animum oculos manum intendit, ne vacua mens audita simulacra et inanes sibi metus fingeret. Initio, quale ubique, silentium noctis, dein concuti ferrum, vincula moveri: ille non tollere oculos, non remittere stilum, sed offirmare animum auribusque praetendere: tum crebrescere fragor, adventare, et iam ut in limine, iam ut intra limen audiri: respicit, videt agnoscitque narratam sibi effigiem. Stabat innuebatque digito, similis vocanti: hic contra ut paulum exspectaret manu significat rursusque ceris et stilo incumbit: illa scribentis capiti catenis insonabat: respicit rursus idem quod prius innuentem, nec moratus tollit lumen et sequitur. Ibat illa lento gradu, quasi gravis vinculis: postquam deflexit in aream domus, repente dilapsa deserit comitem: desertus herbas et folia concerpta signum loco ponit. Postero die adit magistra-

tus, monet ut illum locum effodi iubeant. Inveniuntur
ossa inserta catenis et inplicita, quae corpus aevo terraque
putrefactum nuda et exesa reliquerat vinculis: collecta
12 publice sepeliuntur. Domus postea rite conditis manibus caruit. Et haec quidem adfirmantibus credo: illud 5
adfirmare aliis possum. Est libertus mihi, non inlittera-
tus. Cum hoc minor frater eodem lecto quiescebat. Is
visus est sibi cernere quendam in toro residentem ad-
moventemque capiti suo cultros atque etiam ex ipso
vertice amputantem capillos. Ubi inluxit, ipse circa 10
13 verticem tonsus, capilli iacentes reperiuntur. Exiguum
temporis medium, et rursus simile aliud priori fidem
fecit. Puer in paedagogio mixtus pluribus dormiebat:
venerunt per fenestras (ita narrat) in tunicis albis duo
cubantemque detonderunt, et qua venerant recesserunt. 15
Hunc quoque tonsum sparsosque circa capillos dies
14 ostendit. Nihil notabile secutum, nisi forte quod non
fui reus, futurus, si Domitianus, sub quo haec acciderunt,
diutius vixisset. Nam in scrinio eius datus a Caro de
me libellus inventus est; ex quo coniectari potest, quia 20
reis moris est summittere capillum, recisos meorum capillos depulsi quod imminebat periculi signum fuisse.
15 Proinde rogo eruditionem tuam intendas. Digna res
est quam diu multumque consideres: ne ego quidem
16 indignus cui copiam scientiae tuae facias. Licet etiam 25
utramque in partem, ut soles, disputes, ex altera tamen
fortius, ne me suspensum incertumque dimittas, cum
mihi consulendi causa fuerit ut dubitare desinerem.
Vale.

82. (XXXIII.)

C. PLINIUS TACITO SUO S.

Pliny wishes to be immortalized in the histories of Tacitus.

Auguror, nec me fallit augurium, historias tuas immor- 1
tales futuras; quo magis illis, ingenue fatebor, inseri
cupio. Nam si esse nobis curae solet ut facies nostra 2
ab optimo quoque artifice exprimatur, nonne debemus
5 optare ut operibus nostris similis tui scriptor praedicatorque contingat? Demonstro ergo, quamquam dili- 3
gentiam tuam fugere non possit, cum sit in publicis
actis, demonstro tamen, quo magis credas iucundum mihi
futurum, si factum meum, cuius gratia periculo crevit,
10 tuo ingenio, tuo testimonio ornaveris. Dederat me se- 4
natus cum Herennio Senecione advocatum provinciae
Baeticae contra Baebium Massam, damnatoque Massa
censuerat ut bona eius publice custodirentur. Senecio,
cum explorasset consules postulationibus vacaturos, con-
15 venit me et 'qua concordia' inquit 'iniunctam nobis
accusationem exsecuti sumus, hac adeamus consules petamusque ne bona dissipari sinant quorum esse in custodia
debent.' Respondi 'cum simus advocati a senatu dati, 5
dispice num peractas putes partes nostras senatus cogni-
20 tione finita.' Et ille 'tu quem voles tibi terminum
statues, cui nulla cum provincia necessitudo nisi ex
beneficio tuo, et hoc recenti: ipse et natus ibi et quaestor
in ea fui.' Tum ego 'si fixum tibi istud ac deliberatum, 6
sequar te, ut, si qua ex hoc invidia, non tantum tua.'
25 Venimus ad consules, dicit Senecio quae res ferebat: 7
aliqua subiungo. Vixdum conticueramus, et Massa
questus Senecionem non advocati fidem sed inimici ama-

8 ritudinem inplesse, impietatis reum postulat. Horror omnium: ego autem 'vereor' inquam, 'clarissimi consules, ne mihi Massa silentio suo praevaricationem obiecerit, quod non et me reum postulavit.' Quae vox et statim excepta et postea multo sermone celebrata est. 5
9 Divus quidem Nerva (nam privatus quoque attendebat his quae recte in publico fierent) missis ad me gravissimis litteris non mihi solum verum etiam saeculo est gratulatus, cui exemplum (sic enim scripsit) simile anti-
10 quis contigisset. Haec, utcumque se habent, notiora 10 clariora maiora tu facies: quamquam non exigo ut excedas actae rei modum. Nam nec historia debet egredi veritatem et honeste factis veritas sufficit. Vale.

LIBER OCTAVUS.

83. (II.)

C. PLINIUS CALVISIO SUO S.

How Pliny shared the loss with the buyers of his vintages when the crop failed.

Alii in praedia sua proficiscuntur, ut locupletiores 1
revertantur, ego, ut pauperior. Vendideram vindemias
certatim negotiatoribus ementibus. Invitabat pretium,
et quod tunc et quod fore videbatur. Spes fefellit. 2
5 Erat expeditum omnibus remittere aequaliter, sed non
satis aecum. Mihi autem egregium in primis videtur,
ut foris ita domi, ut in magnis ita in parvis, ut in alienis
ita in suis, agitare iustitiam. Nam si paria peccata,
pares etiam laudes. Itaque omnibus quidem, ne quis 3
10 mihi non donatus abiret, partem octavam pretii quo quis
emerat concessi: deinde eis qui amplissimas summas
emptionibus occupaverant separatim consului. Nam et
me magis iuverant et maius ipsi fecerant damnum.
Igitur eis qui pluris quam decem milibus emerant ad 4
15 illam communem et quasi publicam octavam addidi
decimam eius summae qua decem milia excesserant.
Vereor ne parum expresserim; apertius calculos osten- 5
dam. Si qui forte quindecim milibus emerant, hi et
quindecim milium octavam et quinque milium decimam
20 tulerunt. Praeterea, cum reputarem quosdam ex debito 6
aliquantum, quosdam aliquid, quosdam nihil reposuisse,

nequaquam verum arbitrabar, quos non aequasset fides
7 solutionis, hos benignitate remissionis aequare. Rursus
ergo eis qui solverant eius quod solverant decimam re-
misi. Per hoc enim aptissime et in praeteritum singulis
pro cuiusque merito gratia referri, et in futurum omnes 5
cum ad emendum tum etiam ad solvendum allici vide-
8 bantur. Magno mihi seu ratio haec seu facilitas stetit,
sed fuit tanti. Nam regione tota et novitas remissionis
et forma laudatur. Ex ipsis etiam, quos non una, ut
dicitur, pertica sed distincte gradatimque tractavi, quanto 10
quis melior et probior tanto mihi obligatior abiit, expertus non esse apud me ἐν δὲ ἰῇ τιμῇ ἠμὲν κακὸς ἠδὲ καὶ ἐσθλός.
Vale.

84. (IV.)

C. PLINIUS CANINIO SUO S.

Caninius is to write a poem on the Dacian wars.

1 Optime facis quod bellum Dacicum scribere paras.
Nam quae tam recens, tam copiosa, tam lata, denique 15
tam poëtica, et quamquam in verissimis rebus, tam fabu-
2 losa materia? Dices inmissa terris nova flumina, novos
pontes fluminibus iniectos, insessa castris montium
abrupta, pulsum regia, pulsum etiam vita regem nihil
desperantem; super haec, actos bis triumphos, quorum 20
alter ex invicta gente primus, alter novissimus fuit.
3 Una sed maxima difficultas, quod haec aequare dicendo
arduum inmensum, etiam tuo ingenio, quamquam altissime adsurgat et amplissimis operibus increscat. Non
nullus et in illo labor ut barbara et fera nomina, in 25
4 primis regis ipsius, Graecis versibus non resultent. Sed
nihil est quod non arte curaque, si non potest vinci,

mitigetur. Praeterea, si datur Homero et mollia vocabula et Graeca ad levitatem versus contrahere, extendere, inflectere, cur tibi similis audentia, praesertim non delicata sed necessaria, non detur? Proinde iure vatum 5
5 invocatis dis, et inter eos ipso cuius res opera consilia dicturus es, immitte rudentes, pande vela, ac si quando alias, toto ingenio vehere. Cur enim non ego quoque poëtice cum poëta? Illud iam nunc paciscor: prima 6 quaeque ut absolveris, mittito, immo etiam ante quam
10 absolvas, sicut erunt recentia et rudia et adhuc similia nascentibus. Respondebis non posse perinde carptim 7 ut contexta, perinde incohata placere ut effecta. Scio. Itaque et a me aestimabuntur ut coepta, spectabuntur ut membra extremamque limam tuam opperientur in
15 scrinio nostro. Patere hoc me super cetera habere amoris tui pignus ut ea quoque norim quae nosse neminem velles. In summa, potero fortasse scripta tua magis 8 probare laudare, quanto illa tardius cautiusque, sed ipsum te magis amabo magisque laudabo, quanto celerius
20 et incautius miseris. Vale.

85. (VII.)

C. PLINIUS TACITO SUO S.

Tacitus has sent one of his books to Pliny for criticism.

Neque ut magistro magister neque ut discipulo discipu- 1 lus (sic enim scribis), sed ut discipulo magister (nam tu magister, ego contra; atque adeo tu in scholam revocas, ego adhuc Saturnalia extendo) librum misisti. Num po- 2
25 tui longius hyperbaton facere atque hoc ipso probare eum esse me qui non modo magister tuus sed ne discipulus quidem debeam dici? Sumam tamen personam magistri

exseramque in librum tuum ius quod dedisti, eo liberius quod nihil ex meis interim missurus sum tibi in quo te ulciscaris. Vale.

86. (VIII.)

C. PLINIUS ROMANO SUO S.

The source of the Clitumnus.

1 Vidistine aliquando Clitumnum fontem? Si nondum (et puto nondum; alioqui narrasses mihi), vide, quem 2 ego (paenitet tarditatis) proxime vidi. Modicus collis adsurgit, antiqua cupresso nemorosus et opacus. Hunc subter exit fons et exprimitur pluribus venis sed inparibus, eluctatusque quem facit gurgitem lato gremio patescit purus et vitreus, ut numerare iactas stipes et 3 relucentis calculos possis. Inde non loci devexitate sed ipsa sui copia et quasi pondere inpellitur. Fons adhuc et iam amplissimum flumen atque etiam navium patiens, quas obvias quoque et contrario nisu in diversa tendentes transmittit et perfert, adeo validus ut illa qua properat ipse, quamquam per solum planum, remis non adiuvetur, idem aegerrime remis contisque superetur adversus. 4 Iucundum utrumque per iocum ludumque fluitantibus, ut flexerint cursum, laborem otio, otium labore variare. Ripae fraxino multa, multa populo vestiuntur, quas perspicuus amnis ut mersas viridi imagine adnumerat. Rigor aquae 5 certaverit nivibus, nec color cedit. Adiacet templum priscum et religiosum: stat Clitumnus ipse amictus ornatusque praetexta: praesens numen atque etiam fatidicum indicant sortes. Sparsa sunt circa sacella complura totidemque dei. Sua cuique veneratio, suum nomen, quibusdam vero etiam fontes. Nam praeter illum quasi parentem

ceterorum sunt minores capite discreti; sed flumini miscentur, quod ponte transmittitur. Is terminus sacri profanique. In superiore parte navigare tantum, infra 6 etiam natare concessum. Balineum Hispellates, quibus 5 illum locum divus Augustus dono dedit, publice praebent, praebent hospitium. Nec desunt villae, quae secutae fluminis amoenitatem margini insistunt. In summa, ni- 7 hil erit ex quo non capias voluptatem. Nam studebis quoque; leges multa multorum omnibus columnis, om- 10 nibus parietibus inscripta, quibus fons ille deusque celebratur. Plura laudabis, nonnulla ridebis; quamquam tu vero, quae tua humanitas, nulla ridebis. Vale.

87. (XVI.)

C. PLINIUS PATERNO SUO S.

Pliny's kindness to his slaves.

Confecerunt me infirmitates meorum, mortes etiam, et 1 quidem iuvenum. Solacia duo nequaquam paria tanto 15 dolori, solacia tamen: unum facilitas manumittendi; videor enim non omnino inmaturos perdidisse quos iam liberos perdidi; alterum, quod permitto servis quoque quasi testamenta facere eaque ut legitima custodio. Mandant rogantque quod visum; pareo ut iussus. 2 20 Dividunt, donant, relincunt, dumtaxat intra domum. Nam servis res publica quaedam et quasi civitas domus est. Sed quamquam his solaciis adquiescam, debilitor 3 et frangor eadem illa humanitate quae me ut hoc ipsum permitterem induxit. Non ideo tamen velim durior fieri. 25 Nec ignoro alios eiusmodi casus nihil amplius vocare quam damnum eoque sibi magnos homines et sapientes

videri. Qui an magni sapientesque sint nescio, homines
4 non sunt. Hominis est enim adfici dolore, sentire, resistere tamen et solacia admittere, non solaciis non egere.
5 Verum de his plura fortasse quam debui, sed pauciora quam volui. Est enim quaedam etiam dolendi voluptas, 5
praesertim si in amici sinu defleas, apud quem lacrimis tuis vel laus sit parata vel venia. Vale.

88. (XVII.)

C. PLINIUS MACRINO SUO S.

A flood on the Tiber.

1 Num istic quoque inmite et turbidum caelum? Hic adsiduae tempestates et crebra diluvia. Tiberis alveum
2 excessit et demissioribus ripis alte superfunditur. Quamquam fossa quam providentissimus imperator fecit exhaustus, premit valles, innatat campis, quaque planum solum, pro solo cernitur. Inde quae solet flumina accipere et permixta devehere velut obvius sistere cogit, atque ita alienis aquis operit agros quos ipse non tangit. 15
3 Anio, delicatissimus amnium ideoque adiacentibus villis velut invitatus retentusque, magna ex parte nemora quibus inumbratur fregit et rapuit: subruit montes et decidentium mole pluribus locis clausus, dum amissum iter quaerit, impulit tecta ac se super ruinas eiecit atque 20
4 extulit. Viderunt quos excelsioribus terris illa tempestas deprehendit alibi divitum apparatus et gravem supellectilem, alibi instrumenta ruris, ibi boves aratra rectores, hic soluta et libera armenta, atque inter haec arborum truncos
5 aut villarum trabes, varie lateque fluitantia. Ac ne illa 25
quidem malo vacaverunt quae non ascendit amnis. Nam

pro amne imber adsiduus et deiectis nubibus turbines, proruta opera quibus pretiosa rura cinguntur, quassata atque etiam decussa monimenta. Multi eiusmodi casibus debilitati, obruti, obtriti, et aucta luctibus damna. Ne quid 6
5 simile istic pro mensura periculi vereor teque rogo, si nihil tale, quam maturissime sollicitudini meae consulas, sed et si tale, id quoque nunties. Nam paulum differt patiaris adversa an exspectes; nisi quod tamen est dolendi modus, non est timendi. Doleas enim quantum
10 scias accidisse, timeas quantum possit accidere. Vale.

89. (XX.)

C. PLINIUS GALLO SUO S.

The floating islands of Lake Vadimonis.

Ad quae noscenda iter ingredi, transmittere mare sole- 1 mus, ea sub oculis posita neglegimus, seu quia ita natura comparatum ut proximorum incuriosi longinqua sectemur, seu quod omnium rerum cupido languescit, cum facilis
15 occasio, seu quod differimus tamquam saepe visuri quod datur videre, quotiens velis cernere. Quacumque de 2 causa, permulta in urbe nostra iuxtaque urbem non oculis modo sed ne auribus quidem novimus, quae si tulisset Achaia, Aegyptos, Asia aliave quaelibet miraculorum
20 ferax commendatrixque terra, audita perlecta lustrata haberemus. Ipse certe nuper quod nec audieram ante 3 nec videram audivi pariter et vidi. Exegerat prosocer meus ut Amerina praedia sua inspicerem. Haec perambulanti mihi ostenditur subiacens lacus nomine Vadimo-
25 nis: simul quaedam incredibilia narrantur. Perveni ad ipsum. Lacus est in similitudinem iacentis rotae cir- 4 cumscriptus et undique aequalis: nullus sinus, obliquitas

nulla, omnia dimensa, paria et quasi artificis manu cavata
et excisa. Color caerulo albidior, viridior et pressior, sulpuris odor saporque medicatus, vis, qua fracta solidantur.
Spatium modicum, quod tamen sentiat ventos et fluctibus
5 intumescat. Nulla in hoc navis (sacer enim), sed inna- 5
tant insulae, herbidae omnes harundine et iunco, quaeque
alia fecundior palus ipsaque illa extremitas lacus effert.
Sua cuique figura ut modus: cunctis margo derasus, quia
frequenter vel litori vel sibi inlisae terunt teruntur que.
Par omnibus altitudo, par levitas; quippe in speciem 10
6 carinae humili radice descendunt. Haec ab omni latere
perspicitur eademque suspensa pariter et mersa. Interdum iunctae copulataeque et continenti similes sunt, interdum discordantibus ventis digeruntur, non numquam
7 destitutae tranquillitate singulae fluitant. Saepe minores 15
maioribus velut cumbulae onerariis adhaerescunt, saepe
inter se maiores minoresque quasi cursum certamenque
desumunt; rursus omnes in eundem locum adpulsae, qua
steterunt promovent terram, et modo hac modo illa lacum
reddunt auferuntque; ac tum demum, cum medium te- 20
8 nuere, non contrahunt. Constat pecora herbas secuta sic
in insulas illas ut in extremam ripam procedere solere
nec prius intellegere mobile solum, quam litori abrepta
quasi inlata et inposita circumfusum undique lacum pa-
veant; mox quo tulerit ventus egressa, non magis se 25
9 descendisse sentire, quam senserint ascendisse. Idem
lacus in flumen egeritur, quod, ubi se paulisper oculis
dedit, specu mergitur alteque conditum meat, ac si quid,
10 antequam subduceretur, accepit, servat et profert. Haec
tibi scripsi, quia nec minus ignota quam mihi nec minus 30
grata credebam. Nam te quoque, ut me, nihil aeque ac
naturae opera delectant. Vale.

LIBER NONUS.

90. (VI.)

C. PLINIUS CALVISIO SUO S.

Pliny is bored by the races in the Circus.

Omne hoc tempus inter pugillares ac libellos iucun- 1
dissima quiete transmisi. 'Quemadmodum' inquis 'in
urbe potuisti?' Circenses erant, quo genere spectaculi
ne levissime quidem teneor. Nihil novum, nihil varium,
5 nihil quod non semel spectasse sufficiat. Quo magis 2
miror tot milia virorum tam pueriliter identidem cupere
currentes equos, insistentes curribus homines videre.
Si tamen aut velocitate equorum aut hominum arte tra-
herentur, esset ratio non nulla: nunc favent panno, pan-
10 num amant, et si in ipso cursu medioque certamine hic
color illuc, ille huc transferatur, studium favorque tran-
sibit, et repente agitatores illos, equos illos, quos procul
noscitant, quorum clamitant nomina, relinquent. Tanta 3
gratia, tanta auctoritas in una vilissima tunica, mitto
15 apud vulgus, quod vilius tunica, sed apud quosdam graves
homines; quos ego cum recordor in re inani frigida ad-
sidua tam insatiabiliter desidere, capio aliquam voluptatem, quod hac voluptate non capior. Ac per hos dies 4
libentissime otium meum in litteris conloco, quos alii
20 otiosissimis occupationibus perdunt. Vale.

91. (VII.)

C. PLINIUS ROMANO SUO S.

Tragedy and Comedy, Pliny's villas on the Lake of Como.

1 Aedificare te scribis. Bene est: inveni patrocinium; aedifico enim iam ratione, quia tecum. Nam hoc quoque non dissimile, quod ad mare tu, ego ad Larium lacum.
2 Huius in litore plures villae meae, sed duae maxime ut delectant ita exercent. Altera inposita saxis more 5 Baiano lacum prospicit, altera aeque more Baiano lacum
3 tangit. Itaque illam Tragoediam, hanc appellare Comoediam soleo; illam, quod quasi cothurnis, hanc, quod quasi socculis sustinetur. Sua utrique amoenitas et utra-
4 que possidenti ipsa diversitate iucundior. Haec lacu 10 propius, illa latius utitur: haec unum sinum molli curvamine amplectitur, illa editissimo dorso duos dirimit: illic recta gestatio longo limite super litus extenditur, hic spatiosissimo xysto leviter inflectitur: illa fluctus non sentit, haec frangit: ex illa possis dispicere pis- 15 cantes, ex hac ipse piscari hamumque de cubiculo ac paene etiam de lectulo ut e naucula iacere. Hae mihi causae utrique quae desunt adstruendi ob ea quae super-
5 sunt. Sed quid ego rationem tibi? apud quem pro ratione erit idem facere. Vale. 20

92. (X.)

C. PLINIUS TACITO SUO S.

About combining the service of Minerva and Diana.

1 Cupio praeceptis tuis parere; sed aprorum tanta penuria est ut Minervae et Dianae, quas ais pariter colen-

das, convenire non possit. Itaque Minervae tantum 2
serviendum est, delicate tamen, ut in secessu et aestate.
In via plane non nulla leviora statimque delenda ea
garrulitate qua sermones in vehiculo seruntur extendi.
5 His quaedam addidi in villa, cum aliud non liberet.
Itaque poëmata quiescunt, quae tu inter nemora et lucos
commodissime perfici putas. Oratiunculam unam alteram 3
retractavi; quamquam id genus operis inamabile, inamoenum
magisque laboribus ruris quam voluptatibus
10 simile. Vale.

93. (XV.)

C. PLINIUS FALCONI SUO S.

Not even in the country is leisure undisturbed.

Refugeram in Tuscos, ut omnia ad arbitrium meum 1
facerem; at hoc ne in Tuscis quidem: tam multis undique
rusticorum libellis et tam querulis inquietor, quos
aliquanto magis invitus quam meos lego; nam et meos
15 invitus. Retracto enim actiunculas quasdam, quod post 2
intercapedinem temporis et frigidum et acerbum est. Rationes
quasi absente me negleguntur. Interdum tamen 3
equum conscendo et patrem familiae hactenus ago, quod
aliquam partem praediorum, sed pro gestatione percurro.
20 Tu consuetudinem serva nobisque sic rusticis urbana acta
perscribe. Vale.

94. (XIX.)

C. PLINIUS RUSONI SUO S.

The epitaph of Verginius Rufus.

Significas legisse te in quadam epistula mea iussisse 1
Verginium Rufum inscribi sepulcro suo,

Hic situs est Rufus, pulso qui Vindice quondam
imperium adseruit non sibi sed patriae.

Reprehendis quod iusserit, addis etiam melius rectíusque Frontinum, quod vetuerit omnino monumentum sibi fieri, meque ad extremum quid de utroque sentiam consulis. 5
2 Utrumque dilexi, miratus sum magis quem tu reprehendis, atque ita miratus ut non putarem satis umquam posse laudari cuius nunc mihi subeunda defensio est.
3 Omnes ego qui magnum aliquid memorandumque fecerunt non modo venia verum etiam laude dignissimos 10 iudico, si immortalitatem quam meruere sectantur victurique nominis famam supremis etiam titulis prorogare
4 nituntur. Nec facile quemquam nisi Verginium invenio cuius tanta in praedicando verecundia quanta gloria ex
5 facto. Ipse sum testis, familiariter ab eo dilectus pro- 15 batusque, semel omnino me audiente provectum ut de rebus suis hoc unum referret, ita secum aliquando Cluvium locutum 'scis, Vergini, quae historiae fides debeatur: proinde si quid in historiis meis legis aliter ac velis, rogo ignoscas.' Ad hoc ille 'tune ignoras, Cluvi, ideo me 20 fecisse quod feci, ut esset liberum vobis scribere quae
6 libuisset'? Agedum, hunc ipsum Frontinum in hoc ipso in quo tibi parcior videtur et pressior comparemus. Vetuit exstrui monimentum: sed quibus verbis? 'inpensa monumenti supervacua est: memoria nostri dura- 25 bit, si vita meruimus.' An restrictius arbitraris per orbem terrarum legendum dare duraturam memoriam suam quam uno in loco duobus versiculis signare quod
7 feceris? Quamquam non habeo propositum illum reprehendendi, sed hunc tuendi: cuius quae potest apud te 30 iustior esse defensio, quam ex conlatione eius quem prae-

tulisti? Meo quidem iudicio neuter culpandus, quorum 8
uterque ad gloriam pari cupiditate, diverso itinere contendit, alter, dum expetit debitos titulos, alter, dum mavult videri contempsisse. Vale.

95. (XXI.)

C. PLINIUS SABINIANO SUO S.

Intercession for a penitent freedman.

5 Libertus tuus, cui suscensere te dixeras, venit ad me 1
advolutusque pedibus meis tamquam tuis haesit. Flevit multum, multum rogavit, multum etiam tacuit, in summa, fecit mihi fidem paenitentiae. Vere credo emendatum, quia deliquisse se sentit. Irasceris, scio, et irasceris 2
10 merito, id quoque scio: sed tunc praecipua mansuetudinis laus, cum irae causa iustissima est. Amasti hominem 3
et, spero, amabis: interim sufficit ut exorari te sinas. Licebit rursus irasci, si meruerit, quod exoratus excusatius facies. Remitte aliquid adulescentiae ipsius, remitte
15 lacrimis, remitte indulgentiae tuae: ne torseris illum, ne torseris etiam te. Torqueris enim, cum tam lenis irasceris. 4
Vereor ne videar non rogare sed cogere, si precibus eius meas iunxero. Iungam tamen tanto plenius et effusius, quanto ipsum acrius severiusque corripui, destricte
20 minatus numquam me postea rogaturum. Hoc illi, quem terreri oportebat, tibi non idem. Nam fortasse iterum rogabo, impetrabo iterum: sit modo tale ut rogare me, ut praestare te deceat. Vale.

96. (XXIII.)

C. PLINIUS MAXIMO SUO S.

The fame of Tacitus and Pliny.

1 Frequenter agenti mihi evenit ut centumviri, cum diu se intra iudicum auctoritatem gravitatemque tenuissent, omnes repente quasi victi coactique consurgerent lauda-
2 rentque; frequenter e senatu famam, qualem maxime optaveram, rettuli: numquam tamen maiorem cepi vo- 5 luptatem, quam nuper ex sermone Corneli Taciti. Narrabat sedisse se cum quodam Circensibus proximis: hunc post varios eruditosque sermones requisisse 'Italicus es an provincialis?' se respondisse 'nosti me, et
3 quidem ex studiis.' Ad hoc illum 'Tacitus es an Pli- 10 nius?' Exprimere non possum quam sit iucundum mihi quod nomina nostra, quasi litterarum propria, non hominum, litteris redduntur, quod uterque nostrum his
4 etiam ex studiis notus quibus aliter ignotus est. Accidit aliud ante pauculos dies simile. Recumbebat mecum 15 vir egregius, Fadius Rufinus, super eum municeps ipsius, qui illo die primum venerat in urbem; cui Rufinus, demonstrans me, 'vides hunc?' Multa deinde de studiis
5 nostris. Et ille 'Plinius est' inquit. Verum fatebor, capio magnum laboris mei fructum. An, si Demosthe- 20 nes iure laetatus est quod illum anus Attica ita noscitavit, οὗτός ἐστι Δημοσθένης, ego celebritate nominis mei
6 gaudere non debeo? Ego vero et gaudeo et gaudere me dico. Neque enim vereor ne iactantior videar, cum de me aliorum iudicium, non meum profero, praesertim 25 apud te, qui nec ullius invides laudibus et faves nostris. Vale.

97. (XXIV.)

C. PLINIUS SABINIANO SUO S.

Success of Pliny's intercession for the freedman.

Bene fecisti quod libertum aliquando tibi carum redu- 1
centibus epistulis meis in domum, in animum recepisti.
Iuvabit hoc te: me certe iuvat; primum, quod te tam
tractabilem video ut in ira regi possis, deinde, quod
5 tantum mihi tribuis ut vel auctoritati meae pareas vel
precibus indulgeas. Igitur laudo et gratias ago. Simul
in posterum moneo ut te erroribus tuorum, etsi non fuerit qui deprecetur, placabilem praestes. Vale.

98. (XXXIII.)

C. PLINIUS CANINIO SUO S.

Wonderful tale of a tame dolphin.

Incidi in materiam veram, sed simillimam fictae dig- 1
10 namque isto laetissimo, altissimo, planeque poëtico ingenio, incidi autem, dum super cenam varia miracula hinc
inde referuntur. Magna auctori fides: tametsi quid
poëtae cum fide? Is tamen auctor cui bene vel historiam scripturus credidisses. Est in Africa Hipponensis 2
15 colonia, mari proxima: adiacet navigabile stagnum: ex
hoc in modum fluminis aestuarium emergit, quod vice
alterna, prout aestus aut repressit aut inpulit, nunc
infertur mari nunc redditur stagno. Omnis hic aetas 3
piscandi, navigandi, atque etiam natandi studio tenetur,
20 maxime pueri, quos otium lususque sollicitat. His gloria
et virtus altissime provehi: victor ille qui longissime ut
litus ita simul natantes reliquit. Hoc certamine puer 4

quidam audentior ceteris in ulteriora tendebat. Delphinus occurrit, et nunc praecedere puerum, nunc sequi, nunc circumire, postremo subire, deponere, iterum subire, trepidantemque perferre primum in altum, mox 5 flectit ad litus redditque terrae et aequalibus. Serpit 5 per coloniam fama: concurrere omnes, ipsum puerum tamquam miraculum aspicere, interrogare, audire, narrare. Postero die obsident litus, prospectant mare et si quid est mari simile. Natant pueri: inter hos ille, sed cautius. Delphinus rursus ad tempus, rursus ad 10 puerum venit. Fugit ille cum ceteris. Delphinus, quasi invitet et revocet, exsilit, mergitur variosque orbes 6 inplicitat expeditque. Hoc altero die, hoc tertio, hoc pluribus, donec homines innutritos mari subiret timendi pudor. Accedunt et adludunt et appellant, tangunt 15 etiam pertrectantque praebentem. Crescit audacia experimento. Maxime puer qui primus expertus est adnatantis insilit tergo, fertur referturque, agnosci se, amari putat, amat ipse: neuter timet, neuter timetur: huius 7 fiducia, mansuetudo illius augetur. Nec non alii pueri 20 dextra laevaque simul eunt hortantes monentesque. Ibat una (id quoque mirum) delphinus alius, tantum spectator et comes. Nihil enim simile aut faciebat aut patiebatur, 8 sed alterum illum ducebat reducebatque, ut puerum ceteri pueri. Incredibile, tam verum tamen quam priora, del- 25 phinum gestatorem conlusoremque puerorum in terram quoque extrahi solitum harenisque siccatum, ubi inca- 9 luisset, in mare revolvi. Constat Octavium Avitum, legatum pro consule, in litus educto religione prava superfudisse unguentum, cuius illum novitatem odorem- 30 que in altum refugisse nec nisi post multos dies visum languidum et maestum, mox redditis viribus priorem

lasciviam et solita ministeria repetisse. Confluebant 10
omnes ad spectaculum magistratus, quorum adventu et
mora modica res publica novis sumptibus atterebatur.
Postremo locus ipse quietem suam secretumque perde-
5 bat. Placuit occulte interfici ad quod coibatur. Haec 11
tu qua miseratione, qua copia deflebis, ornabis, attolles!
Quamquam non est opus adfingas aliquid aut adstruas:
sufficit ne ea quae sunt vera minuantur. Vale.

99. (XXXVI.)

C. PLINIUS FUSCO SUO S.

Pliny's manner of life at his Tuscan villa.

Quaeris quemadmodum in Tuscis diem aestate dispo- 1
10 nam. Evigilo cum libuit, plerumque circa horam primam, saepe ante, tardius raro: clausae fenestrae manent.
Mire enim silentio et tenebris ab eis quae avocant ab- 2
ductus, et liber et mihi relictus, non oculos animo sed
animum oculis sequor, qui eadem quae mens vident, quo-
15 tiens non vident alia. Cogito, si quid in manibus, cogito
ad verbum scribenti emendantique similis, nunc pauciora
nunc plura, ut vel difficile vel facile componi tenerive potu-
erunt. Notarium voco et die admisso quae formaveram
dicto: abit rursusque revocatur rursusque dimittitur.
20 Ubi hora quarta vel quinta (neque enim certum dimen- 3
sumque tempus), ut dies suasit, in xystum me vel cryptoporticum confero, reliqua meditor et dicto. Vehiculum
ascendo. Ibi quoque idem quod ambulans aut iacens.
Durat intentio mutatione ipsa refecta: paulum redormio,
25 dein ambulo, mox orationem Graecam Latinamve clare et
intente, non tam vocis causa quam stomachi lego: pari-

ter tamen et illa firmatur. Iterum ambulo, ungor, exer-
4 ceor, lavor. Cenanti mihi, si cum uxore vel paucis, liber legitur: post cenam comoedus aut lyristes: mox cum meis ambulo, quorum in numero sunt eruditi. Ita variis sermonibus vespera extenditur, et quamquam longissimus 5
5 dies cito conditur. Non numquam ex hoc ordine aliqua mutantur. Nam si diu iacui vel ambulavi, post somnum demum lectionemque non vehiculo sed, quod brevius, quia velocius, equo gestor. Interveniunt amici ex proximis oppidis partemque diei ad se trahunt interdumque 10
6 lasso mihi opportuna interpellatione subveniunt. Venor aliquando, sed non sine pugillaribus, ut, quamvis nihil ceperim, non nihil referam. Datur et colonis, ut videtur ipsis, non satis temporis, quorum mihi agrestes querellae litteras nostras et haec urbana opera commendant. Vale. 15

100. (XXXIX.)

C. PLINIUS MUSTIO SUO S.

Restoration of a temple.

1 Haruspicum monitu reficienda est mihi aedes Cereris in praediis in melius et in maius, vetus sane et angusta,
2 cum sit alioqui stato die frequentissima. Nam Idibus Septembribus magnus e regione tota coit populus, multae res aguntur, multa vota suscipiuntur, multa redduntur, 20 sed nullum in proximo suffugium aut imbris aut solis.
3 Videor ergo munifice simul religioseque facturus, si aedem quam pulcherrimam exstruxero, addidero porticus aedi, illam ad usum deae, has ad hominum. Velim ergo emas quattuor marmoreas columnas, cuius tibi videbitur 25 generis, emas marmora, quibus solum, quibus parietes

excolantur. Erit etiam vel faciendum vel emendum 4
ipsius deae signum, quia antiquum illud e ligno quibusdam sui partibus vetustate truncatum est. Quantum ad 5
porticus, nihil interim occurrit quod videatur istinc esse
5 repetendum; nisi tamen ut formam secundum rationem
loci scribas. Neque enim possunt circumdari templo;
nam solum templi hinc flumine et abruptissimis ripis
hinc via cingitur. Est ultra viam latissimum pratum, 6
in quo satis apte contra templum ipsum porticus explica-
10 buntur; nisi quid tu melius inveneris, qui soles locorum
difficultates arte superare. Vale.

C. PLINI CAECILI SECUNDI

AD TRAIANUM IMPERATOREM

TRAIANI IMPERATORIS

AD PLINIUM

EPISTULARUM

LIBER.

101. (I.)

C. PLINIUS TRAIANO IMPERATORI.

Congratulations to the Emperor upon his accession.

1 Tua quidem pietas, imperator sanctissime, optaverat ut quam tardissime succederes patri; sed dei inmortales festinaverunt virtutes tuas ad gubernacula rei publicae 2 quam susceperas admovere. Precor ergo ut tibi et per te generi humano prospera omnia, id est digna saeculo 5 tuo contingant. Fortem te et hilarem, imperator optime, et privatim et publice opto.

102. (II.)

C. PLINIUS TRAIANO IMPERATORI.

Thanks for the grant of the ius trium liberorum.

1 Exprimere, domine, verbis non possum quantum mihi gaudium attuleris, quod me dignum putasti iure trium liberorum. Quamvis enim Iuli Serviani, optimi viri 10 tuique amantissimi, precibus indulseris, tamen etiam ex

rescripto intellego libentius hoc ei te praestitisse, quia pro me rogabat. Videor ergo summam voti mei consecu- 2 tus, cum inter initia felicissimi principatus tui probaveris me ad peculiarem indulgentiam tuam pertinere; eoque 5 magis liberos concupisco, quos habere etiam illo tristissimo saeculo volui, sicut potes duobus matrimoniis meis credere. Sed dei melius, qui omnia integra bonitati tuae 3 reservarunt. Malui hoc potius tempore me patrem fieri quo futurus essem et securus et felix.

103. (LI.)

C. PLINIUS TRAIANO IMPERATORI.

Thanks for a favor.

10 Difficile est, domine, exprimere verbis quantam per- 1 ceperim laetitiam, quod et mihi et socrui meae praestitisti ut adfinem eius Caelium Clementem in hanc provinciam transferres. Ex illo enim mensuram bene- 2 ficii tui penitus intellego, cum tam plenam indulgentiam 15 cum tota domo mea experiar, cui referre gratiam parem ne audeo quidem, quamvis maxime possim. Itaque ad vota confugio deosque precor ut eis quae in me adsidue confers non indignus existimer.

104. (LXV.)

C. PLINIUS TRAIANO IMPERATORI.

The foundlings in Bithynia.

Magna, domine, et ad totam provinciam pertinens 1 20 quaestio est de condicione et alimentis eorum quos vocant

2 θρεπτούς. In qua ego auditis constitutionibus principum, quia nihil inveniebam aut proprium aut universale quod ad Bithynos ferretur, consulendum te existimavi quid observari velles. Neque enim putavi posse me in eo quod auctoritatem tuam posceret exemplo esse conten- 5
3 tum. Recitabatur autem apud me edictum quod dicebatur divi Augusti, ad Anniam pertinens: recitatae et epistulae divi Vespasiani ad Lacedaemonios et divi Titi ad eosdem et ad Achaeos, et Domitiani ad Avidium Nigrinum et Armenium Brocchum proconsules, item ad 10 Lacedaemonios: quae ideo tibi non misi, quia et parum emendata et quaedam non certae fidei videbantur et quia vera et emendata in scriniis tuis esse credebam.

105. (LXVI.)

TRAIANUS PLINIO S.

Trajan's answer.

1 Quaestio ista quae pertinet ad eos qui liberi nati expositi, deinde sublati a quibusdam et in servitute educati 15 sunt saepe tractata est, nec quicquam invenitur in commentariis eorum principum qui ante me fuerunt, quod ad
2 omnes provincias sit constitutum. Epistulae sane sunt Domitiani ad Avidium Nigrinum et Armenium Brocchum, quae fortasse debeant observari: sed intra eas provin- 20 cias de quibus rescripsit, inter quas non est Bithynia; et ideo nec adsertionem denegandam iis qui ex eiusmodi causa in libertatem vindicabuntur puto neque ipsam libertatem redimendam pretio alimentorum.

106. (LXXIV.)

C. PLINIUS TRAIANO IMPERATORI.

Callidromus is sent to tell his adventures to the Emperor.

Appuleius, domine, miles, qui est in statione Nicome- 1
densi, scripsit mihi quendam nomine Callidromum, cum
detineretur a Maximo et Dionysio pistoribus, quibus
operas suas locaverat, confugisse ad tuam statuam per-
5 ductumque ad magistratus indicasse servisse aliquando
Laberio Maximo captumque a Susago in Moesia et a
Decebalo muneri missum Pacoro, Parthiae regi, pluribusque annis in ministerio eius fuisse, deinde fugisse
atque ita in Nicomediam pervenisse. Quem ego per- 2
10 ductum ad me, cum eadem narrasset, mittendum ad te
putavi; quod paulo tardius feci, dum requiro gemmam,
quam sibi habentem imaginem Pacori et quibus ornatus
fuisset subtractam indicabat. Volui enim hanc quoque, 3
si inveniri potuisset, simul mittere, sicut glebulam misi
15 quam se ex Parthico metallo attulisse dicebat. Signata
est anulo meo, cuius est aposphragisma quadriga.

107. (LXXXVIII.)

C. PLINIUS TRAIANO IMPERATORI.

Birthday congratulations.

Opto, domine, et hunc natalem et plurimos alios 1
quam felicissimos agas aeternaque laude florentem vir-
tutis tuae gloriam incolumis et fortis aliis super alia
20 operibus augeas.

108. (LXXXIX.)

TRAIANUS PLINIO S.

Trajan's answer.

1 Agnosco vota tua, mi Secunde carissime, quibus precaris ut plurimos et felicissimos natales florente statu rei publicae nostrae agam.

109. (XCVI.)

C. PLINIUS TRAIANO IMPERATORI.

Pliny asks for instructions how to treat the Christians in his province.

1 Sollemne est mihi, domine, omnia de quibus dubito ad te referre. Quis enim potest melius vel cunctationem 5 meam regere vel ignorantiam instruere? Cognitionibus de Christianis interfui numquam: ideo nescio quid et 2 quatenus aut puniri soleat aut quaeri. Nec mediocriter haesitavi sitne aliquod discrimen aetatum an quamlibet teneri nihil a robustioribus differant, detur paenitentiae 10 venia an ei qui omnino Christianus fuit desisse non prosit, nomen ipsum, si flagitiis careat, an flagitia cohaerentia nomini puniantur. Interim in eis qui ad me tamquam 3 Christiani deferebantur hunc sum secutus modum. Interrogavi ipsos an essent Christiani. Confitentes iterum 15 ac tertio interrogavi, supplicium minatus: perseverantes duci iussi. Neque enim dubitabam, qualecumque esset quod faterentur, pertinaciam certe et inflexibilem obsti-4 nationem debere puniri. Fuerunt alii similis amentiae quos, quia cives Romani erant, adnotavi in urbem remit- 20

tendos. Mox ipso tractatu, ut fieri solet, diffundente se crimine, plures species inciderunt. Propositus est libel- 5 lus sine auctore multorum nomina continens. Qui negabant esse se Christianos aut fuisse, cum praeeunte me 5 deos appellarent et imagini tuae, quam propter hoc iusseram cum simulacris numinum adferri, ture ac vino supplicarent, praeterea male dicerent Christo, quorum nihil posse cogi dicuntur qui sunt re vera Christiani, dimittendos esse putavi. Alii ab indice nominati esse se Chris- 6 10 tianos dixerunt et mox negaverunt; fuisse quidem, sed desisse, quidam ante plures annos, non nemo etiam ante viginti. Hi quoque omnes et imaginem tuam deorumque simulacra venerati sunt et Christo male dixerunt. Adfirmabant autem hanc fuisse summam vel culpae suae 7 15 vel erroris, quod essent soliti stato die ante lucem convenire carmenque Christo quasi deo dicere secum invicem, seque sacramento non in scelus aliquod obstringere, sed ne furta, ne latrocinia, ne adulteria committerent, ne fidem fallerent, ne depositum appellati abnegarent: qui- 20 bus peractis morem sibi discedendi fuisse, rursusque coëundi ad capiendum cibum, promiscuum tamen et innoxium; quod ipsum facere desisse post edictum meum, quo secundum mandata tua hetaerias esse vetueram. Quo magis necessarium credidi ex duabus ancillis, quae 8 25 ministrae dicebantur, quid esset veri et per tormenta quaerere. Nihil aliud inveni quam superstitionem pravam inmodicam. Ideo dilata cognitione ad consulendum te decucurri. Visa est enim mihi res digna consultatione, 9 maxime propter periclitantium numerum. Multi enim 30 omnis aetatis, omnis ordinis, utriusque sexus etiam, vocantur in periculum et vocabuntur. Neque civitates tantum sed vicos etiam atque agros superstitionis istius

contagio pervagata est; quae videtur sisti et corrigi
10 posse. Certe satis constat prope iam desolata templa
coepisse celebrari et sacra sollemnia diu intermissa repeti
pastumque venire victimarum, cuius adhuc rarissimus
emptor inveniebatur. Ex quo facile est opinari 5
quae turba hominum emendari possit, si sit paenitentiae
locus.

110. (XCVII.)

TRAIANUS PLINIO S.

Trajan's answer.

1 Actum quem debuisti, mi Secunde, in excutiendis causis
eorum qui Christiani ad te delati fuerant secutus es.
Neque enim in universum aliquid quod quasi certam for- 10
2 mam habeat constitui potest. Conquirendi non sunt: si
deferantur et arguantur, puniendi sunt, ita tamen ut qui
negaverit se Christianum esse idque re ipsa manifestum
fecerit, id est supplicando deis nostris, quamvis suspectus
in praeteritum, veniam ex paenitentia inpetret. Sine 15
auctore vero propositi libelli in nullo crimine locum
habere debent. Nam et pessimi exempli nec nostri saeculi
est.

ABBREVIATIONS IN THE NOTES

A. & G.	Allen and Greenough's Latin Grammar.
B.	Bennett's Latin Grammar.
Cagnat	Cours d'Épigraphie Latine.
Cowan	Letters of Pliny, Books I. and II. London, 1889.
C.I.L.	Corpus Inscriptionum Latinarum.
Class. Dict. . .	Any dictionary of Classical Antiquities, especially Harper's Dictionary of Classical Literature and Antiquities, edited by Peck.
Crit. App. . . .	Critical Appendix to this volume.
H.	Harkness's Latin Grammar.
Kraut	Ueber Syntax und Stil des jüngeren Plinius; Prof. K. Kraut. Programm des Kgl. Würtemb. Seminars Schönthal. Fues, Tübingen, 1872.
Lagergren . . .	De Vita et Elocutione C. Plinii Caecilii Secundi. Upsala, 1872.
Lewis	Translation of Pliny's Letters. London, 1879.
Mayor	Letters of Pliny, Book III. London, 1889.
Melmoth	Translation of Pliny's Letters. London, 1746–1810.
Merivale	History of the Romans under the Empire.
Mommsen . . .	Index Nominum, in large edition of Keil's Pliny.
Paneg.	Pliny's Panegyric.
Pr. & B.	Prichard and Bernard's Selected Letters of Pliny. Oxford, 1891.
Roby	Grammar of the Latin Language from Plautus to Suetonius.
Smith, Dict. . .	Smith's Dictionary of Greek and Roman Biography and Mythology.

NOTES

BOOK I

Page 1. Letter 1. This first letter serves as a dedication of the collection, or at least of the first book, to the author's friend. Septicius is with some probability identified with the C. Septicius Clarus who was *praefectus praetorio* under Hadrian, 119–121 A.D., and was afterward deprived of the office by the same emperor; see Ael. Spart. *vita Hadriani* 9; 11; 15. To him are addressed Epp. I. 15; VII. 28; and VIII. 1. Suetonius dedicated to him his *Lives of the Twelve Caesars;* cf. Roth, *Suetonius*, Praef. p. ix. Pliny describes him, Ep. II. 9. 4, *C. Septicium, quo nihil verius, nihil simplicius, nihil candidius, nihil fidelius novi.* Pliny's intimate and friendly relations with the whole family of Septicius are evident from Epp. II. 9; VII. 28; VIII. 1.

1\. **paulo curatius**: here in a word we have expressed the conscious, artificial character of these letters, composed and arranged for publication.

3\. **non servato temporis ordine**: this is to be regretted, but there is some question as to how far the expression is to be literally understood. In regard to the chronology of the letters and of Pliny's life, see Appendix I.

4\. **Superest**, etc.: *it only remains for you not to repent*, etc.

5\. **consilii**: *of your advice* to publish the letters. **obsequii**: *of my compliance.*

7\. **addidero**: i.e., if I compose any more than those already written.

Letter 2. Caninius Rufus was a townsman of Pliny, a citizen of Comum. To him is addressed Ep. III. 7; simply to Caninius, Epp. II. 8; VI. 21; VII. 18; VIII. 4; IX. 33. In Ep. VIII. 4, he is about to write a poem on the Dacian wars, showing that he was a kindred spirit with Pliny in the matter of interest in literature.

8. Quid agit: informal personification; the same expression is used of inanimate objects in Ep. II. 11. 25. **Comum**: now Como, on the lake of the same name, Pliny's birthplace. **suburbanum**: sc. *praedium;* a country estate near a town.

9. porticus: *colonnade, cloister.*

10. platanon: *grove of plane trees;* the plane was a favorite shade tree. **eurīpus**: *canal;* as a proper name it is applied to the channel between Euboea and Boeotia. **viridis et gemmeus**: *green and sparkling*, or, possibly, *with green and flowery banks.*

11. subiectus et serviens lacus: *the charming lake below;* i.e., the Lacus Larius, Lake of Como. See Crit. App.

12. solida: *firm;* it had to be hard enough to give a solid foothold to the bearers of a litter, but was not so hard as to jolt unpleasantly the person carried. **gestatio**: *promenade, exercising ground*, for riding in a litter or on horseback. **balineum**: an elaborate bath was at this period a part of every Roman country house of importance. See Harper's Classical Dictionary, article *Balneae.*

13. sol . . . circumit: cf. Ep. II. 17. 8. **triclinia**: *dining rooms;* τρικλίνιον, a couch running around three sides of a table. See Class. Dict.

14. popularia: *for large parties;* cf. Ovid, *Metam.* VI. 198. **paucorum**: *intended for a few guests.* **cubicula**: *rooms, apartments*, especially the small ones used for sleeping. Like the modern Southern Europeans, the Romans took a *siesta* in the hot part of the day. Pliny also uses the word in the sense of *salon*, without an epithet; e.g., Ep. II. 17.

Page 2. **2. intentione . . . obeundae**: *by reason of your careful attention to your property;* thrift was a virtue peculiarly respected by the Romans.

3. si minus: *if not;* see note on *si non*, page 37, line 15.

4. unus ex multis: *like other people;* cf. Hor. *Sat.* I. 9. 71, *unus multorum.* **Quin**: *why . . . not?*

5. alto . . . pinguique secessu: *deep, calm retreat. Pinguis*, in this figurative sense, is untranslatable, but reminds us of a similar use of *gras* in the expression *dormir la grasse matinée.* **te . . . adseris**: *devote yourself.* The proper meaning of *adserere* is seen in the phrase *adserere in libertatem*, to claim as free by a suit at law a person held in slavery. Caninius is to claim his freedom from other occupations in order to give his whole attention to literature.

7. in his . . . reponatur: *on these let your waking and even your sleeping hours be spent.* Notice *vigilia*, instead of *vigiliae* which would be more in accordance with classical usage.

8. exclude: *hatch out;* but on the meaning of this word consult Crit. App.

9. reliqua rerum tuarum: partitive genitive with neuter adjective, instead of *reliquae res tuae;* cf. *reliquum diei*, Livy XXV. 38. 23, where the phrase matches *maior pars noctis.*

10. sortientur: *will fall to the lot of.*

Letter 3. Pompeia Celerina, perhaps the wife of Vettius Proculus, Ep. IX. 13. 13, was by a former marriage the mother of Pliny's second wife. She is mentioned, Ep. III. 19. 8; Ep. VI. 10. 1; *ad Trai.* 51.

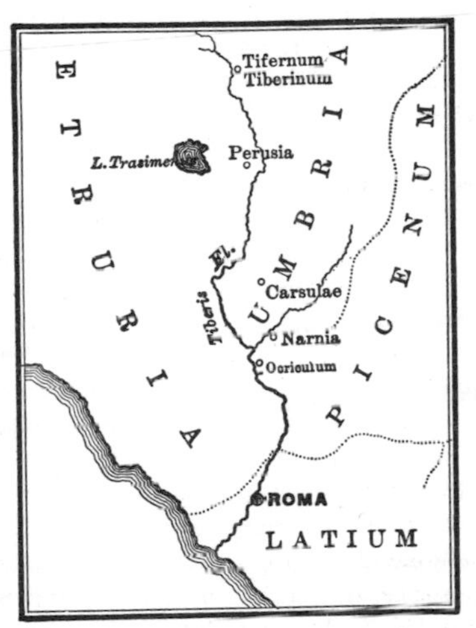

14. copiarum: *conveniences.* **Ocriculano**, etc.: country houses at Ocriculum, Narnia (Nequinum), and Carsulae, in Umbria, and at Perusia in Etruria; see map. The adjectives, in neuter, agree with *praedio*, understood.

16. Ex epistulis meis, etc.: we must suspect a corruption of the text here, but, taking it as it stands, it seems to mean: *one old letter of mine, a short one, shows my knowledge of the charms of your villas and that I have no need that you should write me a description of them.* But the sentence is a very lame one.

18. hoc: adverbial accusative.

19. tui . . . mei: sc. *servi.*

21. nostra: sc. *praedia.*　**deverteris**: *you come to lodge.*

22. ac: *as.*

24. mitium: how *mitis* Pliny was is shown, e.g., in Ep. V. 19; also in Ep. VIII. 16.

25. novitatibus: notice the plural abstract; the sense is semi-concrete, 'new things.'

26. probari: *to please;* lit. 'to approve themselves'; passive with middle force. This use of the passive is rather characteristic of Silver Latin. Cf. Quintus Curtius's mannerism of using the active with *se* for the passive. Curtius probably wrote about two generations earlier than Pliny. See Introduction II. § 9. *c.*

27. ipsos: sc. *dominos.*

Page 3. Letter 4. This letter appears to have been written after January 1, 97, but before the death of Nerva. An account of (C. Licinius) Voconius Romanus (cf. C.I.L. II. 386 C. 3865 a) is given in Ep. II. 13. From this letter, and from *ad Trai.* 4, it appears that he was Pliny's fellow-student and comrade in arms, that he was an advocate, a flamen of Hither Spain (see note on Ep. II. 13. 4), that Pliny obtained for him the *ius trium liberorum* from Nerva, and the *latus clavus* from Trajan. Epp. I. 5; III. 13 are addressed to Voconius Romanus; Epp. II. 1; VI. 15; VI. 33; VIII. 8; IX. 7; IX. 28 to Romanus. Demogeot (*Pline le Jeune, Lettres Choisies*) says that Romanus became a friend of Hadrian, who composed his epitaph: *Lascivus versu, mente pudicus erat.*

1. M. Regulo: M. Aquilius Regulus rose to great wealth and power under Nero by 'delation.' Accused at the beginning of Vespasian's reign, he was defended in the senate by his half-brother, the eloquent L. Vipstanus Messalla. Tac. *Hist.* IV. 42. The charges against him detailed by Tacitus tend to confirm our belief in the justness of Pliny's opinion. Martial's effusive compliments to Regulus, Epig. I. 12; 82; 111; IV. 16, count for nothing as testimonials to his character. He stands almost alone as an object of open scorn and detestation to Pliny, who is nearly always mild and charitable in his judgments. Pliny tells three scandalous stories about him, Ep. II. 20; describes his tasteless and hypocritical mourning at his son's death, Ep. IV. 7; but after his death mourns his loss to the legal profession, Ep. VI. 2. **timidiorem humiliorem**: Regulus feared punishment for his crimes, after the death of his patron Domitian. But in dealing with informers, as in many other respects, the government of Nerva showed itself moderate, not to say feeble. Observe the asyndeton; this is a noticeable feature of Pliny's style, but the same may be said of many authors who labor much after striking effects.

3. tectiora: the free comparison of participial adjectives, which marks the Silver Age of Latin, is already noticeable in Livy.

5. Rustici Aruleni: L. Junius Arulenus Rusticus, a Stoic, pupil of Paetus Thrasea, was put to death in A.D. 93 for writing a panegyric on Thrasea and Helvidius Priscus; the book was publicly burned; cf. Suet. *Domit.* 10; Tac. *Agr.* 2; Pliny's opinion of Rusticus is expressed in Epp. I. 14; II. 18. **periculum foverat**: *had promoted* *the prosecution.* Cowan translates: *had fostered the dangers*, and remarks upon the exceptional use of *foverat* in a bad sense.

6. **librum**: *speech.*

7. **Stoicorum simiam**: *ape of the Stoics;* the scornful epithet reflects the unpopularity of the Stoics with Domitian's courtiers.

8. **Vitelliana cicatrice stigmosum**: *marked with a Vitellian scar*, i.e., branded with disgrace by the scar of a wound received in Vitellius's service; referring probably to the occasion described in Tac. *Hist.* III. 80, when Rusticus was sent as envoy to the troops of Vespasian, as they were about to enter Rome in 69 A.D. **Stigmosum**: this hybrid, with a Greek basis and Latin suffix, is a rare and late word; it is used by Petronius, § 109. **eloquentiam**: *style;* it is not clear whether this is meant as a sneer at Regulus's language. In Ep. IV. 7. 4, however, we find a severe criticism of his oratorical abilities.

9. **Lacerat**: *defames;* so we speak of 'tearing a reputation to tatters.' **Herennium Senecionem**: another friend of Pliny and his colleague in the prosecution of Baebius Massa on behalf of the Baetici; cf. Epp. VII. 33; III. 11. 3; Tac. *Agr.* 2; put to death by Domitian on the accusation of Metius Carus, for writing a life of Helvidius Priscus at the request of the latter's widow, Fannia.

10. **Metius Carus**: one of the most noted of the informers; his name became proverbial in literature; cf. Tac. *Agr.* 45; Juv. I. 36; also Ep. VII. 19. It was he who lodged against Pliny the information which was found among Domitian's papers after his murder. Ep. VII. 27. 14.

11. **meis mortuis**: he means the victims of his accusations. **molestus sum**: *interfere with, annoy.* **Crasso**: M. Licinius Crassus, brother of the Piso adopted by Galba, was accused by Regulus and put to death by Nero; Tac. *Hist.* I. 48; IV. 42. **Camerino**: Sulpicius Camerinus, proconsul of Africa, accused under Nero, but acquitted; Tac. *Ann.* XIII. 52. Apparently he was subsequently less fortunate.

14. **recitaret**: i.e., to his friends. **non adhibuerat**: *had not invited.*

15. **quam capitaliter**: *with what deadly hostility. Capitaliter* is a late word, used first by Pliny, so far as we know. **centumviros**: for an explanation of the centumviral court, see Introduction, page xvi.

19. **relegatus**: *relegatio* was a milder form of banishment than *deportatio*, for it did not involve loss of property or civil *status*, nor was it always for life. **tibi**: ethical dative.

27. pietate: *loyalty.*

Page 4. **5. laqueis**: *in the toils.*

6. Nunc: i.e., since Nerva's accession. **Caecilium Celerem**. cf. Ep. VII. 17; perhaps the same as the governor of Celtiberia, Martial VII. 52.

7. Fabium Iustum: to him are addressed Ep. I. 11 and perhaps Ep. VII. 2; Tacitus's *Dialogus* also is dedicated to him.

8. Spurinnam: an account of him is found in Epp. II. 7 and III. 1; to him are addressed Epp. III. 10; V. 17. He was highly respected by Pliny.

10. sed plane mane: *yes, very early;* the assonance is unfortunate, though this is not a case of strict *homoioteleuton;* plānē mānĕ.

12. efficias ne: *efficere* with *ne* is rare; as it denotes the accomplishment of a result, it is naturally followed by *ut non.*

13. venio: *I'm coming.* **Immo**: *nay;* courtesy on the part of the younger man.

14. porticu Liviae: see Middleton, Remains of Ancient Rome, I. 338, 381; Augustus, in honor of Livia, his wife, built on the Esquiline hill a spacious piazza surrounded by colonnades. It was on the way from Pliny's house to the Forum; cf. Martial X. 19, the epigram which is quoted in Ep. III. 21. In Ep. V. 1. 9, Pliny meets a man at the Temple of Concord, built by Livia herself on this piazza.

16. parce: adverb; observe its emphatic position.

17. quid renuntiandum: *what answer should be returned.*

18. Mauricum: Junius Mauricus, brother of Arulenus Rusticus; cf. introductory note to Ep. I. 14. Banished by Domitian, in 93 A.D.; recalled by Nerva in 96 A.D. His character was similar to that of his brother. To him are addressed Epp. I. 14; II. 18; VI. 14; and he is mentioned in Ep. III. 11. 3. Cf. also Tac. *Hist.* IV. 40; *Agr.* 45; Plutarch, *Galba*, 8. Martial V. 28, says, *licet vincas . . . aequitate Mauricos, oratione Regulos.* His friendship with Nerva and Trajan is referred to in Ep. IV. 22. 3, 4.

22. convenit: *met.* **in praetoris officio**: *while attending upon the praetor;* i.e., in the suite of friends attending the new magistrate on his assumption of office. *Officium* meant either a voluntary courtesy or an obligatory service; from the former meaning developed the post-Augustan one of a ceremony at which such courtesy was rendered.

23. secretum: *a private interview.* **animo meo**: strict classical usage would require *in.*

24. penitus haereret: *rankled.*

25. Satrio Rufo: mentioned in Ep. IX. 13. 17.

27. eloquentia saeculi nostri: cf. Tac. *Dial.* 19. This is a sneer at Pliny, who venerated Cicero as his model.

28. maligne: *sneeringly, spitefully.*

29. honorificum: *complimentary.*

Page 5. **3. quamvis palleat**: the post-Augustan writers developed the practice of using *quamvis* with the subjunctive to concede a fact, as the classical writers used *quamquam* with the indicative.

5, 6. qui . . . dissimulet: a clause of characteristic with accessory causal force. **scripsit**: sc. *Modestus.*

8. Regulus . . . nequissimus: Modestus was apparently quoting from Cic. *de Domo sua*, 18. 48, *hoc ministro omnium non bipedum solum sed etiam quadrupedum impurissimo.* (Gierig.) See Wölfflin's *Archiv für Lexicog. und Gramm.* IV. 139, for an ingenious explanation of the wit of this passage, a punning use of the word *Regulus.*

11. dum . . . venit: we should expect the imperfect subjunctive; the present indicative is colloquial in such a sequence as this.

12. δυσκαθαίρετον: *hard to overturn.*

13. locuples: cf. Ep. II. 20. 13; Martial I. 12; VII. 31. **factiosus**: *influential;* i.e., he had a strong following (*factio*). **curatur a multis**: this is shown by Martial's epigrams cited *supra.* Martial was needy and venal, Pliny was benevolent and independent. We cannot doubt which gives the true picture of Regulus. There is a similar contrast between the portraits of Fouquet, as given by Dumas in his *Vicomte de Bragelonne* and as given in history.

14. quod: viz., being feared.

15. ut haec concussa labantur: *that this fabric* (of influence) *may be shaken and fall in ruins.* **gratia**: *popularity.*

20. ratio constabit: *I shall be justified*, lit. *the account will balance;* an idiom of the language of book-keeping. **aecum**: adjectives and nouns in *-quos, -quom* changed these terminations to *-cus, -cum* about the close of the Ciceronian age. The terminations *-quus, -quum*, though regularly given in our grammars, did not become current till after Pliny's time. B., Appendix to *Lat. Gr.* 57. 1. *d*), 2.

Letter 5. Cornelius Tacitus, the great historian, Pliny's intimate friend. There are ten other letters addressed to him, viz., Epp. I. 20; IV. 13; VI. 9; VI. 16; VI. 20; VII. 20; VII. 33; VIII. 7; IX. 10; IX. 14. This letter is one of the best illustrations of the author's 'graceful pedantry,' a delightfully frank account of a characteristic bit of affectation on the part of this *poseur.*

23. Ego ille: note the double pronoun, proper where *ille* is used with the first or second person; cf. the German usage with the relative *ich der ich*, etc.; *Vater unser der du bist*, etc.

24. et quidem pulcherrimos: Cowan remarks upon the frequent omission of the pronoun before *quidem* in Pliny and also in Cicero; here we might expect *et eos* or *et illos quidem*. There are several instances in Tacitus of this usage, but there is said to be only one in Quintilian. Kraut, § 31.

25. inertia: = *otium*, which does not necessarily mean idleness, but often the quiet pursuit of literature or science. The Romans did not consider literary labor as work, but only a dignified form of idleness. **non . . . discederem**: *and that, too, without at all departing.*

26. retia: *nets*, surrounding a part of the wood into which the game was driven by beaters. Hunting methods with the Romans seem to have been very unsportsmanlike.

27. pugillares: sc. *tabellae*, small memorandum tablets, to hold in the shut hand (*pugnus*), formed of leaves of ivory or wood, covered with a film of wax (*cera*), on which the Romans wrote with a *stilus*, an instrument pointed at one end for writing, and provided at the other with a flat blade or a round knob for erasures. **meditabar . . . enotabamque**: iterative; *I would think and make notes.*

Page 6. **1. vacuas**: i.e., without game.

2. ceras: note-book, another word for *pugillares;* cf. Ep. IX. 36. 6, *venor aliquando, sed non sine pugillaribus*, etc. **Non est quod**: *there's no reason why.* **hoc studendi genus**: here Pliny is unfaithful to his teacher, who does not approve of this sort of study. Cf. Quint. *Inst. Orat.* X. 3. 22. (Cowan.)

4. undique: adjectival use of adverb. **ipsumque illud**: the order is the reverse of the normal one; see Crit. App.

5. cogitationis incitamenta: *aids to reflection.*

6. auctore me: *upon the strength of my example.*

7. lagunculam: *wine flask;* diminutive of *laguna* or *lagena.*

8. non Dianam, etc.: cf. Ep. IX. 10. 1, *cupio praeceptis tuis parere: sed aprorum tanta penuria est, ut Minervae et Dianae, quas ais pariter colendas, convenire non possit.* **montibus**: dative instead of *in montibus.*

Letter 6. To Minutius Fundanus are addressed Epp. IV. 15; VI. 6. In the former he is spoken of as likely to become consul the next year. Ep. V. 16 is in praise of his young daughter, who had just died. He appears to have been proconsul of Asia under Hadrian.

10. Mirum est, etc.: *strange what a good account we can give, or think we can give, of each separate day spent in the city.* (Cowan.) The use of *quam* here is unusual. Ordinarily *quam* (instead of *ut*, 'how') is employed only when it limits an adjective or adverb, or, at least, in some way denotes degree of intensity. **ratio . . . constet**: cf. note on *ratio constabit*, page 5, line 20.

11. pluribus iunctisque: *several successive days*, taken together. **non constet**: in English we do not repeat the verb, but simply employ the negative. In Latin the repetition of the verb is necessary.

13. officio togae virilis: *at a coming of age;* on *officio*, see note on page 4, line 22. The assumption of the *toga virilis*, which was all white, in place of the purple-bordered one (*praetexta*) of childhood, was the most striking feature of the ceremonies which marked the coming of a young Roman to man's estate. The age varied from fourteen to seventeen.

14. frequentavi: *I have attended.* **ille**: *so and so, such an one.* **ad signandum**: i.e., as a witness, seven being required by law; *signare* is to seal, not sign, which is *subscribere.* Under the strict *jus civile* neither was necessary; under the praetorian law, sealing was required; under the law of the emperors, both sealing and signing by the witnesses, whose number was the same under all systems. For the different ways of making wills, see Harper's Class. Dict., article *Testamentum*, or Sandars's *Justinian*, Bk. II., Tit. 10, *De testamentis ordinandis*.

15. in advocationem: to support in a legal trial, by one's opinion, one's presence and sympathy, sometimes by one's testimony, or even by addressing the court. **in consilium**: *for advice* in private, if a suitor; but if a judge, it is a request *to act as his assessor* (*associate*) in a trial.

17. inania: *useless, petty, insignificant.* **cum secesseris**: i.e., into the country.

18. frigidis rebus: *trifles, trivial things;* cf. Ep. IV. 17. 4.

19. postquam . . . lego, etc.: *whenever I read*, etc.; *evenit* is iterative in sense, expressing what is his usual experience. **Laurentino**: his favorite villa at Laurentum, on the coast of Latium, described in Ep. II. 17. He says, Ep. IV. 6. 2, *ibi enim plurimum scribo.*

20. corpori vaco means the same as *corpus curo*, attend to physical comfort — meals, bath, exercise, etc.

23. sinistris . . . carpit: *slanders.*

25. rumoribus: *gossip.* **inquietor**: a late word.

27. sinceram: *genuine.*

Page 7. **2. μουσεῖον**: *abode of the Muses.*

3. strepitum: cf. Hor. *Car.* III. 29. 12, *fumum et opes strepitumque Romae.*

4. multum: *very.* Hor. *Car.* I. 25. 5; *Sat.* I. 3. 57.

5. Satius est enim: notice *enim* in third place.

6. Atilius: Atilius Crescens, a lifelong and intimate friend of Pliny, with some reputation as a wit. He is quoted again in Ep. II. 14. 2. Cf. also Ep. VI. 8, concerning his studious tastes and small means; Cic. *de Off.* III. 1. 1, Scipio's saying, *numquam se minus otiosum esse quam cum otiosus, nec minus solum quam cum solus esset;* Seneca, *de Brev. Vitae* 12. 2, *non otiosa vita . . . sed desidiosa occupatio.*

7. otiosum esse: *to have nothing to do.* **nihil agere**: *to be (busy) doing nothing.* Pliny's occupations in the country were anything but rural; everywhere he was, first of all, a man of letters. Collignon says, "*Il appartient à la race de ces gens dont parle Du Bellay:*

'Toujours par quelque endroit le style vous démange.'

Pellisson, *les Romains.*"

Letter 7. Fabius Justus, consul suffectus 102 A.D. Cf. note on page 4, line 7. Ep. VII. 2 is perhaps addressed to him.

8. Olim = *iamdudum, iampridem:* mostly post-Augustan in this sense; *for a long time you have sent me no letters.*

10. priores: *the ancients, our fathers;* poetic.

11. si vales, etc.: this formula was so stereotyped that it was commonly written with initials only, S. V. B. E. E. V. Cf. Sen. *Ep.* 15. 1, *mos antiquis fuit usque ad meam servatus aetatem, primis epistulae verbis adicere, si vales bene est, ego valeo.*

12. Ludere: *jesting.*

13. quid agas: *how you are.*

Letter 8. For information about Calestrius Tiro see Epp. VII. 16; VII. 32. To Tiro are addressed Epp. VI. 1; VI. 22; IX. 5. He and Pliny served together in the army, were colleagues in the quaestorship, and, though Tiro was the first to obtain the tribuneship of the plebs, again in the praetorship. Tiro became proconsul of Baetica. He and Pliny often visited each other.

15. si iactura, etc.: *if loss is a strong enough word* for the occasion; *iactura* was originally the throwing overboard of part of a cargo to save a ship in a storm.

16. Corellius Rufus: the husband of Hispulla and father of Corellia Hispulla, § 3, *infra;* of senatorial rank, Ep. VII. 31. 4.

cf. Dio 68. 2 ; his advice often asked by Pliny, Epp. V. 1. 5 ; IX. 13. 6 ; praised Pliny to Nerva, Ep. IV. 17. 8 ; praised after his death, Epp. III. 3. 1 ; IV. 17. 1, 4 ; VII. 11. 3 ; IX. 13. 6. Pliny showed his gratitude by kindness to Corellia after her father's death.

18. quae : strictly speaking, the antecedent is *genus*, not *mortis*, but the confusion is a natural one. **fatalis** : *necessary*.

19. utcumque : *somehow or other;* see Introduction II. § 5. *b*. **finiuntur** : this sense of the word is poetic and post-Augustan.

20. arcessita : *voluntary*, i.e., invited ; men ordinarily wait till death comes to them naturally.

Page 8. **1. sapientibus** : *to philosophers*.

2. quamquam . . . habentem : when thus used with a participle or adjective, *quamquam* is elliptical and has the sense of *quamvis*, which is an adverb as well as a conjunction. Earlier writers ordinarily use *quamvis* in such cases. Kraut, § 39.

5. pignora : this word in the figurative sense generally applies to children. A similar figure occurs in the famous sentence of Bacon, Essay VIII., 'He that hath wife and children hath given hostages to fortune.' Here the word is used of relatives in general, as in Tac. *Ann.* XVI. 26. **longa . . . iniqua** : *tedious . . . painful*.

6. valetudine : notice that in consequence of usage *valetudo* oftener means ill health than good. **pretia** = *praemia : rewards of living*, and so *motives for living*.

8. ipsum audiebam : see Crit. App.

9. Patrius : *hereditary*.

11. quoad viridis aetas : *as long as he was in the prime of life*.

13. indignissima : *the most cruel*.

16. iacentem : i.e., ill in bed.

17. hoc moris : *this custom ;* partitive genitive. **intrasset** : iterative subjunctive after *quotiens*, instead of the indicative, which was regular in the Ciceronian age. B. 288. 3. a ; A. & G. 316. a. 2 ; H. 518. 1 ; Roby 1716.

18. quamquam . . . capacissima : cf. note on *quamquam . . . habentem*, line 2, above.

19. Circumtulit oculos : people had to be on their guard in Domitian's time against spies even in the household.

21. scilicet : *of course*. **latroni** : i.e., Domitian. **Dedisses** : conditional without *si ;* indefinite subject. Cowan quotes as parallel Hor. *Sat.* I. 3. 15–17,

deciens centena dedisses
Huic parco, paucis contento, quinque diebus
Nil erat in loculis.

22. fecisset quod optabat: i.e., would have helped to kill Domitian.

23. cuius ille compos: *which he realizing.* **securus liberque**: i.e., by the death of the tyrant before his own.

25. valetudo: *his illness.* See note on line 6 above.

28. Hispulla: probably not identical with Calpurnia Hispulla, the aunt of Pliny's third wife. **C. Geminium**: perhaps the person addressed in Epp. VII. 1; VII. 24; VIII. 5; VIII. 22; IX. 11; IX. 30. It is doubtful, however, whether the name of that person is Geminus or Geminius.

31. perveneram . . . cum nuntiat: an instance of *cum inversum;* hence the indicative in the *cum*-clause, B. 288. 2; A. & G. 325. b; Roby 1733.

32. Iulius Atticus: this may or may not be the person to whom Martial addressed Epigr. VII. 32.

Page 9. **2. sane**: *indeed.*

3. κέκρικα: *I have decided.*

4. reliquit: an instance of zeugma, probably unconscious. The remark really *excited* admiration and *left* regret.

12. testem: *an interested spectator;* cf. Ep. IV. 17.

13. contubernali: first, a tent companion, then any close comrade or associate.

14. Calvisio: *C. Calvisius Rufus*, a *decurio* of Comum, Ep. V. 7. 3, 4. In Ep. IV. 4. 1 he is called *contubernalem meum.* To him are addressed Epp. II. 20; III. 1; III. 19; V. 7; VIII. 2; IX. 6.

17. quae audierim numquam: *such as I have never heard;* subjunctive in a clause of characteristic. Pliny does not appear to disapprove of suicide under certain circumstances. It was a morbid fashion, a symptom of a moribund civilization, when much of the real interest of living had departed.

Letter 9. Sosius Senecio was the son-in-law of Sex. Julius Frontinus and the father-in-law of Q. Pompeius Falco. He is probably the person addressed in Ep. IV. 4. He was *consul ordinarius* in A.D. 102 and in 107; *consul suffectus* in 98 and 99. Trajan respected him highly and erected a statue to him, Dio 68. 16. To him Plutarch dedicated his famous 'Lives.'

20. proventum: *crop*, or, if this word be thought insufficiently respectful, *harvest.* The highly educated nobility of this time, being zealously excluded from active politics, devoted themselves in great numbers to literature, for occupation and amusement. It was a period of 'overproduction' on the part of authors.

21. Aprili: cf. Juv. III. 9, where it is August, and Ep. VIII. 21. 2, where it is July. The occasion here referred to was a time of year long before people went out of town. **quo non recitaret aliquis**. it was a custom, said to have originated with Asinius Pollio, to recite one's poetical, historical, or rhetorical compositions to one's friends, at one's house; or to larger audiences, sometimes in public places, sometimes in rooms hired for the purpose. The great number of these recitations rendered attendance upon them a very burdensome social obligation; cf. l. 23, below: *pigre coitur*. What had been originally intended as a safeguard, viz., the submission of literary works, before publication, to competent critics, had developed into a custom which most people evidently regarded as a nuisance. *Quo non recitaret* is a clause qualifying *dies; aliquis* is rendered emphatic by its position, last in the sentence.

22. studia: *literary pursuits, learning.*

24. stationibus: *places of assembly, public resorts*, where people lounged and met their friends. Such were the various *fora, porticus*, and especially the halls in the great public baths. **sedent**: i.e., outside the audience. **fabulis**: *conversation, gossip.*

25. subinde: said to have been used in prose first by Livy.

26. praefationem: *preliminary remarks*, not part of the work to be recited. Cf. Martial III. 18,

Perfrixisse tuas questa est praefatio fauces.
Cum te excusaris, Maxime, quid recitas?

27. evolverit: the *liber*, a long strip of papyrus, rolled upon a stick was unrolled as the reading proceeded. The question therefore means: *whether he has nearly finished his manuscript.* **tunc quoque**: *even then.*

Page 10. **3. simpliciter**: *without any attempt at disguise.* **libere**: *without embarrassment.*

4. Claudium Caesarem: this emperor had literary ambition, and was somewhat of a historian: he was a curious combination of imbecility and erudition. **spatiaretur**: *was walking up and down.*

6. Nonianum: M. Servilius Nonianus, consul in 35 A.D., died in 59; a historian in the time of Claudius. Cf. Quintil. X. 1. 102; Tac. *Dial.* 23; *Ann.* XIV. 19. **subitum**: adjective for adverb.

9. quia . . . perdidisse: a good example of the paradoxical statement of which our author is fond. His manner of saying a thing is often more important than the thing he says.

13. plerique: *very many;* this sense is common in Pliny, while in early writers the word usually means 'most.' **studia**: sc. *amat.*

16. aliquid quod non recitem: *not something to recite.*

18. creditor: i.e., in order to put the readers under obligation to listen to me in turn.

Letter 10. For information about Junius Mauricus, see note on page 4, line 18. In Ep. II. 18, Pliny has been asked to select an instructor for the nephews of Mauricus; in Ep. VI. 14, he accepts an invitation to visit Mauricus in his country house at Formiae.

20. fratris: Arulenus Rusticus; see note on page 3, line 5.

21. mihi potissimum: *me rather than any one else.*

22. summum: *great.*

Page 11. **1. ex quo nasci**: in expressions of source, the preposition *ex* regularly accompanies the ablative of pronouns, otherwise it is unusual with the designation of a father.

3. Minicius Acilianus: we have no information about him, outside of this letter. **ut iuvenis iuvenem**: see Crit. App.

6. vobis: i.e., you and your brother. **Brixia**: a Roman *municipium* (free town), with the civil rights of a *colonia*, on the road from Comum to Aquileia, eighteen miles west of the Lago di Garda, Lacus Benacus, now Brescia. It had been a city of the Insubrians, and then of the Cenomani. The citizens of a *colonia* had the same private rights as Roman citizens in regard to property, but not the public rights of suffrage and eligibility to office at Rome.

7. nostra Italia: Transpadana. The same character is here attributed to it, as was traditionally ascribed to Livy's birthplace, Patavium, *rusticitas* being here used in a good sense.

8. antiquae: *good old;* often used with this connotation.

9. Minicius Macrinus: elsewhere simply Macrinus; Epp. II. 7; III. 4; VII. 6; VII. 10; VIII. 17; IX. 4, are addressed to him; he lived thirty-nine years with his wife Acilia, until her death, Ep. VIII. 5. To him Persius addressed his second Satire. **equestris ordinis princeps**: *a chief man of the equestrian order*, perhaps one of the more select class of *equites* (*illustres* or *splendidi*), not merely one of those whose property amounted to 400,000 sesterces. Equites who possessed the senatorial census of 800,000, 1,000,000, or 1,200,000 sesterces (the amount was different at different times), and who were eligible for a senatorial career, were sometimes called *illustres* or *splendidi.*

10. quia nihil altius voluit: this assigns the reason, not why Macrinus was *princeps ordinis equestris*, but, by implication, why he was merely of equestrian rank. Maecenas was another *eques* who *nihil altius voluit*. **adlectus inter praetorios**: i.e., given the rank and privileges of an ex-praetor, without having actually been praetor, involving, *inter alia*, the right to sit in the senate. *Adlectio inter quaestorios* also was common under the empire.

11. huic nostrae, etc.: Pliny himself had risen from the equestrian to the senatorial order.

12. ambitioni: *show, display*.

13. Serranam Proculam: not otherwise known. **e municipio Patavino**: Patavium (Padua), Livy's birthplace, the former capital of the Veneti. It was also the birthplace of Paetus Thrasea.

14. loci mores: they remained the same as in Livy's time.

15. quoque: *even*. **Contigit**: *he is fortunate in having*.

16. ei: i.e., to Minicius Acilianus. **P. Acilius**: perhaps the person addressed in Ep. III. 14. He must be Minicius's mother's brother, and we have here an instance of the usage of the time as to *cognomina* taken from the mother's family. See Introduction, pages viii, ix.

20. ac . . . remisit: *has already relieved you of the need of canvassing for him;* there was only one more office, the consulship, to obtain, and that was in the gift of the emperor.

21. facies liberalis: *the look of a gentleman*.

25. Nescio an adiciam: *I don't know whether to add*.

27. imaginor: a late word.

28. publicos mores: cf. Juvenal III. 160,

> *Quis gener hic placuit censu minor atque puellae*
> *Sarcinulis impar? quis pauper scribitur heres?* etc.

29. leges civitatis: i.e., such laws as those which fixed the property qualifications and privileges of senators, knights, and municipal magistrates. **quae . . . arbitrabantur**: the use of this verb constitutes a striking and bold personification of *leges*.

31. posteris: this word, which ordinarily means 'descendants' in general, here has the very unusual sense of *children*, and so is equivalent to *liberis*. **et his**: sc. *posteris*. **pluribus** = *compluribus*.

32. in condicionibus deligendis: *in choosing partners*. **ponendus est calculus**: *this consideration is to be weighed*. *Calculi* were pebbles used as counters in reckoning; hence our word 'calculate.'

Page 12. **2. quam**: connect with *supra*, line 1, a virtual comparative. **sustulisse**: *that I have exalted.*

5. onerare: i.e., by making people expect too much of him.

Letter 11. About Septicius Clarus, see note introductory to Ep. I. 1. Pliny playfully charges his friend, who has failed to come to dinner, with having gone elsewhere to get finer entertainment.

7. promittis: sc. *te venturum.* **Dicitur ius**: *I pronounce judgment on you.* **ad assem**: *to the last farthing.*

9. lactucae: *lettuce.* **cochleae**: *snails.* **ova**: eggs were eaten at the beginning of a meal; Hor. *Sat.* I. 3. 6, *ab ovo usque ad mala.* **alica**: *spelt*, made into broth.

10. mulso: a mixture of wine and honey. **nive**: snow was used as we use ice.

11. in ferculo: the tray on which dishes were brought in, sometimes the dishes themselves. **betacei**: *beet-root.* **cucurbitae**: *gourds.*

12. bulbi: *onions.* **mille**: cf. *sescenti*; i.e., an indefinitely large number. Numerous examples of the latter are found in Plautus, Terence, and Cicero, but *mille* was common as early, at least, as the Augustan age.

13. lectorem: not a *recitator* of his own productions, and yet a witty French editor thinks this may have frightened Septicius away.

14. nescio quem: here, as usually, implying a certain contempt or disparagement. **ostrea**, etc.: these are all expensive luxuries. **vulvas**: *sows' matrices.* **echinos**: *sea-urchins.*

15. Gaditanas: sc. *saltatrices; dancing girls from Cadiz.*

16. invidisti: *you have been niggardly, you have begrudged a pleasure.*

17. studuissemus: this inducement of 'literary amusement' is omitted from Horace's invitation to Torquatus, Ep. I. 5, and from Martial's to Toranius, Epig. V. 78.

18. apparatius: *more elaborately.*

19. simplicius: *with more abandon.* **incautius**: *with less reserve.* **nisi . . . excusaveris**, etc.: *if you don't after that prefer to decline the invitations of others, decline mine forever.*

Page 13. Letter 12. Sex. Erucius Clarus was the son of Erucius Clarus and Septicia, sister of C. Septicius Clarus. See introductory note on Ep. I. 1. We cannot be sure whether this letter is addressed to the son or to the father. Both are mentioned in Ep. II. 9, where it appears that the son had been quaestor and hoped to become tribune of the plebs. While legate of Trajan in the Parthian war, he captured Seleucia, Dio 68. 30. He was *praefectus urbi*, and consul for the second time in 146 A.D.; Aul. Gell. VII. 6. 12; XIII. 18. 2; *Vita Severi* 1. 3.

1. Pompeium Saturninum: to him were addressed Epp. I. 8; and (to Saturninus simply), V. 21; VII. 7; VII. 15; IX. 38. It appears that he wrote orations, history, and poetry, also that he was a comrade in arms of Neratius Priscus, Epp. VII. 7; VII. 8; VII. 15. **hunc . . . nostrum**: *my countryman of that name*, unless it means simply *our friend;* but in Ep. I. 8, it is Pliny's speech to the people of Comum, which he sends to Saturninus for criticism.

3. flexibile: *versatile.* **multiplex**: *many-sided.*

4. tenet, habet, possidet: a legal phrase, like the English 'to have and to hold.' Its triple character reminds us of Cicero, Pliny's constant model. See Introduction II. § 10. *o*.

6. meditata . . . subita: *prepared . . . extempore.* *meditata* has a passive sense; Roby 734. **sententiae**: *aphorisms.*

7. gravis et decora constructio: *dignified and graceful periods.* **sonantia . . . antiqua**: *his words have a classic ring about them.* (Cowan.)

8. Omnia . . . retractentur: *all this is wonderfully pleasing as it flows on in a kind of impetuous stream, pleasing also when you return to it.*

11. cuilibet veterum: Pliny was an ardent admirer of the *veteres.*

13. brevitate . . . sublimitate narrandi: *by his conciseness, clearness, or gracefulness, or even by the splendor and elevation of his diction.*

14. contionibus: the harangues embodied in his histories.

15. orationibus: *his own actual speeches.* **pressior . . . adductior**: *more restrained, chastened, compressed;* but it is hardly possible to put into English three words each embodying the same idea in a different metaphor.

16. Catullus aut Calvus: cf. Ep. IV. 27. 4,

> *Canto carmina versibus minutis*
> *his olim quibus et meus Catullus*
> *et Calvus veteresque.*

These were the poets most admired by Pliny and his set; cf. Hor. *Sat.* 1 10. 19, *nil praeter Calvum et doctus cantare Catullum;*

Ep. I. 2. 2, concerning Calvus as an orator; he was a follower of the 'New Attic' School.

17. leporis . . . amoris: *what strokes of wit, what sweetness of numbers, what pointed satire, what touches of the tender passion.*

18. data opera: *intentionally.* **lēvibus**: not *lĕvibus.*

19. duriusculos: *a little harsh;* to serve as "foils" to the other verses, or to give an archaic air to his style. **quasi** = *sicut.*

21. metro solutum: *in prose;* cf. Cic. *de Or.* iii. 12. 45, and Rolfe, *Diction of Roman Matrons, Class. Rev.* XV. 452.

24. tam doctam politamque: *so finished a scholar.*

25. Est . . . mecum: *his works are in my hands.*

27. non tamquam eundem: i.e., he seems ever new.

Page 14. **1. obesse**: *to be prejudicial, to be an objection;* cf. Martial's squib on a man who admired none but dead authors (VIII. 69).

5. pravum malignumque: *perverse and ungenerous.*

8. verum etiam: *verum* is stronger than *sed;* Roby, § 2209; B. 343. 1; A. & G. 156. b. See Cowan's note and Kraut, § 27. Pliny is fond of this instead of *sed etiam.*

Letter 13. C. Suetonius Tranquillus, the historian, biographer of the Twelve Caesars. He was ten or fifteen years younger than Pliny. To him were written Epp. III. 8; V. 10; IX. 34. He declines a military tribuneship, Ep. III. 8; is urged by Pliny to publish his writings, Ep. V. 10; Pliny obtains for him the *ius trium liberorum,* Epp. *ad Trai.* 94, 95, and calls him there, as in Ep. I. 24, his comrade in arms. There is further information about him in the *Vita Hadriani* 11.

10. dilationem: *adjournment, postponement.* **pauculos . . . excusem**: *beg for a delay of a few days or at least of one day.* Pliny's position as a leader of the bar was such that a request coming from him was likely to be granted.

11. proximum: sc. *diem.*

12. καὶ γάρ τ' ὄναρ, etc.: *for a dream is from Zeus.* Homer, *Il.* I. 63. **eventura**: substantive use of future participle; *things which are going to happen;* some dreams are interpreted naturally, others by contraries. Pliny seems inclined to believe in dreams and to interpret them by contraries.

13. an: there is no *-ne* or *utrum* to balance it; Cowan says this occurs 40 times in Pliny: *utrum — an,* 5 times; *ne — an,* 9 times; *utrumne — an,* only once; Kraut, § 26. b. **somnium meum**: *a dream of mine,* many years before.

15. Susceperam cum, etc.: '*cum inversum*'; cf. page 8, line 31, and note. *Iuni Pastoris:* Martial addressed Epig. IX. 22 to a man named Pastor.

16. socrus mea: probably the mother of Pliny's first wife, whose name is not known; probably not Pompeia Celerina, mother of his second wife, for he was *adulescentulus adhuc.* He began as an advocate at nineteen, but this was apparently not his first case.

18. in quadruplici iudicio: of the centumviral court; see Introduction, page xvi. The case in question was one of great importance, hence the four sections or chambers of the court were sitting together.

19. Caesaris: i.e., of Domitian. **Caesaris amicos**: this term has a quasi-technical force, much like 'privy councillors.' Suetonius often uses it in this way. We find an enumeration of some of Domitian's *amici* in the famous 'Council of the Turbot,' Juv. IV. **quae singula**: *each of which facts alone, any one of which.*

20. excutere mentem: *disturb my composure.*

21. λογισάμενος: *considering.*

22. εἷς οἰωνὸς, etc.: *one omen is best, to fight for our own country,* Hector's words to Polydamas. Homer, *Il.* XII. 243.

23. patria . . . videbatur: lit., *appeared to be my country or whatever (if there be anything) is dearer;* i.e., *as sacred as my country or, if possible, more so.* **fides**: *my promise,* to defend the cause.

24. adeo illa: *just that, that very.*

Page 15. **3. aliquam stropham**: *some pretext, evasion, excuse.*

6. ratio: *position, circumstances, situation.*

Letter 14. Romatius Firmus was a *decurio* of Comum, addressed also in Ep. IV. 29.

9. Municeps: *fellow-townsman,* of Comum.

13. centum milium: 100,000 sesterces (between $4000 and $5000) was the property qualification for the office of *decurio.*

14. nos: i.e., *Comenses.* **apud nos**: i.e., at Comum. **Igitur**: in the strictly classical prose (excepting Sallust) *igitur* is regularly placed after the first word of a sentence. Its initial position is one of the marks of post-Augustan authors. **te . . . perfruamur**: *may enjoy seeing you.*

15. decurione . . . equite: in predicate relation to *te; as decurion . . . knight.*

16. facultates: *fortune;* by the *lex iudiciaria* of Gracchus, 122 B.C., persons with a fortune of 400,000 HS. virtually became *equites,* obtaining the right as such to act as jurors in certain trials. In 67 B.C.

such persons gained the privilege of occupying the first fourteen rows, behind the senators, at the theatres. Similarly, Augustus introduced a senatorial *census* of 800,000, 1,000,000, or 1,200,000 HS. **trecenta milia**: for an *eques* the minimum was 400,000 HS.

18. spondet: *is surety for, guarantees;* a law term.

20. facturum: sc. *te;* see Crit. App. **quam modestissime** *with all possible discretion.*

Page 16. Letter 15. Catilius Severus is addressed also in Ep. III. 12. He was proconsul of Asia; under Hadrian, legate of the province of Syria (*vita Hadriani* 5); *consul ordinarius* for the second time in 120 A.D.; *praefectus urbi* (*vita Hadr.* 24); became an enemy of Hadrian (*vita Hadr.* 15, 24) by aiming at the empire for himself. The emperor Marcus Aurelius was his great-grandson.

1. haereo: *I have been detained.* **attonitus**: *in great alarm.*

2. valetudo: see note on page 8, line 6. **Titi Aristonis**: to him were written Epp. V. 3; VIII. 14. He was a Stoic in philosophy and a distinguished jurist, sometimes referred to in Justinian's Digest. It is inferred from Ep. VIII. 14. 12 that he was alive after 105 A.D. See Mommsen in Keil's *Pliny*, page 427.

3. gravius, sanctius, doctius: *more dignified, more virtuous, more learned.*

4. litterae ipsae: *literature itself;* cf. Ep. IX. 22. 3.

6. iuris: all civil law is comprised in 'public' and 'private.'

7. exemplorum: *of precedents.*

11. fides . . . auctoritas . . . cunctatio: *reliability . . . weight . . . caution.* **pressa**: *modest, restrained, chastened.*

13. quas . . . expendit: *which, with his keen and powerful judgment, he traces up to their sources and first principles, distinguishing between them and balancing them.* (Lewis.)

16. cubiculum, etc.: the sleeping-rooms of a Roman house were very small and simply furnished.

20. non . . . sed ex facto: in accordance with the Stoic doctrine that virtue is its own reward.

21. sapientiae: *of philosophy.*

22. praeferunt: *display, show off;* they got themselves up carefully, with long beard, staff, and mantle, to look like philosophers. The beards of the philosophers are the subject of frequent allusions in literature, some respectful, some of them rather satirical; e.g., Ep. I. 10. 6; Hor. *Sat.* II. 3. 35; Pers. I. 133.

23. sectatur: *frequents.*

25. advocatione . . . consilio: *by assistance in court . . . by advice* (in private). *Advocati* were sympathizers, witnesses, and especially legal counsellors as well as what we call advocates.

27. etiam: construe with *fortitudine*, not with *primo loco*; Kraut, § 27, gives a large number of examples of this use of *etiam* by Pliny, after an asyndeton of two or more members. **primo loco cesserit**: *would yield the first place*; *loco* is ablative.

Page 17. **1. interesses**: *if you were present.*

2. differat: *puts off*, delays the satisfaction of his thirst.

3. opertus: *covered with bed-clothing*, to cause perspiration. **transmittat**: *bears*, lit., *lets pass*; cf. Epp. VI. 4. 2; IX. 6. 1.

5. summa valetudinis: *the outcome of his illness.*

6. sponte exiret e vita: see note on page 9, line 17.

12. commune cum multis: i.e., many may commit suicide under the influence of a sudden impulse; few do so after calm deliberation.

13. expendere: *to weigh, balance.*

14. vitae mortisque: in English, 'life *or* death.'

16. superest ut . . . deus: *it remains for God to*, etc.

20. adsidenti: *sitting by his bed*; sc. *mihi.*

Letter 16. Q. Pompeius Falco, son-in-law of Q. Sosius Senecio, at this time *tribunus plebis designatus.* His career seems to have been a distinguished one; a very interesting collection of facts about him is found in Mommsen's Index Nominum in Keil's *Pliny*, page 422. To Falco are addressed also Epp. IV. 27; VII. 22; IX. 15.

25. Consulis: *you ask my advice.* **an**: for *num.*

Page 18. **1. inanem umbram**: as the emperor himself was always invested with the *tribunicia potestas*, the annually elected tribunes were reduced to insignificance. The real importance of the office now consisted in the fact that either it, or the aedileship, was a necessary qualification for those who wished to pass on to the higher offices of praetor and consul. **sine honore**: attributive to *nomen.*

2. sacrosanctam: the person of a tribune was sacred; an injury or affront to him was therefore a sacrilege; this adjective is a technical term expressing this fact. **in ordinem cogi**: *to be humbled, degraded*, to be reduced to the level of others, when one is a magistrate; originally, perhaps, of an officer 'to be degraded to the ranks': cf. Ep. II. 6. 5, where it is used of the appetite; also Livy III. 51. 13; VI. 38. 12; XXV. 3. 19; XLIII. 16. 9.

3. cum tribunus essem: cf. Introduction, page xiii. **erra**

verim: *I may have been mistaken;* the potential subjunctive referring to the past is rather unusual. Kraut, 46. c.

4. me aliquid: *that I was somebody.* Pliny was something of an antiquarian in politics, and took a rather serious view of the old republican offices, which survived under the empire only as traditional forms.

5. deforme: *unseemly.*

6. loco cedere: cf. note on page 16, line 27.

7. stare: the advocate stood, the judges sat. **iubere . . . quemcumque**: Metellus Nepos's silencing of Cicero at the close of his consulship is an instance of how far the tribunes had carried the power of veto; see Forsyth's *Life of Cicero* I. 161, and Dio Cass. 37. 38. **quemcumque**: relative with verb omitted, = *quemvis.*

8. clepsydra: a kind of water-clock, a water-glass on the principle of the sand-glass. It was ordinarily emptied in fifteen or twenty minutes. An advocate's time of speaking was strictly limited; hence he was said to be allowed so many clepsydras. **interfari** = *interpellare;* used by Vergil and Livy in this sense: *interrupt.*

11. aestus: *perplexity;* the idea is of wavering to and fro; the basis of the metaphor is the ebb and flow of the tide, or the tossing of waves, or the seething, boiling of water in violent agitation. **appellasset**: *should appeal* to me in my quality of tribune. The tribune's power of interference with the acts of other magistrates was called *intercessio.* This was the earliest function of the office after its creation as a magistracy of the whole *populus* at the time of the first secession of the plebs, 494 B.C.

12. quem contra: anastrophe of the preposition. **intercederem . . . an quiescerem**: for omission of first interrogative particle, cf. note on page 14, line 13. *Quiescere* means 'to make no movement'; *silere*, 'to utter no word.'

13. eiurato magistratu: *abdicating my office. Eiurare* was said because it was usual for one quitting an office to swear that he had administered it legally. Thus he 'swore himself out' of office, as nowadays men are 'sworn in.'

16. Sed tu: *tu* emphasized by its position — *as for you.* **plurimum interest quid . . . putes**, etc.: *your notion of the tribuneship has the most important bearing on what rôle*, etc. The clause *quid . . . putes* forms the subject of the impersonal *interest.*

19. ut perferatur: a clause of purpose explanatory of *ita*, — *ought to be assumed with this purpose — of wearing it to the end. Perferre* means to carry out consistently to the end.

Letter 17. About Baebius Hispanus we have no information, nor do we know whether he is identical with the Hispanus addressed in Ep. VI. 25.

20. Tranquillus: Suetonius, the historian; see note introductory to Ep. I. 18.

21. venditare: *to be anxious to sell;* such is the force of the intensive verb. **quanti aecum est**: *for a fair price;* on *aecum*, see note on page 5, line 20.

23. mala emptio: *a dear bargain.*

25. stomachum . . . sollicitant: *tempt the fancy.* (Cowan.)

26. mediocritas: *the moderate size, smallness.*

27. modus ruris: *the (limited) extent of the estate;* cf. *Hoc erat in votis: modus agri non ita magnus*, Hor. *Sat.* II. 6. 1. **avocet**: *divert, amuse.*

Page 19. **1. distringat**: *distract, worry.* **Scholasticis . . . dominis**: *scholars turned landholders; scholasticus* is post-Augustan.

2. relevare . . . oculos: *refresh the mind, divert the eye.*

3. reptare: *saunter;* cf. Hor. Ep. I. 4. 4, *silvas inter reptare salubris.*

4. viticulas: Pliny is fond of diminutives; cf. *arbusculas* in this line, *praediolum* in line 6.

7. dotibus: *advantages, attractions;* properly *dos* means a 'marriage-portion.' **salubriter**: *advantageously, at a good bargain;* a late use of the word, for *saluber* properly means wholesome; cf. Liv. III. 62. 3.

BOOK II

Page 20. Letter 18. Voconius Romanus is the person addressed in Ep. I. 5; see introductory note there. As to the date of this letter, see Appendix I.

1. Post aliquot annos: i.e., it was several years since an occurrence as memorable as that about to be mentioned. Verginius's death occurred at the end of A.D. 97.

2. publicum funus: a signal honor, voted by the senate; the expense was defrayed sometimes by the public treasury, sometimes by voluntary contributions.

3. Vergini Rufi: the 'grand old man' of that generation, consul for the third time in 97, as colleague of the emperor Nerva; he had been Pliny's guardian. See Introduction, page xi. **perinde felicis**: *not less fortunate.*

4. Triginta annis: ablative of duration of time, a construction which increases in frequency in the post-Augustan age. In both the elder and the younger Pliny it almost entirely supplants the accusative of duration. **gloriae . . . supervixit**: *lived to enjoy his fame.*

5. historias: in this connection it is interesting to read Ep. IX. 19, especially § 5.

6. interfuit: *learned the verdict of.*

7. fastigium . . . impleret: a mixed metaphor. **privati hominis**: *of a subject.* **cum principis noluisset**: he had refused the purple after defeating Julius Vindex in 68, again after Galba's accession, the third time after Otho's defeat at Bedriacum in 69. Cf. Juvenal VIII. 221,

quid enim Verginius armis
Debuit ulcisci magis, aut cum Vindice Galba.

8. Caesares: Nero, Galba, Otho, Vitellius, Domitian; the use of a personal direct object of *evadere* is noteworthy.

9. virtutibus: causal. **optimum**: Nerva.

14. citra = *sine;* post-Augustan. **tantum**: *only.*

16. vocem praepararet: *was practising his voice;* better than '*was rehearsing his speech,*' for his speech would not be *liber grandior*, nor would the statement *forte acceperat* be appropriate to it; he seems to have been reading aloud from some other book. Cf. Quint. X. 7. 2. **in consulatu**, etc.: see note at the beginning of this letter: this eulogy of the emperor in the senate was regularly delivered by one of the consuls, for himself and his colleague, on the first day of their term. Pliny's Panegyric was one of these speeches.

18. dum: *as*, rather than, as usual, *while.* **sequitur colligitque**: the verbs are appropriate, for the book was a manuscript roll.

19. per: *along.* **fallente vestigio**: *his foot slipping;* lit., the place where he set his foot betraying him.

20. parum apte collocata: *unskilfully set.*

21. coiit: *knit.*

22. magnum . . . magnum . . . magnum etiam: this use of *etiam* in connection with asyndeton is a marked peculiarity of Pliny's style. See Introduction II. § 6. *a.* Kraut, § 27, has many examples. **ornamentum principi**: the emperor honored himself by honoring such a man as Verginius.

Page 21. **1. Laudatus est**: his funeral oration was spoken from the Rostra in the Forum.

2. Cornelio Tacito: the historian, who was also one of the first orators of his time; the peculiar character of his eloquence is expressed by the adverb σεμνῶς, in Ep. II. 11. 17. The conclusion of the Agricola proves how eloquent Tacitus may have been on this occasion.

4. plenus annis: this is a finer phrase than Virgil's, *Aen.* VII. 53, *plenis annis; plenus* in the best authors is usually constructed with the genitive, but the ablative is frequent and is found even in Cicero. 'Full of the honors he refused' is a fine example of oxymoron.

7. non solum publice, etc.: brachylogy; he evidently means *non solum publice [admirabar, sed etiam privatim] quantum admirabar tantum diligebam.*

8. regio: Transpadana. **municipia finitima**: near to Comum, which was a free town, was the birthplace of Verginius, — perhaps Mediolanum.

10. tutor relictus: i.e., appointed by the will of Pliny's father; a *tutor* was guardian of a boy (or girl) whose father was dead, till the ward reached the age of fourteen (or twelve). A father had the right to name by will a *tutor* for his surviving minor children; otherwise the office devolved upon the nearest agnate kinsman. **adfectum**: this sense of the word is post-Augustan.

11. suffragio: *with his support, influence.* **ad . . . honores**: *on the occasions of my entering office.*

13. officiis: *functions;* cf. page 6, line 13. **sacerdotes**: in this case he means augurs, who formerly had been chosen by the *coöptatio* of the college, but were now nominated by the emperor in his quality of *pontifex maximus;* hence *nominabat* in this sentence means 'recommended to the emperor.' Cf. Ep. IV. 8. 3, where Pliny appears to have been nominated in this way by Frontinus, to whose place he succeeded in the augural college, probably A.D. 103.

16. quinqueviros: a commission of five, appointed by Nerva, to reorganize the public finances and retrench expenses after the extravagance of Domitian's reign; cf. *Paneg.* 62. 2. **minuendis publicis sumptibus**: Prof. Platner (*Am. J. Phil.* ix. 217) says this construction of the gerundive and a noun, equivalent to a clause of purpose, occurs but four times in the letters of Pliny, whereas it is strikingly frequent in Tacitus. B. 339. 7; A. & G. 299. b; H. 544. 2. N. 3; Roby 1156.

19. huius aetatis: about thirty-five. **per quem excusaretur**: this may mean *to take his place* as a substitute, or only *to present his excuses.* The latter view is perhaps the safer one.

20. tibi mandarem: *I would entrust the mission to you* (to Pliny); i.e., the mission expressed in *excusaretur* above.

22. in sinu tuo: *in your (sympathizing) bosom.* **si . . . fas est**, etc.: cf. the so-called epitaph of Naevius, Aul. Gell. I. 24, *Immortales mortales, si foret fas flere*, etc.

23. qua: attracted to gender of predicate accusative *mortem*; the real antecedent is *id*, understood, direct object of *vocare*.

24. Vivit enim: cf. Ennius, in Cic. *Tusc*. I. 15, 34,

> *Nemo me dacrumis decoret nec funera fletu*
> *Faxit. Cur? Volito vivos per ora virum.*

Cf. also the close of Tac. *Agr*. 46.

25. postquam . . . recessit: *now that he has departed.*

28. Verginium cogito: notice the accusative of a person, instead of *de* with ablative; similar instances occur in Tacitus, Quintilian, and Seneca. This idiom is more forcible than the classical *cogitare de aliquo.*

29. recentibus: *vivid, lifelike.*

Page 22. Letter 19. As to Calvina we have no other information than that given in this letter. She appears to have been connected with Pliny by marriage (*adfinitatis officio*, below).

2. an adires, etc.: *whether you should enter upon the inheritance*; by accepting an inheritance an heir rendered himself liable for all claims against the deceased. These might amount to more than the assets of the estate.

3. ductus: for *adductus*; an example of the frequent use of simple for compound verbs in the post-Augustan age.

4. dimissis: *by paying off.* **molestiores . . . diligentiores**: *more importunate . . . more particular, more careful*; cf. Epp. II. 6. 1; IV. 13. 8 for the signification of *diligens.*

6. centum milia: i.e., sesterces, between $4000 and $5000.

7. dixit: *assigned*; *dotem dicere* means 'to constitute a dower.'

8. facilitatis: *leniency.*

9. pignus: *proof.* **famam pudoremque**: *the good name and honor*; it was counted a disgrace to die intestate; cf. Epp. II. 9. 1; III. 20. 4; V. 1. 6; Sal. *Cat*. 16. 2, for this use of *pudor.*

10. suscipere: *defend, rescue from reproach.*

11. acceptum tibi fieri iubebo: *I shall have a release given to you of your father's debt to me. Acceptum ferre* was to enter in the creditor's ledger the receipt of payment from the debtor. This was a written *acceptilatio.* The same result was accomplished by verbal *acceptilatio* according to the prescribed form, which corresponded closely with that of the *stipulatio*, or formal verbal contract. See Crit. App.

12. Nec est quod verearis: *there is no reason why you should fear.*

15. nescio minor an incertior: *about as uncertain as it is small.*

17. ita . . . ne, etc.: the *ne*-clause is final, — *with a view to its not drying up.*

19. ratio constabit: *it will be justified;* cf. *ratio constabit*, page 5, line 20, and note; also *ratio aut constet aut constare videatur*, page 6, line 10.

Letter 20. We cannot be sure whether the person addressed is Julius Avitus or Junius Avitus. Junius Avitus is mentioned in Ep. VIII. 23; at the time of his death he was aedile designate; he had served as tribune of a legion in Germany and in Pannonia, and had been quaestor to several consuls. He is one of the legatees named in the will of a certain Dasumius, A.D. 108 or 109. For the text of this will, see Bruns, *Fontes Juris Romani Antiqui*, Pars II. cap. XIV. Julius Avitus appears to be the brother of Julius Naso, Epp. V. 21. 3; VI. 6. 6; after serving as quaestor he died on his journey home, leaving to mourn him a mother, brother, and sister.

It was a common custom to furnish clients and humble guests with entertainment inferior to that enjoyed in the same room by the host and his privileged guests. Many allusions to it are found in the literature of the period; e.g., Juvenal's fifth satire and Martial I. 20; III. 12; III. 49; III. 60; IV. 85; VI. 11; X. 49. The subject is discussed in Friedlaender's *Sittengeschichte* I[6]. p. 386. Labiche has a modern parallel to this stingy host in his comedy, *Moi.*

20. Longum est altius repetere: *it would be a long story if I should go into the particulars*, lit., 'recall more deeply.' It is interesting to notice how the Latin says *longum est, aequum est*, etc., where the English idiom would lead us to expect *longum sit*, etc.

21. minime familiaris: *slightly acquainted; homo* need not be translated; it is inserted that the adjective may have something to agree with.

22. lautum et diligentem: *at once elegant and thrifty.*

23. sordidum . . . et sumptuosum: *mean and extravagant.*

Page 23. **1. opima**: *dainties.* **minuta**: *bits, scraps.* **ponebat**: for *apponebat.*

2. lagunculis: *bottles;* cf. page 6, line 7, and note.

4. gradatim: *in classes.*

8. ad cenam . . . non ad notam: *to dinner, not to degradation. Nota* was the censor's memorandum on the census list of his reasons for striking off a name from the rolls of senators, knights, or citizens.

10. Etiam: *yes, even so*, or perhaps here only the affirmative repetition of the interrogative *etiamne*.

12. constat: *costs.* **Minime**: *by no means;* negative, not quantitative.

13. liberti . . . liberti: this sentence is a good example of the rhetorical figure 'antimetabole'; cf. Pope's 'A wit with dunces, and a dunce with wits.'

14. si . . . temperes: general sense of second person. **gulae**: *appetite;* Pliny's own table, if we may judge from Ep. I. 15, was very simple.

15. quo: sc. *id*, antecedent of *quo*, object of *communicare*.

16. quasi: the 'apologetic' *quasi*, used to soften the metaphor. **in ordinem redigenda**: *to be kept in order, controlled;* cf. *in ordinem cogi*, page 18, line 2, and note.

19. in mensa: the phrase serves as an adjective modifier to *luxuria*.

20. inponat: quite in the modern sense, *impose upon;* used in this sense by Cicero. Cf. Ep. III. 15. 3; originally some object, such as *fraudem*, was expressed.

21. sub exemplo praemonere: *to give a warning based on the actual case.*

23. novam societatem: *strange combination.*

25. turpius iunguntur: *are more shameful when combined.*

Letter 21. About Caninius Rufus of Comum, see note on Ep. I. 3.

26. Studes: absolute; late use of the verb.

Page 24. **1. studia**: *studies*, quite in the modern sense; a late use of the word.

2. secessus: *retirement;* cf. page 2, line 6.

5. Numquamne, etc.: the sentiment is paralleled in Hor. *Sat.* II. 6. 60, *O rus quando ego te aspiciam?* etc.

6. laqueos: *toils;* cf. the similar sentiment in Ep. I. 10. 9, where Pliny chafes at the demands of his official position, probably in the Treasury. **solvere**: *loosen.* **abrumpam**: cf. Ep. I. 12. 8, *retinacula abrupit.*

7. nec . . . peraguntur: grammatically coördinate, but logically subordinate, *without the earlier ones' being finished.*

9. maius . . . agmen: we are reminded of Goldsmith's

> 'And drags at each remove a lengthening chain.' (*Traveller*, l. 10.)

Agmen is here used in its original sense.

Letter 22. To Domitius Apollinaris is addressed Ep. V. 6, describing Pliny's Tuscan villa. He was a *consul suffectus* in 97 A.D.; when consul designate in the same year, he spoke in the senate, Ep. IX. 13. 13. He was *legatus* of Lycia.

10. petitio: *candidacy*, for tribunate of the *plebs*. **Sexti Eruci**: it is to him or to his father that Ep. I. 16. is addressed; see note on that letter.

12. me altero: *my second self, alter ego.* **alioqui**: *besides*; later, transferred meaning, the original one being 'otherwise.'

14. latum clavum: *the broad purple stripe* on the front of the *tunica*, the badge of the senatorial order, Suet. *Aug.* 38. It was granted to the sons of senators, that they might enter the senate and become familiar with its business. Erucius has held the quaestorship and is following the senatorial *cursus honorum*. **a Caesare nostro**: probably Nerva.

15. suffragio: *support*, influence exerted in his favor. **ius . . . petendi**: *the right of being a candidate*, etc.; the tribunes were elected by the senate upon the nomination of the emperor.

16. nisi obtinet: present for future in conditional clause; the tendency being, as time goes on, to be less precise in tense designation, where the sense is clear. **decepisse**: i.e., by recommending one whom the senators were unwilling to elect.

18. mihi credidit: *believed on my representation.*

19. adiutum . . . cuperem: for the syntax, cf. *Qui te conventum cupit* (Plaut. *Curculio*, 304).

22. tota domo: as evidences of Pliny's intimacy with the whole family, cf. Epp. I. 1; I. 16; VII. 28; and VIII. 1.

23. anticus: *of the good old sort.* Cf. *aecum*, page 5, line 20, and note.

25. C. Septicium: the person addressed in Ep. I. 1; see introductory note on that letter. **nihil verius**, etc.: *no man so genuine, sincere, frank, loyal.*

Page 25. **1. referre gratiam**: *prove my gratitude.*

2. stationes: *lounging-places*, e.g., baths, basilicas, porticoes, places of public resort.

5. tanti: *worth while.*

6. frequentaris: especially at the morning *salutatio* at his house; also when he appeared in public.

Letter 23. If Octavius is Octavius Rufus, he is the friend addressed in Ep. I. 7, where Pliny refuses to defend Gallus against the prosecution of the Baetici, but promises not to appear on their behalf. He may be the Rufus referred to in Ep. IX. 38. He was one of the numerous persons who exemplified "the widely diffused skill, which the age of Trajan possessed in various forms of poetry."

9. patientem: *indifferent, indolent.* **durum**: *hard-hearted.*

10. qui . . . teneas: *since you keep back* from the public. **libros**: apparently some poems.

11. invidebis: *begrudge;* several instances of *invidere*, with abl. *rei* occur in Pliny; cf. Epp. I. 10. 12; II. 20. 8; III. 8. 2; VII. 28. 2; IX. 13. 5; *Paneg.* 86; Kraut, § 18. a; Roby 1331. It is common in other post-Augustan writers; cf. Quint. IX. 3. 1.

12. per ora hominum ferantur: cf. Ennius, cited in note on page 21, line 24, *volito vivos per ora virum;* Cowan cites Verg. *Aen.* XII. 235, *vivusque per ora feretur; Georg.* III. 9, *victorque virum volitare per ora.*

13. lingua Romana: usually *lingua Latina.* Val. Max. II. 2. 2 has an interesting passage on the anxiety of the earlier Romans to extend the use of the Latin language. **spatiis**: Cowan cites as parallel Verg. *Georg.* II. 541, *sed nos immensum spatiis confecimus aequor*, 'a boundless breadth of plain.' (Mackail, *Latin Lit.*)

14. adhuc: *longer*, i.e., in addition.

15. Enotuerunt: post-Augustan and rare (Lex.). See Crit. App.

16. retrahis in corpus: *reunite with the main body;* for the tense, see note on *nisi obtinet*, page 24, line 16.

17. quandoque: *one of these days = aliquando.* **errones**: *vagrants, vagabonds.* **aliquem . . . dicantur**: i.e., some one to whose authorship they will be attributed.

18. adserere: *deliver;* see note on *adseris*, page 2, line 6.

21. viderint: *let my friends see to it*, or perhaps better, *my friends will see to it.* Roby, § 1593.

25. editione: *publication.*

27. olim . . . praesumo: *I have long been anticipating; praesumo = praecipio;* cf. Epp. III. 1. 11; VI. 10. 5; *olim* in this sense occurs in Ep. I. 11. 1. **non temere**: *not without reason.*

Page 26. **1. etiam**: this use of *etiam* combined with asyndeton has already been noted. See note on page 20, line 22; Kraut, § 27.

2. quo: sc. *silentio.*

3. acre et intentum: *one of close attention.*

Letter 24. L. Neratius Priscus was, according to Mommsen, *legatus pro praetore* of Pannonia in A.D. 98. To Priscus were addressed Epp. VI. 8; VII. 8; VII. 19.

10. inpetratum . . . cupio: cf. *adiutum cuperem*, page 24, line 19.

11. Regis exercitum: i.e., as governor of Pannonia; three legions were stationed in that province in the time of Augustus and Tiberius; it was always thought necessary to keep a strong force along the Danube.

12. larga materia: *abundant opportunity.* **longum . . . tempus**: an imperial *legatus* held office during the emperor's pleasure, often for several years; a military tribune was appointed for six months.

13. Convertere: passive in middle sense.

15. unus aut alter: *one or two;* a common phrase at this period.

16. Voconius Romanus: cf. note on Ep. I. 5. **in equestri gradu clarus**: *a distinguished member of the equestrian order.*

17. pietate: *devotion* to the boy. **vitricus**: his step-father's name is not known. **alius** = *alter.*

18. Mater e primis, etc.: this is not very clear; the text is doubtful. See Crit. App.

20. Flamen: sc. *Augustalis.* The worship of the emperor, intended to unite the different parts of the empire in the bonds of common loyalty, was established at various important cities in the provinces, and provincial nobles were appointed as *flamines*, priests of the emperor cult. Or, understanding the passage differently, we may take him to have been one of the *flamines minores* at Rome.

21. simul studeremus: *were students together;* again the late use of the verb, as, e.g., page 24, line 26.

22. seria . . . iocos: cf. *seria ac iocos celebrare*, Livy, I. 4. 9; also Cic. *de Fin.* II. 26, *ioca, seria, ut dicitur.*

25. subtile: *acute.*

27. ut Musas . . . credas: as Varro said, the Muses, if speaking Latin, would have chosen to speak in Plautus's language; Quint. X. 1. 99.

Page 27. **1. vincitur**: sc. *in amore;* cf. Ep. IV. 1. 5, *vinci in amore turpissimum est.*

3. trium liberorum ius: see note on page 121, line 9. **ab optimo principe**: probably Trajan.

4. quamquam . . . daret: i.e., on other occasions; for *quamquam* with the subjunctive, see B. 309. 6; A. & G. 313. *g*; H. 515, III. N. 1. 3; Roby 1697. **parce**: cf. *quam parce haec beneficia tribuam*, Trajan to Pliny, *ad Trai* 95.

6. tueri: *maintain.*

13. capacem: *worthy*, lit., capable of containing.

Letter 25. There are eight other letters in the collection addressed to Maximus: Epp. III. 2; VI. 11; VI. 34; VII. 26; VIII. 19; VIII. 24; IX. 1; IX. 23. In Ep. III. 2 he appears as *legatus* of a province, in command of an army. He was quaestor in Bithynia, tribune of the *plebs*, praetor, legate of the emperor sent to settle the affairs of the free cities, etc. But there are so many Maximi that it is not clear to which of them these facts refer.

18. distringor: *I am kept busy, I am distracted.* **centumviralibus causis**: *by cases in the court of the centumviri;* see Introduction, page xvi.

19. exercent . . . delectant: *give me more work than pleasure, I find more laborious than interesting.*

21. insignis: sc. *causa.*

22. cum quibus iuvet dicere: *with whom I care to plead* (Cowan) either as associates or as opponents.

23. ad declamandum: their declamations were school exercises.

24. transierunt: i.e., from the schools. **inreverenter**: apparently a neologism; cf. *capitaliter*, Ep. I. 5. 4; *eloquentius*, Ep. III. 18. 6; *exultantius*, Ep. III. 18. 10; *custodite*, Ep. V. 16. 3. **Atilius**: cf. page 7, line 6, and note, also Ep. VI. 8.

25. expresse: *aptly, neatly;* post-classical.

26. auspicari: *begin;* cf. Plaut. *Capt.* 766, 767. **ab Homero**: cf. Quint. I. 8. 5; X. 1. 46.

Page 28. 1. ita maiores natu, etc.: Pliny is affecting the style of an old man, but he was not yet forty.

3. nisi . . . producente: *unless introduced by some man of consular rank.*

4. opus: *profession.*

6. Secuntur: for the form, see note on *aecum*, page 5, line 20. **actoribus**: *pleaders, orators;* observe the increasing use of the dative with *similis* in Silver Latin, as compared with the earlier use of the genitive of persons.

7. similes: like the orators in the sense of being worthy of them; the audience is as good as the speakers. **conducti et redempti**: *hired and bought.* **manceps convenitur**: *the agent is met,* i.e., an agreement is made with the agent, who supplies persons for hire to applaud the advocate.

8. basilica: sc. *Iulia.* This was the meeting-place of the centumviral court; a vast open hall, surrounded by triple rows of columns, running along the S.W. side of the Forum; begun by Julius Caesar and finished by Augustus. **sportulae**: lit., *little baskets*, the dole of food or money given by patrons to their poor clients; here, of course, it means bribes for applause. Cf. Quint. XI. 3. 131.

9. ex iudicio in iudicium: *from one court to another.*

10. Σοφοκλεῖς: *σοφῶς = bravo!* cf. Martial I. 3. 7, *grande sophos;* I. 76. 10, *perinane sophos.* This may be intended for a pun, the two meanings being (1) 'Sophocleses,' (2) 'Bravo-shouters.'

12. laudicēni: (*laus, cena*) *who praise for a dinner, good-cheerers;* see Duff's *Juvenal,* 7. 44, and note. This may be an attempt at a pun, on *Laodicēni,* 'Laodiceans,' for which *Laudicēni* is occasionally found. But it seems sorry wit. **foeditas**: *low practice.* (Cowan.)

13. utraque lingua: by the Greek and Latin names just mentioned. **Here**: the Augustan spelling was *heri.* **nomenclatores** slaves employed to tell their master the names of those whom he me

14. sane aetatem: *just the age.*

15. constat: *costs.*

16. numerosa: *crowded;* post-Augustan sense.

17. corona: *a circle* of listeners.

18. cum . . . dedit: note the perf. indic. with *cum.* **mesochorus**: *coryphaeus, chorus-leader;* here leader of the *claque.*

25. Largius Licinus: the man who offered the elder Pliny 400,000 sesterces for his volumes of notes; cf. Ep. III. 5. 17.

26. hactenus . . . corrogaret: *going only, however, to the extent of inviting* — not hiring.

27. Quintiliano: referred to by Pliny as his teacher also in Ep. VI. 6. 3; see Introduction, page xi. **audisse**: notice the perfect infin. with *memini.* This is habitual with Pliny. Roby 1372. Note the omission of the subject, *me.*

28. adsectabar: i.e., as a pupil. **Domitium Afrum**: a famous orator, born at Nemausus (Nîmes) in Gaul. He held high positions under Tiberius, Caligula, Nero, being *consul suffectus* in A.D. 39. By conducting certain unrighteous prosecutions for the government, he sacrificed his character. He died in A.D. 60. Cf. Quint. X. 1. 118; V. 7. 7.

Page 29. **1. Novissime**: *at last.*

2. intermissa causa: *giving up the case.*

3. centumviri: vocative. **hoc . . . perit**: *our profession is done for.*

4. alioqui: *anyhow, besides.*

6. fracta pronuntiatione: *mincing utterance;* cf. Juv. II. 111; Tac. *Dial.* 26; *Ann.* XIV. 20. 7; Quint. I. 10. 31; *Paneg.* 54.

7. teneris: *effeminate, affected;* see Crit. App.

8. Plausus tantum . . . cymbala et tympana: like priests of Cybele or Dionysus; *Only the clapping of hands, or, rather, cymbals and drums, are lacking to this sing-song oratory.* (Cowan.) Quintilian, XI. 3, speaks with contempt of this sort of elocution. **ac potius**: cf. Epp. II. 13. 3; II. 17. 25; VI. 10. 3; VI. 18. 3.

10. theatris quoque: *to the theatres even.* Interest in theatrical exhibitions, and the consequent rivalry of actors, was so intense that even before the close of the republic, actors sought to increase their prestige by hired applause. The partisanship of the spectators often led to riotous scenes. It was following the example of the theatre, then, when the *claque* was introduced into literary recitations and the courts of law. Friedländer, *Sittengeschichte* II.[6] p. 475; III.[5] 375.

11. ratio aetatis: *consideration of my youth.*

13. indignitates: *indecent scenes.* (Cowan.)

Letter 26. Julius Valerianus is probably the same as the person addressed in Epp. V. 4, and V. 13; both letters are on legal matters.

16. Marsi: *estate in the Marsian district;* cf. page 55, line 7, *in Tuscos*, etc.; sc. *tractant* as *infra*, § 2. It was habitual to designate an estate in a given territory by the name of the people of the territory, in the plural; cf. Hor. *Car.* II. 18. 14, *Satis beatus unicis Sabinis.* See Mayor's note on Pliny, Ep. III. 4. 2, *in Tuscos.*

18. aeque . . . quam: cf. I. 20. 1, *aeque . . . ut.*

19. parum commode tractant: *are giving me trouble.* (Cowan.)

21. querellae: cf. Ep. V. 14(15). 8; IX. 36. 6; apparently discontented tenants are the cause of the troubles.

Letter 27. To Asinius Gallus is addressed Ep. IV. 17, if our reading is correct, and to Gallus, Ep. VIII. 20. In Ep. I. 7, we find the Baetici preparing an accusation against Gallus for misgovernment of their province. But the identification in these cases is conjectural.

The Laurentine villa of Pliny has always been a subject of interest and study. Many attempts have been made to draw a satisfactory plan of it. Dr. H. W.

Magoun, *Am. Philol. Ass. Proceedings*, July, 1895, reviews ten such plans, beginning with that of Scamozzi, 1615, and ending with his own, 1894; cf. same, *Proceedings*, Dec, 1894. See pages 164, 165.

23. Laurentinum . . . Laurens: sc. *praedium* or *rus*; alternative forms of the adjective of *Laurentum*, a town on the coast of Latium, between Ostia and Lavinium. The district surrounding it was called the *ager Laurens* or *Laurentinus*.

Page 30. **1. gratiam**: *charm.* **opportunitatem**: *convenience of location*, near Rome. **litoris spatium**: *the breadth of the beach*, or *the extent of the property along the shore.*

2. secessit: *is distant.*

3. salvo iam et composito die: *without losing or leaving unfinished your day's work*; cf. Hor. *Car.* I. 1. 20, *solido . . . die*; *salvo*: 'undiminished'; *composito*: 'completed,' 'disposed of.' After the close of business, about 2 P.M., Pliny could drive, in a couple of hours, to his villa. Ostia is about sixteen English, or seventeen Roman miles from Rome.

6. lapide: the Roman highways were marked at every mile by a stone pillar; distances were counted from the gilded stone in the Forum, *miliarium aureum*; 'all roads lead to Rome.'

7. Utrimque, etc.: *whichever way you go, the rest of the route is somewhat sandy.* **iter**: one quitted the highway (*via*), to follow one of the ordinary unpaved country roads (*iter*). **iunctis**: *for a team*, a harnessed pair of horses or mules.

8. equo: *a saddle-horse.*

9. facies: *the view, the scenery.* **silvis**: Castel Fusano, which is now pointed out as the site of this villa, whether rightly or wrongly, is in a wood, about five miles from Laurentum and two from Ostia, but in the Laurentine district. The shore line has gone out about a mile since Pliny's time.

10. diffunditur et patescit: *spreads out and opens before you.*

11. greges: cf. Juv. I. 107, *si Laurenti custodit in agro conductas Corvinus oves.*

12. hieme depulsa: they came down to enjoy the warmer pastures below during the cold season.

13. nitescunt: *they grow fat*, lit., *sleek.* **usibus capax**: *large enough for convenience.* **non sumptuosa tutela**: ablative of quality; *not expensive to keep up.*

14. atrium: *entrance hall*; originally the sole, then the chief room of the house; in the more elaborate houses of the imperial age, the hall of entrance and reception, a large anteroom for the house

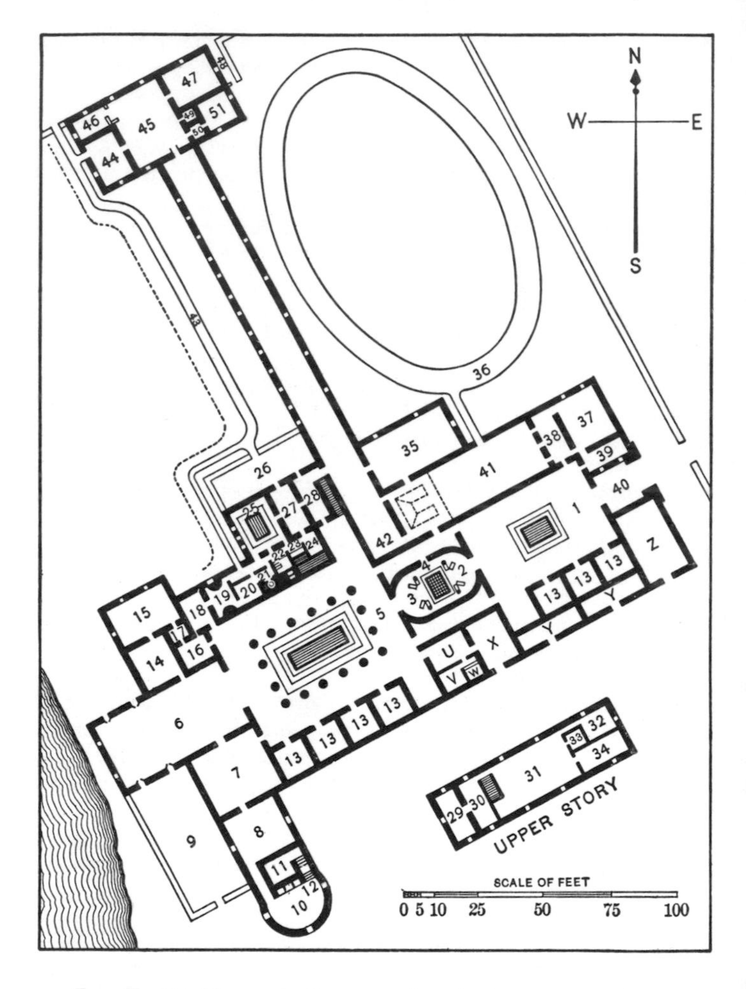

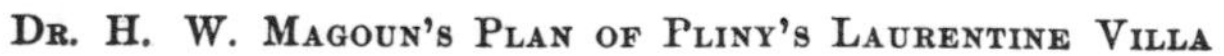

DR. H. W. MAGOUN'S PLAN OF PLINY'S LAURENTINE VILLA

Proceedings of the American Philological Association, Special Session, 1894, page xxxiv.

EXPLANATION OF PLAN

1. atrium
2. 3. porticus
4. area
5. cavaedium
6. triclinium
7. cubiculum (amplum)
8. cubiculum (minus)
9. hibernaculum
10. cubiculum (in hapsida curvatum)
11. dormitorium membrum
12. transitus interiacens
13. *servants' rooms*
14. cubiculum (politissimum)
15. cubiculum (grande)
16. cubiculum (munimentis hibernum)
17. procoeton
18. cubiculum (aliud)
19. cella frigidaria
20. unctorium
21. hypocauston
22. propnigeon
23. caldarium (?)
24. tepidarium (?)
25. piscina
26. sphaeristerium
27. 28. 29. 30. diaetae
31. cenatio
32. cubiculum
33. apotheca
34. horreum
35. triclinium
36. gestatio
37. cenatio
38. 39. diaetae
40. vestibulum
41. hortus (pinguis) [*with* trichila(?)]
42. cryptoporticus
43. xystus
44. heliocaminus
45. cubiculum
46. zotheca
47. cubiculum (noctis)
48. andron
49. hypocauston
50. procoeton
51. cubiculum

U. culina (?)
V. *larder* (?)
W. latrina (?)
X. *kitchen storeroom* (?)
Y. *general storerooms* (?)
Z. stabulum (?)

For description and illustration, see Class. Dict., article *Domus.* **frugi nec tamen sordidum**: *plain but not mean.* (Melmoth.)

15. porticus: *cloister.* **in D litterae similitudinem**: some manuscripts and some plans have O instead of D. Pr. & B. explain that there were two D's, thus: ᗡD, with the area between; taking one D, and understanding the shape as semicircular, which seems most reasonable, we cannot determine whether the straight side was in front or rear.

16. festiva: this may mean *cheerful* or *handsome.*

18. specularibus: *panes* either of glass, which was in use before this date, or of mica or talc (*lapis specularis*), which could be split into very thin sheets. Cf. Pl. *Nat. Hist.* XXXVI. 22; Martial VIII. 14; Juvenal IV. 21. **imminentibus**: *overhanging.* **muniuntur**: the subject is *porticus.*

19. contra medias: *facing the middle of it;* i.e., of the *porticus*, line 15. **cavaedium hilare**: *cheerful inner court*, either because of its decorations or its abundance of light, as it was open to the sky in the centre, being either a kind of second *atrium* or a peristyle (court, surrounded by columns). In its earlier use *cavaedium* apparently = *atrium*, but later, as houses grew larger and more elaborate, it designated a second open chamber or court, meaning, in general, the open interior of the house. Cf. Magoun, cited above. **mox** = *deinde;* post-Augustan. **triclinium**: *dining-room;* see Class. Dict. for description and plan.

20. Africo: the S.W. wind.

21. fractis iam, etc.: *only by the spray of the spent waves.* (Cowan.)

22. valvas: *folding doors*, with two leaves.

24. prospectat: notice the variety of expressions in the context for 'view,' 'outlook,' 'prospect'; it has been remarked that the Romans took infinite pains to secure beautiful views from their houses, and that their chief enjoyment of natural beauty was through their windows. **a tergo**: the visitor looking out to sea would have *behind him* the portions of the villa already described. Turning around, he would see them in the reverse order, as they are here enumerated.

26. retractius paulo: *a little further back;* i.e., not projecting as the *triclinium* did. **cubiculum**: not a bedroom, but a *salon* or *withdrawing-room.*

27. orientem, occidentem: i.e., in winter S.E. and S.W. The allusions to the sun in such connections are very frequent; cf. *infra,*

§§ 7, 8, 13 ; also Epp. I. 3. 1 ; V. 6. 15 ; V. 6. 24. Much dependence was placed on the sun for heating interiors in cold weather.

30. angulus: exposed from S.E. to S.W., sheltered from the other points of the compass. **purissimum**: *brightest.*

31. continet et accendit: *collects and intensifies.* **hibernaculum**: *winter exercise ground*, for Pliny's slaves (*meorum*).

Page 31. **1. nubilum . . . serenum**: sc. *caelum; overcast the sky with clouds and take away fair weather.*

2. cubiculum in hapsida curvatum: *a salon with semicircular wall;* i.e., a bay window. Pliny would have enjoyed sitting with Montaigne in his study, described in Bk. III. ch. 3, on *Les trois Commerces.*

4. armarium: *book-case*, cupboard with shelves, containing Pliny's favorite books.

6. dormitorium membrum: *a sleeping-apartment; dormitorium* is a post-Augustan adjective. **transitu**: *passage*, a *hypocauston*, heated from beneath, by terra-cotta flues (*tubulatum*) laid below its mosaic pavement, which was supported (*suspensum*) on short pillars; cf. § 23, *infra;* Ep. V. 6. 25 ; Sen. Ep. 90. 25. Many such flues have been found in position. Some editors understand *transitu* simply as a 'conduit,' for the pipes.

8. digerit et ministrat: *distributes and supplies.*

9. detinetur: *is appropriated.*

10. plerisque tam mundis: sc. *membris* or *cubiculis* from the sense of *reliqua pars.*

11. politissimum: Cowan translates this *tastefully decorated*, and supposes that this *cubiculum* balanced and corresponded to that described in § 6, *supra*, this one perhaps being intended for guests, that for servants, musicians, etc.

12. cenatio: apparently a less large and formal apartment than the *triclinium* or state dining-room, yet often used as its synonym. **quae plurimo . . . lucet**: *with plenty of sunshine and a wide sea view.* (Cowan.)

13. procoetone: *anteroom* (προκοιτών).

14. altitudine aestivum: *cool in summer* (lit., suitable for use in summer) *because of its high ceiling.*

16. balinei: see Class. Dict., article *Balneae.*

17. effusa: *broad, wide.*

18. duo baptisteria, etc.: *two plunge baths* (cold) of circular form let into semicircular niches in the two opposite walls, or perhaps only of semicircular form and projecting out (*eiecta*) from the walls.

19. si . . . cogites: *considering the nearness of the sea*, which is available for swimming. **unctorium**: *anointing-room*, an important adjunct of the bath.

20. hypocauston: *sweating-room;* called *hypocauston*, because heated from below the pavement. **propnigeon** (πρό, πνιγεύς): a room or passage containing or communicating with the furnace of a bath; Vitruvius calls it *praefurnium*. **duae cellae**: i.e., *caldaria* and *tepidaria*.

22. piscina: *pool* for swimming, warm in this case; cf. Ep. V. 6. 25. **ex qua natantes**, etc.: this implies glazed windows. *Natantes*, 'swimmers,' illustrates the post-Augustan tendency to use the participle for the *nomen agentis*. **mare aspiciunt**: a fine view was an important element in the luxury of private baths.

23. sphaeristerium: *ball-ground*, *tennis-court;* exposed to the afternoon sun, where they exercised before bathing; cf. Epp. V. 6. 27; III. 1. 8.

24. sub qua: i.e., on the ground floor. **diaetae**: *sitting-rooms*, sometimes the word means 'summer house.'

25. in ipsa: i.e., on the second floor. **cenatio**: this dining-room was apparently on the third floor, where the view was most extensive.

27. alia turris: there is no certainty about the location of these towers; the plans show the widest diversity in this respect. **in quo sol nascitur**, etc.: cf. § 6, *supra;* here Pliny is apparently describing the upper story first.

28. apotheca et horreum: *wine closet and storeroom*. The *apotheca* was in the upper part of a house, as the passage of smoke through it was considered beneficial to the wine. Horace invites an *amphora* to descend from the wine closet. *Car.* III. 21. 7.

30. patitur: poetic, *hears;* informal personification. **languidum et desinentem**: *faint and subdued.*

31. gestationem: cf. note on *gestatio*, page 1, line 12.

Page 32. **3. inarescit**: *withers.*

4. vinea: a vine, on a trellis, shading a walk, where the ground was kept soft for barefoot exercise, *ambulatio;* cf. Ep. III. 1. 8. **tenera**: *dainty;* this adjective is a stereotyped epithet of the vine, but it is impossible to translate it satisfactorily; we do not know precisely what aspect of it was especially associated with the noun.

7. malignior: *unfavorable.* **Hac . . . facie**: i.e., the view over the garden.

9. vestibulum: the entrance from the main road, leading into the *atrium.* It may have been a sort of *porte cochère*, as the villa was reached by driving.

10. hortus . . . rusticus: *a fertile kitchen garden;* that previously described was an ornamental garden.

11. cryptoporticus: *covered portico;* a hybrid word, said to be peculiar to Pliny. **prope publici operis**: genitive of quality; *almost big enough for a public building.*

12. fenestrae: i.e., one on the garden side opposite every other one on the side toward the sea. **singulae**: the windows on the garden side were *single*, implying that on the other side they were arranged in pairs or threes. **alternis**: abl. of degree of difference. The meaning seems to be that there was a single window opposite *every other* pair.

13. serenus . . . inmotus: *clear and still;* cf. Tac. *Hist.* I. 86.

16. xystus: *a terrace walk;* sometimes a parterre, divided into flower beds. **violis**: these and roses were the principal flowers cultivated by the Romans. They were much used for garlands at feasts. In general, we remark the very limited variety of flowers and trees then known. **repercussu**: *reflected radiation.*

21. Nam ante meridiem, etc.: in the morning, the sun shone on the N.E. side (*xystus*), and the S.W. side was in shadow; at noon, the interior was, of course, shady; in the afternoon, when the sun shone on the S.W. side of the cryptoporticus, the nearest part of the garden and the *gestatio* on the N.E. side of it were in the shade. *Gestationis proximam partem* may have been the adjoining *vinea.*

27. aëre pigro et manente: *by closeness and lack of circulation of the air.*

28. In capite . . . diaeta est: *at the head of the terrace and portico successively is a garden suite of rooms.* (Cowan.) As terrace and portico were parallel, the rooms at the end of the former extended opposite the end of the latter. **amores mei**: *my favorite*, or *which I am in love with.*

30. heliocaminus: *sun-parlor.*

31. cubiculum: coördinate; *also a room.* Translate: *A sun-parlor which looks on the terrace on one side, the sea on another, and the sun on both; also a room which looks on the cryptoporticus through folding doors, and the sea through a window.*

Page 33. **1. zotheca**: *cabinet* (a small private chamber), *alcove* or *recess.* The word is found only in Pliny and Sidonius Apollinaris; if it means a 'den' for wild beasts, it is used in the same figurative sense as the English word.

2. specularibus: see note on page 30, line 18.

3. cubiculo: i.e., the adjoining room. **cathedras**: *easy chairs.*

5. et distinguit et miscet: you could look at the separate views from the several windows, or you could blend them all into one by taking a sweeping view from the *lectus* in the middle of the room.

6. somni: i.e., to sleep in during the day; genitive of that for which a thing is intended; see Introduction II. § 3. *b.*

9. ratio: *explanation.*

10. andron: *a passage* between two walls; changed from its original Greek meaning — the 'men's apartments.'

13. angusta fenestra: like the register of a modern hot-air flue, whereby heat could be admitted or excluded at will.

16. oblicum: see note on *aecum*, page 5, line 20.

19. Saturnalibus: the *Saturnalia*, according to the enactment of Augustus, lasted three days, December 17–19, but were practically continued eight days, a period of license and noisy merriment on the part of slaves. See Class. Dict.

21. obstrepunt: zeugma; *I do not interrupt their sports by my presence, nor they my studies by their noise.* The latter sense of *obstrepunt* is the proper one.

22. deficitur: *lacks.* We oftener find the active, with the nominative of the thing that is lacking. **aqua salienti**: *running water;* the land is low and there are no hills near by. A number of fountains on Pliny's Tuscan estate are mentioned in Ep. V. 6. 23, 37, 40.

23. ac potius: *or rather;* a favorite phrase, already noted. **in summo**: *close to the surface;* it was not necessary to dig far for water.

25. moveris humum: *dig;* perfect subjunctive. The classical usage is to put the indicative in a 'generalizing clause' after a relative word (*quocumque*) except when the thought is expressed by the indefinite 2nd singular. Kraut, § 46. c.

26. sincerus: *fresh, sweet,* not brackish. **corruptus**: i.e., brackish.

27. ligna: for fuel.

29. vicus: a village on the shore near by.

30. balinea meritoria: *public baths; meritorius* means 'for hire.'

32. calfacere: a loose use of the infinitive instead of the subjunctive with *ut* after *dissuadeat. Suadere* with the infinitive is common in poetry and in Silver prose. Reid's note to Cic. *de Sen.* 32 says: The usual construction after verbs of advising or warning is *ut* with the subjunctive, but, even in Cicero and the other writers of the best period, the infinitive sometimes follows when the advice or warning is *general* and not addressed to any particular person.

Page 34. 1. **continua . . . intermissa**: *close together . . . at long intervals.*

3. **utare**: *look at them from.* **mollit . . . indurat**: in quiet weather the beach grows dry and soft; when washed by the waves it grows firm again.

5. **soleas . . . squillas**: *soles and sea-leeks* (a kind of prawns or shrimps). In Juvenal V. 81, *squilla* = 'lobster,' in Hor. *Sat.* II. 4. 58, 'prawn.'

10. **inhabitare**: post-Augustan for *habitare.* **nimis urbanus**: *too fond of the city.*

12. **villulae**: one of the author's favorite diminutives, manifestly not to be taken literally.

13. **ex tuo contubernio**: *from your sojourn.*

Letter 28. Junius Mauricus is addressed in Epp. I. 14 and VI. 14; cf. notes on page 4, line 18, and on Ep. I. 14.

14. **praeceptorem**: i.e., a public teacher of rhetoric, not a private tutor.

15. **fratris**: Arulenus Rusticus; cf. note on page 3, line 5. **beneficio tuo**: *thanks to you.*

17. **resumo**: poetic and post-Augustan in prose; cf. *praesumo*, page 25, line 28.

20. **ordinis**: i.e., the senatorial. **loquebantur**: sc. *iuvenes*; see Crit. App.

23. **probe discere**: i.e., can learn without having their characters and manners corrupted by their associations.

24. **profitentur**: *teach publicly;* hence our 'professor'; post-Augustan absolute use of the verb; the noun *professor* occurs in Quintilian, Suetonius, and in other authors, as well as in Pliny.

Page 35. 2. **nisi . . . amares**: *if you did not love them more than if they were your own;* hyperbole.

4. **vindicassem**: *I would have claimed.*

5. **suscipiendas**, etc.: *that one must take the risk of offending people.*

6. **simultates**: actual enmities, stronger than *offensas.*

Letter 29. C. Calvisius Rufus was a decurion of Comum, several times spoken of by Pliny as his *contubernalis.* To him were written, besides this letter, Epp. III. 1; III. 19; V. 7; VIII. 2; IX. 6.

9. Assem para: *get your copper ready;* the language of the strolling *improvisatore*, who entertains the crowd in the street and takes up a collection. **fabulas**: *several stories.*

11. Verania: sc. *uxor.* **iacebat**: *was lying ill.*

12. Galba adoptavit: as related in Tac. *Hist.* I. 14, 15, 47; Plut. *Galba* 28; Suet. *Galba* 17. He was murdered four days after his adoption.

13. inpudentiam: sc. *vide*, or else it is simply an exclamatory accusative.

15. Esto, si venit tantum: *let it pass, if he only came.*

17. componit vultum: *componere vultum* is to assume whatever expression is suitable to the context; here it is a look of anxious interest and deep thought. Cf. Ep. III. 16. 5, *composito vultu*; Ep. VII. 1. 6, *vultum composui.*

18. agitat digitos, computat: the Romans were very clever at making elaborate calculations upon their fingers; cf. Mayor's note on Juvenal X. 249, which is too long to quote here. It contains numerous citations from Greek and Latin literature on the subject in question. In general, it may be said that units and tens were counted on the left hand, hundreds on the right.

19. climactericum tempus: *a time of great crisis*, especially the 7th and 9th years or any multiple of either, most of all the 63rd, 7 times 9. Cf. Aul. Gell. III. 10; XV. 7. But here Regulus is pretending to cast her horoscope.

24. codicillos: diminutive of *codex; tablets*, to write upon; as to the legal nature of codicils as testamentary dispositions, see Hunter, *Roman Law*, pp. 825 sqq. The codicil to be made in this case is merely a supplement to the will.

25. clamat . . . hominem nequam: notice this rather free use of the accusative.

Page 36. **2. detestatur**: this verb means to imprecate, to call down the wrath of the gods upon some one. Regulus virtually does this in swearing falsely by the life of his son. Yet he professed extraordinary affection for this son; cf. Ep. IV. 7.

3. novissima valetudine: *last illness;* cf. Ep. II. 1. 9.

5. novis tabulis: *a new will*, not 'a cancellation of debts.' **captare**: *to court, to pay court to; captator* is the regular word for a legacy hunter; cf. Ep. IV. 2. 2; Hor. *Sat.* II. 5.

8. vertit adlocutionem: *changed his tone;* late sense of the word *adlocutio.*

10. bona morte: *an easy death*, like εὐθανασία.

11. tantulum: sc. *legavit.*

12. scholastica lege: *according to the rule of rhetoricians,* treating each theme under three heads, dividing a speech into three parts, a rule not approved by Quintilian (IV. 5. 3). This is better than to understand 'according to the practice of idle men,' i.e., always asking for another story.

13. Aurelia: cf. Juv. V. 98, *Quod captator emat Laenas, Aurelia vendat.* **ornata**: *distinguished.*

14. pulcherrimas: not because people put on their finest clothes when about to die, but in honor of the ceremony of will-making, a most important act in the opinion of the Romans, and having an almost sacred character.

15. tunicas: plural because two were worn at once, the upper one often of silk, which was 'worth its weight in gold.'

16. leges: *to bequeath;* present subjunctive of *legare.* **ludere**: *that he was joking.*

17. ne multa: sc. *dicam; not to make a long story of it.*

18. quas erat induta: B. 175. 2. *d*; A. & G. 240. *c.* note; H. 377; Roby 1127. 2.

21. hereditates . . . legata. the *heres* was the personal representative of the testator, succeeding to all his rights and liabilities; the *legatarius* merely received a gift from the testator, payable by the heir.

22. Ἀλλὰ τί διατείνομαι: *But why do I trouble myself.* Cowan compares Demos. *de Cor.* 275, Diod. Sic. XIII. 28.

25. ex paupere et tenui: cf. Tac. *Hist.* IV. 42; his father had been banished and his property distributed among his creditors.

26. cum consuleret: i.e., the omens; cf. Ep. VI. 2. 2.

27. sescenties: sc. *centena milia;* 60,000,000 sesterces. **exta duplicia**: cf. Plin. *N. H.* XI. 37; Suet. *Aug.* 95; Valer. Max. I. 6. 9. This was a very lucky omen.

28. quibus portendi: note the subordinate clause of *oratio obliqua* with an infinitive verb; B. 314. 4; A. & G. 336. 2. *c*; H. 524. 1. 1); Roby 1784. *b.* **milies et ducenties**: 120,000,000 sesterces.

30. falsi: *forgery,* of which the most frequent form was the fabrication of wills. The most famous of the laws against forgery was the often-cited *Lex Cornelia* of Sulla. Did Regulus evade legal penalty by *dictating* to the testatrix? Is it not worse than forgery to browbeat a testator into making a will which he does not wish to make?

BOOK III

Page 37. Letter 30. To C. Calvisius Rufus are addressed six letters; cf. introductory note on Ep. II. 20.

2. Spurinnam: Vestricius Spurinna had been a general of Otho against Vitellius in A.D. 69, Tac. *Hist.* II. 11; 18; 23; 36; Plut. *Otho* 5; 7; and consul twice or thrice; under Nerva he was legate of Lower Germany, and was honored for victories over the Bructeri, Ep. II. 7. The poems long attributed to him are undoubted forgeries. Pliny addressed to him Epp. III. 10, and V. 17.

4. distinctius: *more methodical* (Mayor); the day is marked off into definite periods, each with its proper occupation.

5. siderum cursus: cf. Cic. *de Sen.* 77. **disposita**: *well-ordered;* cf. Epp. II. 11. 17; IV. 23. 1.

7. indecent: Mayor says this is ἅπαξ λεγόμενον in this sense.

8. industria: *exertion.*

10. parva haec, etc.: *trifles like the following — trifles but for their daily recurrence* (Mayor); they are important because they form habits.

11. ordine: *routine.*

12. lectulo continetur: *keeps his sofa*, studies on his reading couch. It was not customary to sit upright at a desk. **hora**: $\frac{1}{12}$ of the actual day, hence varying from about $1\frac{1}{4}$ hr. to $\frac{3}{4}$ hr. according to the season. This matter is elaborately discussed, with a table for the various months and days, in Stoffel, *Guerre Civile*, Appendix A. **calceos**: the Romans went about the house with bare feet, or with sandals, *soleae;* cf. Epp. VI. 16. 5, and IX. 17. 3.

13. ambulat: probably in his garden, back and forth. **passuum**: 1 *passus* = 2 *gradus* = 5 *pedes;* hence the Roman mile was 5000 Roman feet = about 4850 English feet.

14. honestissimi: *high-toned;* no vulgarity was permitted.

15. explicantur: *are engaged in.* **si non**: less common than *si* (or *sin*) *minus*, when a verb expressed in the first member of the sentence is omitted in the second. B. 306 2. a; Roby 1563, 1565. **legitur**: by a *lector*, a slave or freedman.

16. si tamen: *provided, of course.* **gravantur**: *object.*

17. considit: probably on a garden seat. **liber**: notice the omission of the verb.

18. uxorem: her name was Cottia; Ep. III. 10. **singularis exempli**: *of unique virtue;* note the genitive of quality attached directly to *uxorem* without an appositive *mulierem;* cf. Livy XXI. 1. 4, *Hannibalem annorum ferme novem;* this species of brachylogy is quite common in Pliny; Kraut, § 14. e; see Introduction II. § 3. *c*.

19. proxime: temporal; his visit to Spurinna was *nuper*.

20. secretum: *privacy, private interview*, as in Ep. I. 5. 11. **quantum . . . antiquitatis**: *what glimpses of old times.* (Mayor.)

21. facta . . . viros: accusative instead of the more usual *de* with ablative.

22. temperamentum: *limit, restraint, measure;* cf. Epp. I. 7. 3; II. 17. 9; III. 20. 12.

Page 38. **1. Peractis septem milibus**: this may be simply driving to and fro in his *gestatio*, or under a *porticus;* cf. note on page 1, line 12.

3. utraque lingua: Latin and Greek.

4. lyrica: *lyric poems;* first used as a noun by Pliny; as to the four fragmentary odes attributed to Spurinna, published in 1613, see Mayor's note on this place, and Teuffel's *Roman Literature* (translation by Warr), § 323, note 5. **doctissima**: *clever;* i.e., they showed great technical skill.

6. nuntiata: a slave was kept near the *solarium* or *clepsydra* to announce the passing of the hours.

7. hieme nona, aestate octava: at Rome, at the winter solstice, the ninth hour began at 1.30 P.M., at the summer solstice the eighth began at 1.15 P.M. Vitruvius, IX. 7, 7, describes the effect of all sun-dials — to divide the day at any season into twelve equal parts. See Class. Dict., art. *Horologium.* **caret**: the subject is vague, *dies* or the like; it is definite in Hor. *Car.* III. 29 23, 24.

caretque
ripa vagis taciturna ventis.

8. movetur pila: *he plays ball; pila* is best taken as ablative; note the reflexive force of *movetur*.

9. pugnat cum senectute: cf. Cic. *de Sen.* 35, *pugnandum tamquam contra morbum sic contra senectutem.*

10. Lotus: from *lavare.*

11. legentem: sc. *aliquem.* **remissius . . . et dulcius**: *light and agreeable.*

14. puro: *plain*, without chasing or embossing; a less simple taste preferred *argentum caelatum.* **Corinthia**: sc. *aera;* Corinthian bronzes were highly prized and very costly; Ep. III. 6. The elder Pliny (*Nat. Hist.* XXXIV. 7, 8) enumerates the different kinds of bronze that were made; one contained a large proportion of silver and resembled silver in appearance. He states that the Corinthian bronze was used for dishes (*ad esculenta*), for bowls, and for lamps. We are rather accustomed to associate it with statues and other purely decorative works of art.

15. quibus delectatur nec adficitur: *for which he has a taste but not a passion.* **Frequenter**: *often;* Silver Latin. **comoedis**: instrumental ablative, of persons, the more appropriate as they are slaves. This was a higher form of entertainment than that ordinarily furnished at dinners by ballet dancers and buffoons.

16. distinguitur: *is enlivened.* **quoque**: *even.* **condiantur**: *may have a flavor of letters.* (Mayor.)

17. aliquid de nocte: cf. Ep. III. 5. 13.

20. vividum: *vigorous.*

21. solaque, etc.: *wisdom is the only symptom of old age.*

22. praesumo: *anticipate, look forward to, forestall. Praecipio* is the classical word; cf. Epp. II. 10. 6; VI. 10. 5.

23. ratio aetatis: *considerations of age.* **receptui canere**: military phrase; *to sound the signal for the retreat.*

24. laboribus: cf. II. 14. 1; busy practice, state trials (Ep. III. 4. 8); his office of *praefectus aerarii Saturni* (Ep. III. 6. 6).

26. provincias: Transpadane Gaul under Otho, Lower Germany under Nerva.

28. apud te subsigno: *I promise you under my hand and seal; I register my vow, my resolution, and leave the record with you.* (Mayor.)

29. in ius voces ad hanc epistulam meam: *you may bring suit against me upon the evidence of this letter of mine.* Note the mixture of metaphors; *cursum, terminum,* and *evehi* drawn from the race-course, the rest of the sentence from the law courts.

Page 39. Letter 31. Baebius Macer appears as consul elect, speaking in the senate in A.D. 103 or 104 (Ep. IV. 9. 16 sqq.), and as praefect of the city in 117 (*Vita Hadriani* 5. 5). This is the only letter in the collection addressed to him.

1. avunculi: for Pliny the Elder, cf. Introduction, pages ix, x, xi, xii. He was born A.D. 23, and perished in the eruption of Vesuvius, Aug. 24, 79. Cf. especially Epp. V. 8. 5; VI. 16; VI. 20.

3. indicis: *index* may mean, as with us, a table of the contents of a book, or a list of books of a given class, or it may be equivalent to *titulus*, the label attached to a volume, giving its name and author.

4. haec . . . cognitio: i.e., of the order in which they were written.

5. De iaculatione equestri: *On throwing the javelin from horseback.*

6. praefectus alae: the command of a cavalry regiment (*ala*) was one step in the equestrian *cursus honorum;* see Egbert, *Latin Inscriptions*, p. 173; Cagnat, pp. 109 sqq.

7. ingenio curaque: *talent and industry.* **Pomponi Secundi**: a poet in the time of Tiberius, Caligula, and Claudius, chiefly celebrated for his tragedies. See Smith, Dict. III. 764. Being a friend of Sejanus, he was imprisoned after the latter's fall, A.D. 31, but was released in 37, and became consul in 41. Afterwards, when legate of Claudius in Germany, he defeated the Chatti in 50, and won triumphal ornaments. Tacitus calls him (*Ann.* V. 8) a man *multa morum elegantia et ingenio illustri.* He was an intimate friend of the elder Pliny, who tells (*N. H.* XIV. 56) how Caligula dined with him, and about his expensive wine.

9. quasi debitum munus: *as a last tribute, so to speak* ('apologetic' *quasi*), or *a duty, as it were, which he owed to the memory of his friend.*

The lost historics of the elder Pliny were one of the sources from which Tacitus drew (*Ann.* I. 69). Suetonius also cites them, *Caligula* 8; cf. also *Vita Plinii* attributed to Suetonius.

12. somnio monitus: cf. the story of Fannius's dream, Ep. V. 5. 6. **Drusi Neronis**: stepson of Augustus, who died B.C. 9 in Germany on the last of his many campaigns.

13. latissime victor: note the adverb used like an adjective; cf. Verg. *Aen.* I. 21, *populum late regem;* Hor. *Car.* III. 17. 9; IV. 4. 23. Drusus conquered Raetia and Noricum, made the Danube a frontier of the empire, and planned to subdue Germany as far as the Elbe, to which he penetrated on one expedition; cf. Vell. Paterc. II. 97.

15. adsereret: *save, vindicate;* cf. *adseris*, page 2, line 6, and note. **Studiosi**: *The Student;* genitive singular. **tres**: sc. *libri.* **volumina**: *rolls, volumes;* a long work was in several *volumina* for convenience, while one roll might contain several short works.

16. ab incunabulis: *from the cradle;* lit. 'swaddling clothes'; cf. Quint. pr. 6. Quintilian begins his scheme of education at birth, *igitur nato filio*, I. 1. 1.

17. Dubii sermonis: *On bad grammar* or *diction*, or else *On ambiguous language.* Considerable fragments of this treatise are extant.

19. erectius: *lofty.* Most of the literature in Nero's reign was of a 'harmless' sort. There was danger in expressing 'elevated' sentiments, such as would be natural in history, philosophy, and poetry. Grammar was safe ground.

20. A fine Aufidi Bassi: sc. *historiarum;* cf. the title of Tacitus's Annals: *ab excessu Divi Augusti;* this work of Pliny probably extended to the reign of Claudius. As to the work of Bassus, which was thus continued, see Teuffel, *Roman Literature* (translation by Warr), § 277; Quint. X. 1, 103. **Naturae historiarum**: commonly called *Naturalis Historia*, dedicated to Titus, the son of Vespasian, a vast work of encyclopaedic character, a mine of information on the greatest variety of subjects; this work alone has survived.

21. triginta septem: the first book consists of a table of contents and a list of sources, including 146 Latin and 327 foreign authors.

23. scrupulosa: *requiring great care.*

26. medium tempus: i.e., between his quitting of practice at the bar and his death. **qua . . . qua**: *as well . . . as.*

27. amicitia principum: i.e., of Vespasian and Titus.

Page 40. **2. Vulcanalibus**: the 23d of August, when sunrise is about a quarter past five; the date chosen for first lighting lamps before daylight, because Vulcan was the god of fire; this was with most persons merely a ceremony (*auspicandi causa*), but Pliny really began to study. **auspicandi causa**: *for luck.*

3. a nocte multa: *long before dawn;* lit., 'from deep in the night'; cf. *ad multum diei:* 'till late in the day.' **hora septima**: the first hour after midnight.

4. octava: the second hour after midnight. **sexta**: midnight. **somni paratissimi**: predicative genitive of quality; Kraut, § 14. e; *sleep came at his bidding*; cf. Ep. VI. 16. 13, where he readily went to sleep in trying circumstances.

5. inter: *during.*

8. relicum: see note on *aecum*, page 5, line 20.

9. cibum: it was customary to take a light luncheon or second breakfast towards noon (*prandium*); the few mouthfuls of food (*ientaculum*) taken on rising could hardly be called a meal. **interdiu**: as opposed to the evening or late afternoon when the heartier *cena* was served.

10. facilem: *easily digestible*, or *easily prepared; simple* would do for either sense.

14. frigida: sc. *aqua.*

15. dormiebat: the siesta was a universal habit, necessary for men who rise in the small hours.

16. cenae tempus: three or four in the afternoon. **Super**: *during* = *inter*. Common in this sense in the Silver Age. Cf. Epp. IV. 22. 6; IX. 33. 1.

17. et quidem: here adversative.

19. revocasse . . . coëgisse: for the perfect infinitive with *memini*, see note on page 28, line 27. **repeti**: *the passage to be repeated.* **avunculum**: *aunculum*, *aunclum*, *oncle*, uncle.

20. nempe: in post-Augustan Latin occasionally used post-positively.

21. decem amplius: B. 217. 3; A. & G. 247. c; H. 417. 1. N. 2. **versus**: *lines* of prose or verse.

23. primam: sc. *horam.*

24. Haec: referring to the whole disposition of the day, described above.

25. In secessu: i.e., on vacation, in the country.

26. de interioribus: *of the time while he was actually in the water;* lit., in the inner rooms. **destringitur**: with a *strigil*, a flesh-scraper. **tergitur**: with a *linteum*, a linen towel.

29. vacabat: *devoted his whole time.* **notarius**: *short-hand writer.* The Romans had an elaborate system of short-hand, specimens of which have been preserved. **libro**: Pliny must have read the book as they went along and dictated to the *notarius*, who put down his words in the note-books (*pugillares*).

30. manicis: *gloves*, or, more precisely, the sleeves of the tunic made long so as to cover the hands.

32. Repeto: *I recall.*

Page 41. **1. correptum**: in pregnant sense, *chidden* ('with the question why, etc.').

2. non perdere: *have avoided losing.*

3. intentione: *application.*

4. electorum: *selections.* **commentarios**: *note-books.*

5. opisthogrăphos: *written on the back*, i.e., on both sides of the papyrus, which was unusual. The word is a late importation from the Greek.

7. procuraret: *was procurator;* note the special technical meaning developed from a general sense. This was an equestrian office; one might become *procurator Caesaris* after being *praefectus alae.* Procurators were either governors of minor imperial provinces (e.g., Pilate, of Judaea) or fiscal agents of the emperor in larger ones, either imperial or senatorial.

8. Largio Licino: to him is attributed, in Ep. II. 14. 9, the foundation of the *claque* in court-rooms. **quadringentis**, etc.: 400,000 sesterces, a knight's fortune.

14. illae occupationes: the official ones.

17. Ego autem tantum: some predicate must be supplied for *ego*, the thought being substantially the same as above in *sum desidiosissimus*.

19. tota vita: another case of duration of time expressed by the ablative. This construction occurs even in earlier writers, especially when the substantive is modified by *totus*.

22. haec: *these details.*

23. grata: *interesting.*

Letter 32. To Annius Severus is addressed one other letter, Ep. V. 1.

26. Corinthium signum: see note on page 38, line 14.

28. modicum: *small.* **festivum et expressum**: *elegant and bold.*

Page 42. **1. quantum . . . sapio**: it seems to have been a part of the Roman *gravitas* to affect an ignorance of the fine arts. Pliny goes on to talk like a connoisseur.

3. vitia: *defects.*

4. laudes: *good points.*

5. etiam: after asyndeton of several members; see note on page 20, line 22.

6. cedentes: *retreating* high on the head, back from the forehead.

7. contracta: *pinched, drawn.*

8. recessit: *has become hollow.* **ut a tergo**: *as far as one can judge from behind;* i.e., so far as the back of the body shows signs of age.

10. artificum . . . imperitorum: *of artists . . . of those who are not connoisseurs.*

11. quamquam: see note on page 8, line 2.

12. tirunculum: *novice.*

14. patria: viz. Comum. **celebri**: *frequented.*

17. omnia: sc. *suscipere.*

18. iam nunc: *right away.* **basim**: *pedestal.*

19. honores: *official titles.*

22. si tamen officii ratio permiserit: *if, that is, the claims of my office* (*praefectus aerarii Saturni*) *permit.*

24. ad paucos dies: *that it will be for only a few days.*

Letter 33. The death of Silius Italicus. For Caninius Rufus, see note at beginning of Ep. I. 3.

27. Silius Italicus (A.D. 25–101): was consul in 68, then, abandoning official life, spent the rest of his days in literary retirement. His chief work was a long epic poem (*Punica*), in seventeen books, on the second Punic war, which is still extant; Teuffel, *Roman Literature* (translation by Warr), § 320. **Neapolitano**: sc. *praedio*; the chief interest of this estate was the fact that on it was situated the tomb of Vergil. What is to-day shown as Vergil's tomb is a very dubious relic. Cf. Martial XI. 48 and 49.

28. inedia: this showed the calm, deliberate nature of the resolution to die; it was the dignified method of suicide. **finisse vitam**: Mayor has an interesting note on this passage, containing a long list of the suicides of Roman authors and a discussion of the views of the ancients regarding the morality of self-destruction.

Page 43. **1. clavus**: *a hard tumor*; sometimes a 'corn' or 'callus.'

2. decucurrit ad mortem: *took refuge in death*; more literally, 'had recourse to death.'

3. minorem ex liberis: they were both sons; this one was named Severus; cf. Martial IX. 86.

4. maiorem: consul probably from Sept. 1, 93; cf. Martial VIII. 66.

5. Laeserat famam, etc.: *He had damaged his reputation* by acting as an informer, or at least so it was believed. He did this *sponte*, not as a public duty at the command of the senate nor on the complaint of an injured province.

6. sponte: note the absence of a possessive adjective. **Vitelli**: emperor for a few months in A.D. 69.

7. Asiae: one of the two senatorial provinces of consular rank, the other being Africa; Silius was its governor under Domitian.

8. industriae: the bad significance of the word is like that in the term *chevalier d'industrie*, 'adventurer.'

9. otio: the retirement in which his later years were spent, devoted to literature. **sine potentia**, etc.: in the time of the Flavian emperors.

11. ex fortuna: *in accordance with his station*, rank or wealth. **frequenti**: agrees with *cubiculo*; his *salon* was crowded.

13. carmina: especially his *Punica*, which Professor Wilkins calls 'the characteristic work of a well-schooled, lifeless age.' He calls Silius 'a slavish imitator of the diction and metre of Vergil,' who 'produced many thousand verses as dull as they were faultless.' **maiore cura quam ingenio**; cf. the expression in Ep. III. 5. 3.

16. adventu . . . principis: Trajan succeeded Nerva on the latter's death, Jan. 28, 98, but did not return to Rome from the Rhine till 99.

17. laus: abstract noun in apposition to the preceding sentence, *ac . . . commotus est.*

19. φιλόκαλος: *a virtuoso.* **emacitatis**: a rare word, *mania for buying.*

20. Plures . . . villas: among them was one at Puteoli which had belonged to Cicero; cf. Martial XI. 48.

21. adamatis: *taking a fancy to.*

24. natalem: sc. *diem;* October 15.

26. annum . . . excessit: the transitive use of *excedere* is post-Augustan; see Introduction II. § 3. *i.*

27. delicato . . . infirmo: a rare use of *delicatus;* his constitution was not strong, but he had no disease.

Page 44. **2. modo modo**: *but yesterday* (Mayor); denoting the immediate past; perhaps colloquial; cf. Petronius, 37; 42; 46. But cf. also Seneca, *ad. Helv. Matr.* II. 5. There is a more developed habit of reduplication in modern Italian.

5. L. Piso: the son of Germanicus's enemy, Cn. Calpurnius Piso. **Pisonis**: murdered A.D. 70 by order of the commander in Africa, Valerius Festus; Tac. *Hist.* IV. 49; 50. **Valerio Festo**: cf. C. I. L. II. 2477.

6. per . . . facinus = modal ablative.

7. consul ipse: he had been consul A.D. 27; hence the word *nuper* is rather striking, as this letter must have been written about seventy-five years later. But the word is often used very loosely; cf. Tac. *Ger.* 2; *Hist.* IV. 17.

9. vivacitas: a post-Augustan word; *vital force, length of life; vivax* means 'strongly clinging to life.'

10. regiae = *regis.*

11. Xerxen: when he reviewed his fleet and army at the Hellespont on the way down to invade Greece. Cf. Herod. VII. 45; Sen. *Brev. Vit.* 16. **obisset oculis**: *surveyed, reviewed.*

12. tam brevis . . . occasus: *so early a death*, an unusual force of *brevis*, which ordinarily means 'of short duration'; here it refers to something that will occur 'within a short time.'

14. futilis et caduci: *vain and fleeting.*

15. aliena manu: i.e., the emperor's. **quatenus** = *quoniam* *since ;* we say 'as long as,' for 'in as much as.' Cf. Juvenal XII. 102 ; Tac. *Ann.* III. 16 ; *Dial.* 5. 19. This use is adopted from poetry.

18. quoque : *even.*

19. Ἀγαθὴ δ' ἔρις : *rivalry is good ;* a reminiscence of Hesiod, *Works and Days*, 24. **invicem se mutuis** : faulty redundancy.

20. exacuunt : *whet.*

Letter 34. Julius Genitor was a rhetorician. He is highly commended in Ep. III. 3. 4–7. To him were written also Epp. VII. 30, and IX. 17.

21. Artemidori : Zeller infers from what is said of him that he was a Stoic.

22. in maius extollat : *exaggerates.* **supra meritum** : the phrase serves as an adjective to *praedicatione.*

24. philosophi . . . summoti : *summovere* is a technical term for the police bidding people 'move on' ; this banishment of philosophers from Rome was a police measure. Domitian gave expression to his hatred and fear of the philosophers, especially the independent outspoken Stoics, by decrees of banishment in 89 and 94. An account of his motives and of the extent to which these edicts were enforced may be read in Merivale, chap. 62.

25. quo notabilius . . . esset : *to make it more conspicuous.*

26. praetor : for A.D. 93 ; these events connected with the banishment of the philosophers took place in the last four months of that year, and in the year following.

Page 45. **1. aes alienum** : *debt.*

2. pulcherrimis : *most creditable.* **mussantibus** : *hesitating ;* lit., whispering in murmurs.

4. septem amicis : all members of one family or connected with it by marriage or friendship ; cf. Boissier, *l'Opposition sous les Césars.*

5. Senecione : see note on page 3, line 9. **Rustico** : see note on page 3, line 5. **Helvidio** : the elder Helvidius Priscus, son-in-law of Thrasea Paetus, was banished by Nero, recalled by Galba, banished and afterwards put to death by Vespasian. He left a son bearing the same name. This is Helvidius the younger, put to death, with Rusticus, by Domitian in A.D. 93. In 97, Pliny prosecuted Publicius Certus, upon whose accusation Helvidius had been condemned.

6. Maurico : see note on page 4, line 18. **Gratilla** : wife of Rusticus, banished by Domitian in A.D. 93 ; see Tac. *Agr.* 45. **Arria** : cf. Ep. III. 16, and notes. **Fannia** : cf. Ep. VII. 19, and notes.

8. augurarer: *I was anticipating.*

11. C. Musonium: sc. *Rufum*; of Etruria, a Roman knight and Stoic philosopher; cf. Tac. *Ann.* XIV. 59; XV. 71. He was banished in A.D. 65 for an alleged share in the conspiracy of Piso, but in Tac. *Hist.* III. 81, he is back again in Rome (A.D. 69). He was not exiled with the other philosophers in A.D. 71. **quantum . . . aetatem**: *considering the difference in our ages.*

13. cum . . . militarem: cf. Introduction, page xiii. Notice the subjunctive mood, though *tum* precedes.

14. indolis: *natural ability.*

15. specimen: *proof, evidence.* **sapientem aut proximum**, etc.: the absolute sage was ideal, not actually to be found; cf. Cic. *de Amic.* V. 18, *eam sapientiam interpretantur, quam adhuc mortalis nemo est consecutus*, etc. **simillimumque sapienti**: see note on page 28, line 6, and Introduction II. § 3. *f.*

19. iuxta: as in Livy and other authors = *pariter.*

20. nihil . . . tribuat: *makes no concession.*

24. adsectatoribus: *adherents.* It was common in antiquity for a man of importance to choose his son-in-law from among the young men who might be considered his followers and probable successors.

30. versatur: *is wont to fall into.*

Page 46. Letter 35. About Catilius Severus, cf. introductory note to Ep. I. 22.

1. expedita: *simple, easily despatched.*

2. Socraticis . . . sermonibus: *philosophical talk*, but bright and cheerful as Socrates's talk is in Xenophon and Plato; humor is one of its chief characteristics.

3. officia antelucana: *early visits of ceremony, salutations at daybreak;* clients and dependents often went before dawn to pay their duty to their patrons. Cf. Ep. III. 5. 9. Pliny did not wish to be out so late as to meet early risers on his way home.

5. Caesar . . . reprehendit: in his *Anti-Cato*, which he wrote in reply to Cicero's eulogy of Cato Uticensis.

6. ebrii: genitive; Mayor quotes Hor. *Car.* III. 21. 11 and 12:

> *Narratur et prisci Catonis*
> *Saepe mero caluisse virtus.*

Sen. *Tranq.* XVII. 4. *Cato vino laxabat animum curis publicis fatigatum.* **retexissent**: *had uncovered;* Cato had covered his head with his toga in order not to be recognized.

8. deprehensos: *detected.*

11. modus constet: *let moderation characterize*, etc.; lit., 'let a limit be set.'

Letter 36. About Voconius Romanus, cf. introductory note to Ep. I. 5, and for Pliny's high opinion of him, cf. especially Ep. II. 14. To him are addressed eight letters of the collection.

13. Librum: *speech*; the name Panegyricus, given to it later, is found in two Mss. and in Sidonius Apollinaris, Ep. VIII. 10. A proper title would be *gratiarum actio*. Cf. Introduction, pages xiv, xv. **optimo**: this was decreed as a formal title of Trajan by the senate, but not till A.D. 114. **consul . . . egi**: in the senate, Sep. 1, 100.

14. misi: *I send*; epistolary perfect. **missurus**: equivalent to the apodosis of *etsi . . . exegisses*.

15. pulchritudinem materiae: *the nobility of the theme*.

18. securusque, etc.: in the absence of any suspense in regard to the subject-matter of the speech, the whole attention is fixed upon the manner. **elocutioni**: *diction*.

20. utinam . . . spectarentur: *I only wish . . . received their due attention*; the implication is that they do not, hence the use of the imperfect subjunctive. **ordo**: *arrangement*; Gierig, before his edition, and Dierauer (Büdinger's *Untersuch. zur röm Kaisergeschichte*), have analyses of the Panegyric. **transitus**: *transitions* from point to point. **figurae**: *rhetorical figures*; Gierig's edition has an enumeration of those occurring in the speech.

21. invenire praeclare, enuntiare magnifice: *fine thoughts, noble expression*.

22. disponere apte, figurare varie: *suitable arrangement, variety of figures*.

Page 47. **2. elata et excelsa**: *high and lofty*.

4. summittere . . . attollere: *to lower . . . to raise the tone of*.

Letter 37. Nepos is probably P. Metilius Sabinus Nepos, named among the Arval Brothers in 105 A.D., whose successor was appointed in 118. To Nepos are addressed also Epp. II. 3; IV. 26; VI. 19. In the heading of Ep. IV. 26, he appears, if we follow the reading of the *codex Riccardianus*, as Maecilius Nepos, and in that letter is spoken of as *maximae provinciae praefuturus*.

9. clariora . . . maiora: *more famous . . . more meritorious*. The thesis on Arria's character is illustrated by three incidents, *scholastica lege*. Cf. Ep. II. 20. 9.

10. Fanniae: the wife of Helvidius Priscus. Mommsen gives the *stemma* of this famous family as follows:

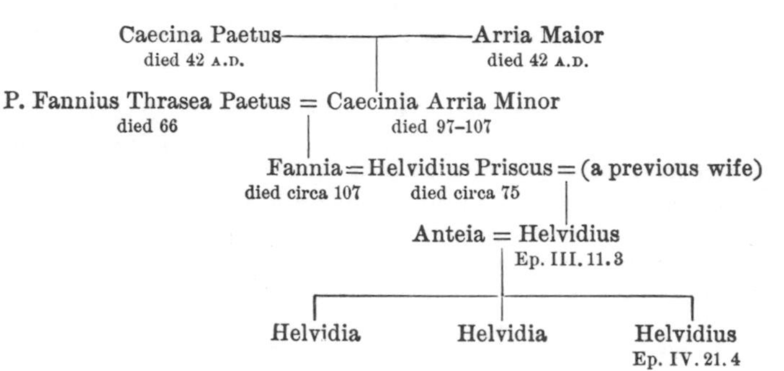

Arriae: Arria Maior, who died in 42, as told below, refusing to survive her husband.

12. obscuriora: *less well known.*

15. mortifere: post-Augustan; occurs here only in Pliny; also in Dig. 9. 2. 36. 1.

16. pulchritudine, etc.: note the ablatives of quality attached directly to *filius;* we should expect some appositive to *filius*, as *puer;* Draeger, *Hist. Syntax* I². 541–2.

18. funus: the funeral arrangements in general. **exequias**: the actual procession.

19. quotiens . . . intraret: iterative subjunctive, common in Silver Latin, especially in Suetonius; B. 287. 2. a; H. 518. 1; Roby 1716.

20. commodiorem: *better, more comfortable.*

21. persaepe: this word occurs here only in Pliny. **quid ageret**: *how he was.*

23. Cum . . . vincerent prorumperentque: see note on *quotiens . . . intraret*, line 19.

25. Composito vultu: it makes no practical difference whether we understand this to mean *with tranquil look*, or *with an assumed expression* (*of cheerfulness*); cf. *componit vultum*, page 35, line 17, and note.

26. foris: *outside* her husband's sick-room.

Page 48. **3. 'Paete, non dolet'**: Martial's epigram (I. 14) on this famous saying reads:

Casta suo gladium cum traderet Arria Paeto,
Quem de visceribus strinxerat ipsa suis,
"Si qua fides, vulnus quod feci non dolet," inquit,
"Sed quod tu facies, hoc mihi, Paete, dolet."

6. matrem . . . agere: *still to act the mother*, when she was a mother no longer.

7. Scribonianus: M. Furius Camillus Scribonianus, consul A.D. 32, revolted in 42, while legate of Illyricum; Tac. *Ann.* VI. 1; XII. 52; *Hist.* I. 89; II. 75; Suet. *Claud.* 13.

8. in partibus: i.e., the party of Scribonianus.

15. apud Claudium: i.e., before the emperor Claudius at the trial.

17. audiam: present subjunctive, of course. **et vivis**: she is excited; the disjointed syntax is appropriate. The absence of *tu*, which is emphatic, is noteworthy. See Crit. App.

19. Thrasea: son-in-law of Caecina Paetus, cf. diagram above, note on page 47, line 10; a native of Patavium, a friend of the poet Persius, who was a relative of his wife; active in the senate, A.D. 58–63, accused of *maiestas* (high treason) in 66, and condemned to suicide. The closing chapters of Tacitus's *Annals* contain a dramatic account of his death, though, unfortunately, it is incomplete. The literature of the period is full of references to this Cato of his generation. He used to say 'Nero may kill me but cannot harm me.'

21. filiam: Arria Minor; when Paetus's time came to die, he persuaded her to live for their daughter's sake.

24. attentius: this word occurs here only in Pliny.

26. male: *in a painful manner.*

27. cathedra: *arm chair*, cushioned, especially for women's use; cf. Martial III. 63. 7. The same name was given to a professor's chair; hence our phrase '*ex cathedra.*'

28. Focilata: *revived, resuscitated.*

Page 49. Letter 38. It is a question whether Curius Severus is identical with Vibius Serenus, to whom Ep. IV. 28 was written.

4. principi gratias agerem: another reference to the Panegyric. See note on page 46, line 13.

5. ad rationem: *according to the exigency.*

6. spatiosius et uberius: *at greater length and with greater fulness.*

8. Suae: note the exceptional reference to the indirect object of the verb in its own clause.

9. sub exemplo: cf. the same phrase in Ep. II. 6. 6. It is interesting to notice that in the Panegyric, while ostensibly only praising Trajan's virtues, Pliny read him an elaborate lecture on the duties of a prince.

15. idem utilitatis: note substantive *idem*, with limiting genitive.

17. codicillos: *letters* or *notes* on wax tablets. **libellos**: *notices* in writing, circulars as opposed to private letters; ordinary means of collecting an audience.

18. si valde vacaret: *if you should really have plenty of time.*

20. foedissimis . . . tempestatibus: the bad weather would have furnished a good excuse for staying at home.

21. per biduum: *for two days* in succession.

24. studiis: *literature;* again the late sense of the word, often noted above. Robert (*Pline le Jeune; Lettres Choisies*) suggests that Pliny might well have added *an principi.*

26. gravari: *grow weary.*

Page 50. **1. puncto**: ablative of time within which.

2. triduo: ablative of duration of time; see note on page 20, line 4.

3. eloquentius: a neologism.

6. studium: *enthusiasm.*

7. audientium: on the use of the participle rather than the *nomen agentis*, see note on page 31, line 22.

8. severissima: *the most chaste in style, the simplest.* **Memini quidem**, etc.: *I am, of course, mindful that I recited to a small number of persons, what I wrote for the general public;* i.e., he admits that he fears the general public may not be as appreciative as the select audience.

9. recitasse: see note on page 28, line 27.

11. hac severitate aurium: *severe taste.* As a disciple of Quintilian, Pliny revolted against the bombastic rhetoric of Seneca's school, and desired to revert to the simpler and chaster models of the Ciceronian age. **sicut olim theatra male**, etc.: he puts the responsibility of bad performances and of bad taste in the performer upon the public; *theatra* means, of course, theatrical audiences; there is an implied comparison with the audiences who listened to the recitations of literary works.

16. laetioris stili constare rationem: *a more florid style is justified;* see note on page 5, line 20.

17. pressius et adstrictius: *subdued and restrained.*

18. hilarius . . . exultantius: *gay . . . exuberant.*

19. arcessita: *far-fetched.* **inducta**: *irrelevant, out of keeping;* cf. our colloquial 'lugged in.' **segnius**: *less earnestly.*

20. venerit: *I hope it has already arrived!*

21. blanda: *smooth.*

22 iusta possessione: a legal phrase; panegyric is a field which might be considered as fairly occupied by the representatives of the florid style. **decedant**: the construction with both ablative and dative is worth noting. **acta mea**: *an account of my doings.*

Letter 39. About Calvisius Rufus, see introductory note to Ep. II. 20.

26. Adsumo . . . in consilium, cf. Ep. IV. 22. 1. **rei familiaris**: *property.*

27. inserta: *running into;* certain angles projected into Pliny's land, or certain parts were enclosed by it.

Page 51. **1. sollicitant**: *tempt.*

2. iungendi: *annexation.*

3. voluptuosum: the first known occurrence of this word, which is found nowhere else in Pliny. (Mayor.) **eadem opera, eodem viatico**: *at the same time and at the expense of one journey.* (Lewis.)

4. procuratore: this agent, or steward, often a freedman.

5. actoribus: *managers, sub-agents;* often trusted slaves.

6. tueri: *keep in repair;* cf. Ep. II. 17. 4.

7. supellectilis: *furniture.* **atriensium**: i.e., the major-domo and his assistants, who kept the interior of the house in order. **topiariorum**: *fancy gardeners*, who trimmed box and other evergreens into ornamental patterns, and laid out parterres. The Romans would have admired the gardens of Louis XIV., the formalism of which was as oppressive as the etiquette of his court. They were unfortunately imitated extensively in England and in Germany.

8. venatorii instrumenti: *equipment for the chase.*

12. incerta . . . experiri: *to guard against uncertainties of fortune by locating one's property in different places.*

14. inter sua: see Crit. App.

15. caput: *the chief consideration.*

16. campis, vineis, silvis: *constare*, 'to consist of,' is construed with *ex* (Cicero), *de*, *in*, or the simple ablative without a preposition. **materiam**: *lumber;* fire-wood is *lignum.*

17. statum: *regular;* fr. *sisto.*

18. imbecillis: perhaps *feeble* financially, or perhaps the word merely describes their lack of energy and ability. The class of small farmers had nearly perished in Italy. The peasants were reduced to the position of tenants, holding their land by leases from the great landlords. In central Italy, grazing had taken the place of tillage, and the country was depopulated. Matters were not so bad in the fertile Cisalpine, where Pliny's land was situated, near Comum.

cultoribus: note the dative of agent with a simple tense of the passive; cf. Ep. IV. 13. 9, *oppidis petantur;* B. 189. 3; A. & G. 232. b But Kraut. § 18. d, and Mayor call it ablative of instrument.

19. pignora: *chattels;* this word is chosen because the tenant's farming-stock was *pledged* to secure the rent and liable to seizure if it was unpaid. **reliqua**: *balance due, arrears.*

21. Sunt . . . mancipiis: *therefore they must be provided with slaves and at greater expense, for these must be good ones.*

22. instruendi: sc. *agri* or *coloni;* the farms or the tenants must be provided for. **quod frugi**: for the omission of the verb of the *quod*-clause, sc. *sunt instruendi*, cf. Ep. VI. 20. 3, *quia solitus Campaniae.*

23. vinctos: *in fetters, chain-gangs.*

24. videantur: sc. *agri.* **sestertio tricies**: 3,000,000 sesterces; ablative of price, as if *sestertium* were nom. sing. neut. instead of gen. plur. masc. limiting *centena millia* understood. **non quia non**, etc.: cf. Epp. I. 20. 22; V. 8. 1; B. 286. 1. b. c; A. & G. 321. R; H. 516. II. 2; Roby 1744.

25. hac penuria colonorum: *owing to this poverty of the tenant farmers.*

28. sum: *my fortune is invested.*

30. socru: Pompeia Celerina, to whom Ep. I. 4 is addressed, mother of his second wife. This wife appears to have died in A.D. 97. Ep. IX. 13. 4, and 13. **cuius arca**, etc.: cf. Catullus 10. 31, 32; *arca* occurs here only in Pliny.

31. non moveat: *non* is irregularly used for *ne; moveat* is jussive. **si cetera non refragantur**: *if other considerations do not oppose, if there are no other objections. Refragari* occurs also in Ep. II. 5. 5.

Page 52. Letter 40. Messius Maximus is addressed also in Ep. IV. 25, which is a sequel to this letter. There are ten other letters in the collection addressed simply to Maximus, but we cannot be sure as to the identity of all the Maximi. The name was a common one. See Mommsen in Keil's *Pliny*, page 418, and Smith's *Dict. of Biog. and Mythol.* II. 998.

4. legisse: see note on page 28, line 27.

5. lex tabellaria: *ballot law.* Several *leges tabellariae* are enumerated in Hunter, *Roman Law*, page 63. Elections were transferred by Tiberius from the *comitia* to the senate, and there the ballot was at first not used. **latori**: A. Gabinius, tribune of the plebs B.C. 139, introduced the first *lex tabellaria*, substituting the ballot for open voting in elections. But we do not know certainly which law is meant here.

7. comitiorum: not the assembly but the *elections*.

8. tabellas: *ballots*, in the form of waxed tablets.

9. contionum: *public meetings*, not organized assemblies, which would be *comitia*.

11. custodiebatur: *was observed;* a Silver Latin meaning.

13. agmina . . . circuli: *large crowds . . . small knots.*

17. hunc ordinem: *the following manner of conducting.* **citato nomine**: *when the name was announced.*

20. cui quaestor fuerat: the relation of a consul to his quaestor was quasi-paternal; cf. Cic. *Phil.* II. 71.

23. preces: Ep. II. 9 is an example of such *preces*.

24. natales: *birth;* Silver Latin in this sense. **annos**: i.e., alleging that the candidate is under the legal age; the *leges annales* fixed the minimum age for each office.

26. gratiosi: *influential*, or *popular*.

Page 53. **2. vereor**: this fear appears as realized in Ep. IV. 25.

4. quoto cuique: *how few have!*

7. beneficio tabellarum: *thanks to the ballot.* This post-Augustan use of *beneficio* is paralleled in Tac. *Dial.* 8. 7.

8. reciperatoriis iudiciis: *trials before recuperatores. Recuperatores* were not a standing tribunal nor taken from a fixed list, but chosen for each case when it arose; probably first employed in cases where an alien was a party. Their procedure was comparatively summary. Cf. Rein, *Criminalrecht* 873–7; Hunter, *Roman Law;* Sandars, *Justinian;* Class. Dict. The point of the comparison here lies in the phrase *repente apprehensi.*

10. sinceri: *impartial.* **scripsi**: epistolary perfect.

14. illa vulgaria: sc. *audiemus* or some similar verb. **'ecquid commode vales?'** *are you sure you're quite well?*

17. unius: i.e., Trajan's.

19. Salubri temperamento: *by a wholesome dispensation.* The idea of this passage is that although the supreme direction of affairs is fortunately in the hands of the emperor, enough freedom is still left to warrant a patriotic interest in the government on the part of good citizens.

Letter 41. This is the only letter to Cornelius Priscus. He appears in the senate as a consular in A.D. 105 or 106, Ep. V. 20. 7, and in 120 was proconsul of Asia. See Mommsen in Keil's *Pliny*, page 407.

23. Valerium Martialem: the chief epigrammatic poet of Rome, born about A.D. 40 in Spain, where he also died not before 101 or 102. His epigrams, about 1550 in number, are extant. See Appendix I. Pliny's harmless vanity gives the epigram written in his honor another chance of surviving by incorporating it into his letter, a precaution which Martial's fame has rendered unnecessary.

24. ingeniosus acutus acer: *able, sagacious, subtle.*

25. salis . . . fellis . . . candoris: *wit . . . satire . . . frankness* (or *good-nature*). Martial uses the first two words and the adjective *candidiora* in Epig. VII. 25. Mr. Mackail, *Latin Lit.* 194, says, "The 'candor' noted in him by Pliny is simply that of a sheet of paper, which is indifferent to what is written upon it, fair or foul. He may claim the merit — nor is it an inconsiderable one — of being totally free from pretence."

26. Prosecutus eram viatico: *I had presented him with a sum of money for his journey.* **secedentem**: *on his departure* (for Spain). This must have been about A.D. 98.

Page 54. **1. qui . . . laudes**: Mayor has an interesting note on the substantial rewards bestowed upon authors, instancing among others Ennius, Quintilian, Isocrates, and Aristotle. Alexander the Great was especially generous in his favors to literary men.

2. honoribus: not, as usually, *offices* specifically, but *honors* in general.

7. nisi . . . tenerem: *if I did not remember.* Ep. IV. 27 forms an interesting parallel.

9. Esquiliis: *on the Esquiline Hill;* construed like the name of a town, without a preposition; plural, because the hill had several summits. An aristocratic quarter after the improvements of Maecenas in the reign of Augustus.

11. sed ne tempore, etc.: Martial X. 19. **non tuo**: *inappropriate;* cf. line 23 of the epigram, *haec hora est tua*, etc. The metre is Phalaecian (hendecasyllabic); A. & G. 371. 11; H. 629. 1.

13. tetricae: *austere.*

14. centum . . . virorum: the centumviral court, in which Pliny practised much; see Introduction, page xvi. **studet auribus hoc**: Mayor says, "No other example of this construction is cited; *auribus* is *dativus commodi*, and no other accusative than *nihil* or a neuter pronoun or adjective would be allowed."

16. Arpinis . . . chartis: i.e., the speeches of Cicero, who was a native of Arpinum. This is especially flattering to Pliny, who worshipped Cicero.

19. rosa: i.e., the garlands on the heads of the revellers.

20. rigidi . . . Catones: Cato of Utica was the ideal of stern propriety; cf. Ep. III. 12. 2, 3. The plural is 'generic'; it does not mean several Catos, but Cato as a type of a certain class of men.

25. At non erunt: *at* here, as often, introduces an imaginary objection of an opponent to what has just been said; cf. the elliptical *at enim*.

BOOK IV

Page 55. Letter 42. Calpurnius Fabatus was the paternal grandfather of Pliny's third wife, Calpurnia. To him were written also Epp. V. 11; VI. 12; VI. 30; VII. 11; VII. 16; VII. 23; and VIII. 10. Besides, he is mentioned in Epp. V. 14. 8; VIII. 11. 3; VIII. 20. 3. An inscription shows that he had an extensive military career and held civil office, being also *flamen Augusti* at Comum. He lived to an advanced age, and died in A.D. 112; *ad Trai.* 120.

1. neptem: the writer's third wife, Calpurnia.

2. mutuo: adv.; a very brief way of saying, 'we reciprocate your feelings.'

5. adeo: *the fact is.* **itineris ratio**: *the circumstances of the journey.*

7. in Tuscos: *to my Tuscan estate*; see note on *Marsi*, page 29, line 16.

10. Tiferni Tiberini: appositional genitive; see Crit. App. A small town on the Upper Tiber, due east of Arretium, close to the Apennines, on the border of Etruria and Umbria; cf. map, page 131. **paene adhuc puerum**: he was eighteen years of age at the time referred to.

11. patronum: *advocate.* **cooptavit**: *elected.*

12. Adventus: *arrivals*; i.e., at Tifernum.

13. honoribus: *elections to public office.*

17. Subsistemus: *we shall stay.*

18. sequenti: sc. *die.* **viam . . . corripiemus**: a poetic phrase found in Vergil, Horace, and Ovid.

19. fortes: *well and strong.*

20. continget hilares: sc. *invenire.*

Page 56. Letter 43. To Attius Clemens was addressed likewise Ep. I. 10, about the philosopher Euphrates. We may suspect that Regulus's grief for his son was less insincere than Pliny would have us believe. However that may be, we cannot commend this letter for good taste.

1. Regulus: the famous advocate and *delator*; cf. notes on Ep. I. 5.

2. nescio an: *I doubt whether*; often so in Silver Latin; the usual meaning in the strictly classical period is 'I rather think.'

3. posset recta sectari: *might have pursued a right course.*

4. referret: *take after.* **emancipavit**: liberated from the *patria potestas*, making him *sui iuris*; a *filius familias*, i.e., a son not emancipated, could not acquire anything for himself by inheritance. **heres matris**: his emancipation by his father may have been a condition attached to his institution as heir by his mother. Women were under certain disabilities in the matter of making wills; Hunter, *Roman Law*, 795–6.

5. mancipatum: *sold* (or *bought*) *into bondage*, just the reverse of *emancipatum*; or else *sold* (or *bought*) *for a consideration*, i.e., the retention of the property in the family. The point is the surprise of reading *mancipatum* where one expects *emancipatum*. The bondage in question was a quasi-slavery. The person *in mancipio* was *servi loco* to his master, but was free in his relations to all other persons and to the state.

7. simulatione: *flattery*, in order to become his son's heir. The emancipated son, after he was fourteen, could institute as heir whomsoever he pleased; thus the father becomes a courtier of his own son. **Regulum cogita**: cf. *Verginium cogito*, page 21, line 28; see Introduction II. § 3. *h*.

8. insane: *extravagantly.* **mannulos**: Gallic *ponies*; *mannus* is a Celtic word.

9. iunctos: *in teams.* **solutos**: *for the saddle.*

10. luscinias, etc.: pet birds appear not seldom in Latin literature; cf. Plaut. *Capt.* 1002, *quasi patriciis pueris aut monerulae aut anites aut coturnices dantur quicum lusitent*; also Statius, *Silvae* II. 4; Catullus 2; Pl. *N. H.* X. 59, 60.

12. Convenitur: i.e., people flocked to offer their condolence.

15. in Regulo demerendo: *in putting Regulus under obligations.* As he was now childless, he was flattered by legacy-hunters.

17. porticibus: cf. Martial I. 12, where, however, the reference is to Regulus's villa at Tibur.

19. gloriosus: *boastful*, *ostentatious.* **Vexat**: i.e., by keeping them in the city to call on him at the unwholesome season.

21. perverse: *with his characteristic inappropriateness.*

24. augurer: *predict.*

Page 57. Letter 44. Nothing is known about Catius Lepidus.

1. vim: *energy.* **Regulo**: cf. notes on Epp. I. 5, and IV. 2. **Mirum est quam**: cf. page 6, line 10, and note.

2. in quod incubuit: *what he takes pains with.*

3. ut nemo: *as no one else ever did.* **imagines**: painted portraits, and medallions in stone or metal.

4. officinis: *studios.* As to the omission of *in*, see Introduction II. § 3. *m.*

6. effingit: *has him portrayed.* **auditorio**: *audience;* properly, however, it is the place, not the people.

7. recitavit tamen: although it was only a boy's life.

8. exemplaria mille: the multiplication of copies was not expensive, being accomplished by slave labor. A publisher had a work dictated to a large number of copyists at once, and the price of an ordinary book was nearer the rate of modern times than one would naturally suppose. Statius, *Silv.* IV. 9. 6–9, describes a pretty little volume bound in purple and costing only ten *asses* (*decussis*).

9. publice: *to the municipal authorities.*

10. decurionibus: the *decuriones* were the members of the municipal senates, the provincial notables. Class. Dict.: articles, *Decuriones, Curiales.* **vocalissimus**: *having a very sonorous voice.*

12. intentio: *energy, earnestness.* **quidquid velis**: cf. *quocumque moveris*, page 33, line 25, and note.

14. bonis . . . malis: may be masculine or neuter.

15. ἀμαθία μὲν θράσος λογισμὸς δὲ ὄκνον φέρει: *ignorance begets confidence, consideration delay;* words of Pericles, Thucyd. II. 40; cf. "And fools rush in where angels fear to tread."

17. Imbecillum . . . inventio: *weak lungs, a stammering voice, an indistinct utterance, a slow imagination. Latus*, meaning the lungs or voice of a speaker, is frequent in Cicero; e.g., *de Senec.* 14.

20. ipso illo: note the order, the reverse of the usual one.

21. Herennius Senecio: cf. note on page 3, line 9. **Catonis illud**: *that well-known saying of Cato*, defining an orator as *vir bonus dicendi peritus;* Quint. XII. 1. 1; Sen. Contr. I. Praef. 9.

22. e contrario vertit: *reversed.*

24. expressit: *defined.*

25. tali epistulae: i.e., this letter, containing so choice a story.

26. ex sodalibus meis: this may indicate that Comum was the home of Catius Lepidus.

27. circulator: one who collects a *circulus*, a *mountebank, peddler, quack;* cf. *assem para*, Ep. II. 20. 1, and note.

Page 58. 1. **ἐπάρας . . . τὴν φωνὴν**, etc.: *lifting up his voice and rejoicing, and shouting with all his might.* Demos. *de Cor.* 291, speaking of Aeschines describing the public misfortunes and triumphing over Demosthenes.

4. **credas . . . puero**: a good example of the studied, striking, epigrammatic sentences with which Pliny is fond of ending letters.

Letter 45. Maturus Arrianus of Altinum, a Roman knight, was a man in whose judgment and integrity Pliny had great confidence; Ep. III. 2. To him are addressed, besides this letter, Epp. I. 2; II. 11; II. 12; IV. 12; VI. 2; VIII. 21.

5. **auguratum**: Pliny solicits the honor of a place in the college of augurs in Ep. *ad Trai.* 13. Mommsen believes this letter to Arrianus was written in 103 or 104. The college of augurs enjoyed great prestige on account of its antiquity, but had no real importance under the empire. The number of members was increased to sixteen by Julius Caesar. They were chosen originally by coöptation, then by popular election, last by imperial nomination.

6. **gravissimi principis**: Trajan.

8. **religiosum**: *sacred.*

9. **sacrum . . . insigne**: *has the peculiar privilege.*

10. **alia**: i.e., other offices.

11. **fortunae hactenus licet**, etc.: *Fortune has no further power than to bestow it;* i.e., this is an office from which one cannot be removed; it is held for life.

12. **possit**: the subject is implied in *hoc*, referring to the office in question. **dari**: viz., by Fortune.

13. **Iulio Frontino**: praetor urbanus in A.D. 70, Tac. *Hist.* IV. 39, three times consul, legate of Bithynia, proconsul of Asia, etc., died in 102 or 103. He was the author of the well-known works on Tactics and on the Roman Aqueducts. Cf. Ep. IX. 19. 6.

14. **nominationis die**: the day of appointment by the emperor, or the day when names were suggested to him for appointment. **per hos continuos annos**: *for the last few years invariably.*

18. **M. Tullius** (Cicero): because Cicero was the great model in the department of oratory, in which Pliny was chiefly active (*aemulari studiis cupio*), Pliny was glad to be like him in other particulars. No doubt their respect for the science of augury was equally sincere. Cicero's remark (*de Divin.* II. 51) about the haruspices is familiar to all: *Vetus autem illud Catonis admodum scitum est, qui*

mirari se aiebat quod non rideret haruspex haruspicem cum vidisset; quota enim quaeque res evenit praedicta ab istis? etc.

21. iuvenior: observe the unusual form; cf. Apul. *Metam.* VIII. 21; Tac. *Germ.* 24; Sen. *Epist.* 26. 7; 66. 34. The *leges annales* under the republic, set a higher age for each office. Pliny, born in 62, consul in 100, was 38. Cicero was 43. Cicero was consul *suo anno*, 43 then being the minimum age for that office. But Pliny might have been consul several years earlier than 100; see Introduction, page xiv.

Page 59. Letter 46. Statius Sabinus is unknown.

1. nos: the writer and the person addressed are co-heirs.

2. nusquam . . . iussisse: it was common to leave slaves a gift of liberty by will. A slave could not acquire property for himself, but only for his master. Hence, one could not leave a legacy to one's own slave, for that would be in effect leaving it to one's heir, who would own the slave, and who was the successor to one's own legal personality. Appointment of a slave as heir involved a gift of liberty by implication; leaving a legacy did not.

4. Contuli: *I have conferred; consulted.* **peritis iuris** = *iuris consultis, iuris prudentibus.*

7. error: *oversight* on the part of the testatrix.

10. custodire: *observe, carry out;* cf. Ep. III. 20. 3.

13. Moretur, etc.: i.e., let him enjoy *de facto* freedom and the legacy.

14. caverit: sc. *Sabina;* B. 307. 1. 2; A. & G. 312. R; H. 513. II. N. 1; Roby 1580.

15. elegit: *since she chose wisely;* this is not a generalization, but a particular case of one who has chosen well; hence the indicative, which often has accessory causal force in relative clauses.

Letter 47. As to Maturus Arrianus, see introductory note to Ep. IV. 8.

16. Egnatium Marcellinum: not otherwise known.

18. provinciam: it is not known which one is meant.

19. scribam: *clerk,* assigned to him and paid by the treasury. **ante . . . tempus**: *before the time when his salary was due by law.*

20. amisisset: i.e., by death.

21. subsidere: *to remain in his hands.*

Page 60. **5. percommode**: *extremely well;* the counsel were very distinguished for so small a case.

6 (C.) Caecilius Strabo: consul designate in A.D. 103 or 104, one of the Arval brotherhood; cf. Ep. IV. 17. 1. **Baebius Macer**: addressed in Ep. III. 5; see introductory note.

7. obtinuit: *prevailed;* absolute use of the verb.

8. Quamvis . . . sufficiat: see Introduction II. § 8. *d.*

13. plurimum tribuat: *attaches the utmost importance.*

14. his: notice the substantive use of neuter pronouns and adjectives in cases other than the nominative and accusative; see Introduction, II. § 2. *c.* **isto usque**: *all the way to you.* Arrianus may have been at his home, Altinum, in Venetia.

Letter 48. On Cornelius Tacitus, cf. introductory note to Ep. I. 6. This letter is a good example of Pliny's generosity and shrewdness — the 'canny' spirit of the north Italian — and is likewise interesting as a picture of education in the provinces.

19. pauculis adhuc diebus: *for the next few days; adhuc; yet,* referring to the future.

20. Tusculano: Pliny's estate near Tusculum; cf. Ep. V. 6. 45. **opusculum**: it would be interesting to know which work.

22. intentionem: *ardor, concentration.*

23. ne quid . . . pereat, etc.: *to satisfy my impatience.* (Lewis.)

24. praecursoria: the word is a neologism and *quasi* apologizes for it.

26. patria: *native town;* viz., Comum.

27. praetextatus: still wearing the bordered toga of boyhood, which was changed for the *toga virilis* at seventeen or a little earlier; cf. note on Ep. I. 9. 2. **studes**: *do you go to school?* How many times this question has been asked of boys by all sorts of persons from Pliny to Mr. Pumblechook!

Page 61. **1. etiam**: *yes.* **Mediolani**: *at Milan,* 30 miles (by rail) south of Como. It was even then an important city and later became an imperial residence.

2. pater eius: sc. *dixit.*

3. praeceptores: *public teachers, professors* of rhetoric.

4. vehementer: this is like our colloquial use of 'awfully' and similar words. **intererat**: *it would be ('twere) to your interest;* for the mood and tense, see B. 304. 3; A. & G. 311. c; cf. Roby 1566.

6. potissimum: i.e., rather than elsewhere.

9. Quantulum est: *What a small matter it would be!* Rhetoricians were first paid by the state under Vespasian. Here is a suggestion that Comum should follow the example of Rome.

10. habitationes . . . viatica: *lodgings and travelling expenses.*

11. peregre: *away from home.*

12. inpenditis: this is the verb of the relative *quod(que)*. **adicere mercedibus**: *apply (add) to the salaries* of the teachers.

14. pro re publica: cf. Introduction, page xx, in regard to Pliny's public generosity.

17. ambitu corrumperetur: *be perverted to private ends.*

19. occurri . . . potest: *can be obviated.*

20. religio: *conscientiousness*, care in proper selection.

21. collationis: *of contribution.*

22. de alieno: *of another man's bounty.*

29. frequentare: *inhabit;* they will not become estranged by absence.

31. oppidis: dative of agent with an uncompounded tense of the passive. B. 189. 3; A. & G. 232. b; H. 388. 1, 3; Roby 1146. **studia . . . petantur**: *instruction be sought.*

Page 62. **1. altius et quasi a fonte**: *from farther back and, so to speak, from their source.*

5. ingenii tui: Robert (*Pline le Jeune: Lettres Choisies*) remarks that so far Tacitus is always spoken of as a great orator, and that only from Bk. VI. onward are his historical works referred to.

7. Omnia . . . libera parentibus: it would have been a refreshing spectacle to see the good people of Comum examining into the qualifications of Tacitus's professor from Rome.

10. illuc: to Comum. **ea lege**: *on this condition.* **ut . . . nihil**: notice the irregular use of the words for *ne . . . quid*, in a final clause; cf. *ne cui . . . astringam*, line 6. **hinc**: from Rome.

11. quam fiduciam: an epigrammatic conclusion.

Prichard and Bernard sum up the information gained from this letter about education in the provinces: two kinds of schools — (1) government schools (*multis in locis*); (2) those established by public subscription where it was possible. It does not appear that teachers started schools as a private venture. Boys came from a distance to attend good schools and lived in lodgings while pursuing their education.

Letter 49. To Valerius Paulinus are addressed Epp. II. 2; V. 19; IX. 3; IX. 37. In Ep. IV. 9. 20, 21, he is mentioned as a consular member of the senate in the year 103 or 104.

13. apud centumviros: see Introduction, page xvi.

14. tribunali: the platform on which the judges sat.

15. cetera: *the rest of the space* — the open centre of the Basilica, devoted to the sessions of the court.

16. ornatus: *noble, distinguished;* cf. page 36, line 13. **scissis tunicis**: two tunics were worn, an upper and a lower. The toga was of heavier, stronger material. This young man had his clothes torn in the press of people eager to hear Pliny.

20. desidiae . . . alienam: *make the indolence of others an excuse for our own.*

This letter is a case of vanity, frank and harmless. Pliny tries to think he is paying the chief honor to the profession of the orator.

Letter 50. Asinius Gallus may be the same as the Gallus addressed in Epp. II. 17, and VIII. 20; cf. introductory note to the former.

23. causam: we cannot say what the nature of the suit was, but we learn, page 64, lines 9 and 10, that it was unusual to bring such a suit against a woman. **Corelliae**: daughter of Corellius Rufus, whose death is the subject of Ep. I. 12. She was, perhaps, a first cousin of Pliny's wife Calpurnia.

24. C. Caecilium: sc. *Strabonem;* cf. Ep. IV. 12. 4, and note.

Page 63. **2. ut sciam**: *that I may know what is to be done.*

5. familiaris: *intimate.*

7. destinatus . . . honor: the consulship.

8. functi sumus: referring to his own consulship, which began Sept. 1, 100.

11. frigida . . . inania: both words are used in Ep. I. 9. 3.

13. graviorem sanctiorem subtiliorem: *of greater dignity and rectitude, of keener judgment.*

14. quod evenire contra solet: i.e., one is apt to like a person first, without knowing why, and afterwards learn to admire him.

15. penitus inspexi: *gained a thorough insight;* cf. Ep. I. 10. 2; *Paneg.* 83.

16. nihil a me, etc.: sc. *habuit.*

19. aequali: i.e., as usual, in point of age.

20. suffragator et testis: cf. Ep. III. 20. 5.

21. deductor: *escort*, usual at inaugurations of magistrates; cf. Ep. II. 1. 8.

23. quamquam: see Introduction II. § 5. *j.* **inbecillus**: *feeble,* physically not mentally.

26. de bonis iuvenibus: Pliny was about thirty-five at the time of this conversation.

Page 64. **3. quidem**: concessive, correlative with *tamen* following, *many indeed, but chiefly*, etc. **ut longiore vita**: *as was natural in a rather long life.*

4. Cornutum: Pliny's colleague in several offices; cf. Ep. V. 14, and Introduction, page xiv.

6. destituisse: *to have disappointed.*

7. subire offensas: *to offend others, to run the risk of offending others.*

9. nova . . . ut feminae: *unusual as being brought against a woman.*

10. haec: i.e., his reasons for espousing the cause of Corellia.

11. in actione: i.e., in the course of his speech to be made at the trial. **latius . . . uberius**: *with greater detail and fulness.* (Lewis.)

12. angustiae: *limits.*

Letter 51. Calpurnia Hispulla was the daughter of Calpurnius Fabatus and the paternal aunt of Pliny's wife Calpurnia. To her was written also Ep. VIII. 11. Allusions to her are found in Epp. IV. 1. 7, and 19; V. 14. 8; *ad Trai* 120; 121.

14. pietatis: *of dutiful affection.* **fratrem**: the father of Pliny's wife.

15. filiam: from the allusions to the early training of Pliny's wife by her aunt, we infer that both her parents died early.

16. adfectum: the sense in which the word is here used is post-Augustan.

17. repraesentes: *display, exhibit;* the word is appropriate to the love of the father who is dead rather than to that of the aunt herself. **non dubito . . . fore**: the infinitive, instead of a *quin*-clause, after *non dubito* is not frequent until the Silver Age. Cf. Corn. Nep. *Praef.* 1.

19. evadere: *that she is turning out.* **acumen**: *intelligence.* **frugalitas**: i.e., she was a good housekeeper, not a *femme savante.*

20. amat me: he was much older than she. **castitatis**: i.e., her thoughts did not run on younger, more attractive men. **Accedit his**: cf. page 60, line 14, and see note on *his*, ibid.

21. mei: objective genitive.

23. acturus: sc. *causam; about to speak in court.*

26. discreta velo: *behind* (lit., 'shut off by') *a curtain.*

Page 65. **1. format**: *sets to music.* **artifice**: *artist.*

9. ex tua praedicatione: *in consequence of what you said of me.*

11. formare: *to train, influence.*

12. ominari: *to predict that I would be.*

14. invicem: *for each other.*

Letter 52. Sempronius Rufus is otherwise unknown.

15. principis optimi: Trajan was in Rome A.D. 103 and 104. **consilium**: the advisory council of the *amici Augusti*, originated by Augustus, and made by Hadrian a formal, official council of state. Pliny alludes to his own participation in the council in Epp. I. 20. 12; VI. 22; VI. 31; cf. Merivale, ch. 67. Juvenal's fourth satire contains the account of the ridiculous 'Council of the Turbot,' said to have been held by Domitian.

16. agon: ἀγών, *contest;* large remains of an amphitheatre are to be seen at Vienne. **Viennenses**: *people of Vienna* (Vienne) on the Rhone, a *colonia* near Lugdunum (Lyons). **ex . . . testamento**: such a bequest was not unusual.

17. Trebonius Rufinus: perhaps the person addressed in Ep. VIII. 18; cf. Smith, Dict. III. 666.

18. duumviratu: the office of the *duumviri* in a *municipium* or *colonia* was analogous to that of the two consuls at Rome; cf. Class. Dict., article *Duumvir.*

20. Egit . . . causam: before the emperor and the *consilium.*

21. actionem: *his speech.*

22. in negotio suo . . . loquebatur: i.e., without having an advocate to represent him.

23. perrogarentur: *asked from each in turn* all around the circle. **Iunius Mauricus**: cf. note on page 4, line 18.

26. Constanter, etc.: *firmly and bravely spoken.*

27. Quidni: *of course.* **hoc**: i.e., this frankness and independence. **a**: *on the part of.*

Page 66. 2. Veiento: a courtier of Domitian, an informer, and a famous scoundrel; details in Smith, Dict. III. 1236. In Ep. IX. 13. 13 he is mentioned as sitting in the senate; cf. also Juv. III. 185. **in sinu**: i.e., his head opposite Nerva's breast as they lay on the couch at dinner.

4. Catullo Messalino: another rascally courtier of Domitian; cf. Smith, Dict. II. 1054. **luminibus orbatus**: cf. Juv. IV. 113 as to the fact; Suet. *Vesp.* 7, for the phrase.

5. mala caecitatis: *faults peculiar to a blind man.*

9. in commune: *generally.*

10. super: *during;* cf. page 40, line 16, and note.

12. nobiscum cenaret: cf. Ep. IX. 13. Nerva was very gentle, not to say feeble, in dealing with the whole class of *delatores;* cf. Merivale, ch. 63. **Longius abii**: *I have digressed considerably.* Doubtless the digression was intended to be the main thing in the letter. **libens tamen**: *but I am not sorry.*

13. infecerat: *had corrupted.*

14. noster hic: i.e., ours at Rome; see Hardy's *Juvenal*, 2d ed.; note on *Sat.* III. 114. **omnium**: i.e., all over the empire.

With the sentiments expressed in this letter it is interesting to compare what Pliny says of public games in Epp. VI. 34; VII. 11. 4; IX. 6.

Letter 53. Of Fabius Valens nothing is known except what may be inferred from this letter. Evidently he was a young friend of Pliny.

18. in quadruplici iudicio: the four sections of the centumviral court were sitting together, as they did to hear the most important cases; cf. Introduction, page xvi.

19. egisse me iuvenem: Pliny's *début* as a pleader was at the age of nineteen. It was not long before he began to practise in the court of the *centumviri*. He still spoke of it in Ep. VI. 12. 2 as *harena mea*; cf. also Martial's epigram, quoted in Ep. III. 21.

20. Processit: *travelled, wandered.*

21. hoc: the one in which he had been engaged *proxime*. **illo**: the one which he *egerat iuvenis*.

22. in utroque: *in both trials.*

23. conversiones: *changes.*

26. otio: *retirement, private life.*

27. civilibus officiis: he means the services which a citizen is ordinarily called upon to render; a good notion of their nature is obtained from Ep. I. 9; *officiis* is dative of purpose.

28. Studiis: *profession* of orator or advocate. **processimus**: *I became prominent, I advanced myself.*

Page 67. **1. periclitati . . . obfuerunt**. these words refer to the later years of Domitian's reign, when all good men who were conspicuous ran the risk of falling victims to the tyrant's suspicion. **rursus . . . iterum**: referring to the return of happier days under Nerva and Trajan.

4. documento: *a lesson, a proof that we should.*

6. tam volubili orbe: *in a cycle so rapidly revolving.*

9. ratio: *the object.*

Letter 54. As to Messius Maximus, see note on Ep. III. 20, which was written to him.

11. Scripseram tibi, verendum esse, etc.: cf. Ep. III. 20, where the evils are described for which voting by ballot was the remedy. **tacitis suffragiis**: i.e., by ballot.

12. vitium: *abuse.* **Proximis**: i.e., the last before writing this letter.

15. suffragatorum: *of the candidate's supporters.*

16. iratum principem: *iratum* is proleptic; *invoked the wrath of the emperor.*

17. comprecatus: like *imprecatus*, the opposite of *deprecatus.*

19. scurriliter: *like a buffoon* (*scurra*). The Romans were especially offended by levity in public.

20. dicax . . . urbanus . . . bellus: *pert . . . witty . . . smart.*

24. scaena et pulpito: *the 'boards' of a (comic) theatre.*

26. Ἀλλὰ ταῦτα τῷ ὑπὲρ ἡμᾶς μελήσει: *these matters will be a care to one above us*, i.e., the emperor; probably a quotation from some lost work.

BOOK V

Page 68. Letter 55. About Annius Severus, see introductory note to Ep. III. 6, which is addressed to him. That letter, also, was about a legacy received by the author.

1. Legatum: from Curianus, mentioned immediately below. **gratius**: because it showed that Curianus appreciated Pliny's honorable conduct in regard to the estate of Pomponia Galla, the mother of Curianus.

2. exheredato: a testator might disinherit a son, but he must have reasonable cause for so doing. Otherwise the will might be successfully contested.

4. splendidos equites: this term is sometimes used for knights with property enough to qualify them for the senatorial order (1,200,000 sesterces), who remained in the equestrian. They wore the *latus clavus*, the badge of senators.

6. praeiudicio: the decision of a preliminary question in a suit at law, which was generally an indication of how the main question would be decided; or a previous decision of an analogous case, a precedent; here it means *example,* implying that the other heirs would imitate Pliny's action.

7. conventione: i.e., he agreed to restore it to Pliny after enjoying the moral effect of his example in inducing the other heirs to hand over their shares.

9. locupleti et orbo: a favor to a rich and childless person would be interpreted as a bid for his inheritance.

11. cessissem: i.e., if Pliny should acknowledge the right of Curianus to be heir, and *surrender* his own claim; in regard to *cessio* *hereditatis*, cf. Hunter, *Roman Law*, pages 881, 882. Sohm, *Institutes of Roman Law* (Ledlie's translation), page 418, foot-note.

12. exheredatum: sc. *eum* = *Curianum*. **liqueret**: *should appear*, lit., 'be clear.' **rogo cognoscas**: see Introduction II. § 8. *e.*

13. cognoscas: Pliny is invited to be judge of his own case.

14. minorem: *less impartial.*

15. iam nunc: *from the start, from now on.*

16. pronuntiandi: gerund serving as genitive of definition with *constantiam; the courage to give judgment;* see Introduction II. § 9. *b.*

17. Adhibui in consilium: it was usual for a *iudex* to have the service of one or more advisers, learned in the law, as 'assessors.'

18. spectatissimos: the superlative is regularly embodied in the relative clause instead of agreeing directly with the antecedent.

19. Corellium: see Ep. I. 12 and notes. **Frontinum**: see Ep. IV. 8. 3 and note. **his circumdatus**: *between these.*

21. qui defunctae pudorem tueretur: *to defend the honor of the deceased*, which was in a sense assailed by the contesting of her will.

22. secessi: *I withdrew* to an inner room. **ex consilii sententia**: *in accordance with the opinion of my assessors. Consilium* was the name given to the legal advisers or assessors of an emperor or of a magistrate.

Page 69. **2. cum ceteris subscripsit**, etc.: *brought an action against the others in the centumviral court. Subscribere*, because the plaintiff signed the notice of the suit which was served on the defendant; the technical phrase was *subscribere (litem) cum aliquo* or *in aliquem*, or even *alicui.*

4. conponere et transigere: *to arrange a compromise;* a kind of verbal hendiadys.

7. capitis rei: *charged with a capital crime*, i.e., facts about them might be elicited in the course of the investigation which would arouse Domitian's suspicion and so endanger their lives.

8. Gratillae: wife of Arulenus Rusticus; see note on page 45, line 6.

9. Rustici: see note on page 3, line 5. Under Domitian it was dangerous to be known as friends of his victims.

10. aedem Concordiae: a large temple at the base of the Capitol rock. Its portico looked S.E. along the Forum. The *podium*, or solid base of masonry, which supported the building at the time of Augustus, is still to be seen.

11. ex parte quarta: the Falcidian law of B.C. 40 enacted that an heir should have at least a clear fourth of the estate, and that not more than three-fourths should be left in legacies to others. If the natural heirs were disinherited for no sufficient reason, they could contest the will by an action called *querela inofficiosi testamenti.* This could be prevented by leaving them one-fourth of what they would have received if the testator had died intestate. Such a fourth was called the *portio legitima.* Cf. Hunter, *Roman Law*, Index, under *Querela inofficiosi testamenti; Quarta Falcidia; Portio legitima.*

12. ex asse: *to the whole estate.* Inheritances and portions thereof were expressed by the *as*, or unit, and the various fractions (*unciae*) of the *as.* Sandars's *Justinian*, Bk. II. Tit. XIV. 5; Hunter, *Roman Law*, page 761.

13. exhausisset: sc. *mater*, the testatrix.

17. usu cepisse: *have acquired by prescription;* two years' adverse possession gave the ownership of 'immovables,' and one year's possession the ownership of all other things. *Res hereditatis*, a special class of things, were thus acquired in one year. Pliny does not make this latter point, viz., that *usucapio hereditatis* was perfected in one year. Sandars's *Justinian*, Bk. II. Tit. VI. pr.; Gaius II. 54; Hunter, *Roman Law*, pages 265 sqq., 269, 270.

20. tantundem: i.e., as much in proportion as Curianus would get from each of the other heirs; that is, one-quarter of what Pliny had received.

23. anticum: cf. Ep. II. 11. 18, *pulchrum et anticum.*

24. omnibus: on the abl. plur. neut. of adjectives as substantives, see note on *his*, page 60, line 14.

27. Neque enim sum, etc.: this naïve confession is highly characteristic of the author.

Page 70. Letter 56. This is the only letter to Calpurnius Flaccus. He was *consul suffectus* in A.D. 97.

1. turdos: *field-fares*, or *thrushes.* They were kept confined in *ornithones*, and fattened for the table. It was customary to send them as gifts on certain days. Martial XIII. 92, says:

Inter aves turdus, si quid me iudice certum est,
Inter quadrupedes mattea prima lepus.

Varro says they cost three *denarii* (half a dollar) apiece. **parem calculum ponere**: *match in value*, lit., 'place an equal counter.' For the method of using *calculi*, cf. Class. Dict. article *Abacus.*

2. urbis copiis: *with city wares;* Pliny was out of town, away from the markets of Rome. **nec maris**, etc.: i.e., the weather was too stormy for fishing.

3. epistulas: note the plural, though the reference is apparently to a single letter. This may be after the analogy of *litterae;* cf. Ep. *ad Trai.* 10. 1. This usage is post-Augustan.

4. steriles et simpliciter ingratas: *barren and frankly unthankful;* i.e., confessing that they are no return for your favor.

5. sollertiam Diomedis: cf. Homer, *Il.* VI. 234 sqq. Diomede proposed to Glaucus that they exchange armor in token of friendship, and Glaucus consented. Diomede's arms of plain bronze had cost nine oxen; Glaucus's, inlaid with gold, one hundred. Hence the proverb: χρύσεα χαλκείων.

Letter 57. To Nonius Maximus was written also Ep. IV. 20.

8. Fannium: a distinguished advocate who wrote a history of the deaths of famous men of the reign of Nero.

9. hominem elegantem: *man of taste.*

11. natura . . . usu . . . veritate: ablatives of cause, of means, of specification.

12. ista: i.e., the points just mentioned. **casus ipsius**: *his own misfortune* in dying under the circumstances described.

13. vetere testamento: an instance of Pliny's loose employment of the ablative of manner; see Introduction II. § 3. *o.* Fannius had made his will so long before, that it did not really express his wishes at the time of his death. **prosecutus est**: *remembered,* as we say of gifts in a will.

14. hoc: the fact of his death. **utcumque**: here virtually an adverb limiting *tolerabile,* — *somehow endurable.*

18. subtiles et diligentes et Latinos: *keen, painstaking, and expressed in pure Latin.*

19. sermonem historiamque: *colloquial style and formal history,* which latter the ancients considered properly rhetorical. The Lives of Suetonius represent a style combining *sermo* and *historia.*

Page 71. **1. acerba**: *cause for bitter regret.*

2. Nam qui voluptatibus, etc.: this sentence is thought to be an echo of Sallust's *multi mortales dediti ventri,* etc. *Catil.* 2. 8.

4. posteros cogitant: *have their thoughts set on posterity;* cf. *Regulum cogita,* page 56, line 7, and note.

7. praesensit: *had a premonition of.* **per nocturnam quietem**: Pliny takes rather a serious view of dreams; cf. Epp. I. 18; III. 5. 4.

8. lectulo: *study-couch.* **habitu studentis**: *the posture of a person engaged in study;* the Romans in reading or writing reclined on a couch.

9. scrinium: a case to hold Ms. rolls. **imaginatus est**: a post-Augustan word.

10. Neronem: who had died in A.D. 68.

11. ediderat: sc. *Fannius.*

12. revolvisse: *unrolled.*

13. tamquam . . . futurus esset: an instance of the substantive *tamquam*-clause; cf. *reum postulavit tamquam . . . praevaricaretur,* Ep. III. 9. 29, and Mayor's note *ad loc.; oculis oberrasse tamquam videret,* Ep. IX. 13. 25. See Bennett, *Wölfflin's Archiv* (1899), 405.

16. exhauserit frustra: i.e., in preparation for the parts not completed.

18. Nec dubito te . . . terreri: see note on page 64, line 17.

19. inter manus: for the usual *in manibus;* Pliny's friend Tacitus says *inter manus,* however; *Dial.* 3. 1; Ann. III. 16; cf. Ep. II. 5. 2.

Letter 58. About Suetonius Tranquillus, the historian, see introductory note to Ep. I. 18.

22. Libera . . . fidem: *fulfil the promise.* **hendecasyllaborum**: Phalaecian metre, lines of eleven syllables; cf. page 54, above, where several lines of Martial, in this metre, are quoted. A. & G. 371. 11; H. 629. I. **qui . . . spoponderunt**: *sponsio* was a solemn form of promise, giving rise to an actionable obligation: Pliny's verses here have gone bail for the appearance of Suetonius's history.

25. ad exhibendum formulam accipere: *to receive a summons to produce in court;* the plaintiff was said *intendere formulam,* the defendant *accipere formulam.* The defendant here is Pliny's 'hendecasyllabics,' personified. Notice that *ad exhibendum* is not an expression of purpose with reference to the verb of the sentence, but a phrase attributive to *formulam;* there were formulas of various kinds and for many purposes.

26. edendo: *publishing.* **quoque**: *even.*

27. vicisti: *you have outdone.*

Page 72. **3. scazontes**: called also *choliambi:* σκάζειν = 'to limp,' hence 'limping iambics.' A. & G. 365. c; H. 622. 4, footnote.

This metre was commonly, though not exclusively, used for satire and invective. An exception is Catullus's tender and beautiful poem on Sirmio; Catull. 31.

4. **lima**: a common metaphor for literary polish. **me . . . mei**: there is an awkward change to *nos . . . nobis* in the next sentence.

5. **vēnire**: from *vēneo.*

Letter 59. To Pontius were written also Epp. VI. 28 and VII. 4.

9. **municipium**: probably Comum.

10. **Cornutum Tertullum**: Pliny's life-long friend, and his colleague in several offices; cf. Introduction, page xiv. At this time he was a *consularis.* The *cura viarum* was given sometimes to *consulares*, sometimes to *praetorii.* Egbert, *Latin Inscriptions*, page 169. **Aemiliae viae**: the principal road of this name (there were three), leading from Ariminum to Placentia, afterward extended to Milan; it was originally built about B.C. 185, by M. Aemilius Lepidus.

12. **meo nomine**: *for my own sake.* **sit licet, sicut est**: *though he be, as in fact he is.*

13. **iucundus**: predicative.

15. **mandatum mihi officium**: i.e., the *cura alvei Tiberis et riparum et cloacarum urbis*, a consular function. As *curatores* Pliny and Cornutus were again in a sense colleagues, though their *curae* were different. Cf. Suet. *Aug.* 37, as to the beginning of the custom of assigning these functions to men of importance.

16. **video**: note the use of present tense with *postquam.*

17. **Cornuto**: ablative.

18. **ad exemplar . . . expressius**: *more vividly true to the ideal.*

19. **fama**: *by reputation.*

21. **Una diligimus, una dileximus omnes**: an accidental hexameter, if we overlook the fact that the third foot is an iambus.

22. **aetas nostra**: *our generation.*

24. **necessitudinis publicae**: *close association in office.*

26. **in praefectura aerarii**: Pliny was in charge of the *aerarium militare* for three years and of the *aerarium Saturni* for four years. Cf. Introduction, page xiv, and Appendix I.

Page 73. 1. **qui** = *qualis.* **altissime inspexi**: cf. *penitus inspexi*, Ep. IV. 17. 4, and note.

5. **ut prius**: referring to the year of Domitian's tyranny.

7. **indulgeam**: *give full play to.* **Praevertor**: *I turn aside.*

9. **prosocero**: Calpurnius Fabatus; see Ep. IV. 1, and introductory note. **amita**: Calpurnia Hispulla. Fabatus was a citizen of Comum. It seems likely that this party of friends was at one of Pliny's country places near Comum.

11. rationes: *accounts.* This extreme distaste for business, which is scarcely in the manner of the fine Romans of the old school, is simply one of Pliny's harmless affectations, supposed to be becoming in a man devoted to *belles lettres.* Cicero was a poor business man in his private affairs, as is evident from his correspondence. Pliny only pretended to be.

12. initiatus: *devoted.* **coeperam etiam**: this is a striking example of one of Pliny's mannerisms, of which there are said to be about one hundred examples in the letters and some thirty in the Panegyric. Here we have *eram . . . eram . . . eram . . . circumibam . . . audiebam . . . legebam . . . coeperam etiam*, seven verbs without *et* or *-que*, the last followed by *etiam.* In Ep. VI. 6. 9, e.g., we have *hoc tempus meum, hoc fides, hoc etiam dignitas.* Numerous examples will be readily observed of this peculiar form of asyndeton, the last member of the connected series of words or phrases being followed by *etiam;* cf. *inter alia*, page 20, line 22, and note. See Introduction, § 6. *a.*

13. angustiis: *shortness.*

14. commeatus: *leave of absence, vacation;* Pliny wrote to Trajan concerning one of thirty days' duration, Ep. *ad Trai.* 8.

16. remittat: i.e., back to the capital; note the subjunctive, without *ut*, depending on *cupio;* see Introduction, II. § 8. *e.*

Letter 60. Marcellinus is addressed also in Ep. VIII. 23. A Claudius Marcellinus is mentioned in Ep. II. 11. 15; an Egnatius Marcellinus in Ep. IV. 12. 1. Whether either is identical with the person here addressed, we do not know.

18. Fundani: C. Minutius Fundanus is addressed in Epp. I. 9; IV. 15; VI. 6; cf. notes on Ep. I. 9.

19. defuncta: *on account of the death of.* Lanciani describes her tomb, *Ancient Rome*, 281. **festivius**: *livelier, sprightlier.*

22. matronalis . . . puellaris: rare words, though not peculiar to Pliny.

23. Ut illa, etc.: *how she used to*, etc.

26. paedagogos . . . praeceptores: the former were slaves who took charge of children at home and escorted them to and from school, the latter were teachers. **suo quemque**: note the invariable order of the words in this collocation.

Page 74. 2. custodite: *cautiously;* first used by Pliny. (Lagergren.)

6. hic: i.e., *vigor animi.*

10. indignius: *more cruel.* **destinata**: *betrothed.*

14. ut multa luctuosa dolor invenit: *as grief finds many mournful details.*

15. margarita: *pearls*, chiefly used for ear-rings. The form *margaritum* is rare, usually the singular is *margarita;* but cf. Tac. *Agr.* 12, *gignit et oceanus margarita.* Pearls and emeralds were the favorite gems among the Romans. They had not the art of cutting diamonds.

16. fuerat erogaturus: *he would have spent.* **hoc . . . inpenderetur**: an object clause depending on *praecipientem;* see note on *remittat*, page 73, line 16.

20. pietatis: *affection; totus* ('absorbed in') with the genitive is an idiom used by Livy in III. 36. 7, and is not unusual in post-Augustan Latin; see Introduction, II. § 3. *a.*

23. referebat: *recalled, reproduced.*

24. exscripserat: cf. *expressius*, page 72, line 19.

26. castigatorium: *implying reproof;* this is one of Pliny's new words; see Introduction, II. § 1. *a.*

29. medentium = *medicorum;* see note on *audientium*, page 50, line 7.

Page 75. Letter 61. P. Calpurnius Macer Caulius Rufus was legate of lower Maesia in A.D. 112, at the time when Pliny was governor of Bithynia; cf. Epp. *ad Trai.* 42; 61; 62; 77.

2. viridibus: post-Augustan; *green things*, trees, etc.

4. felicior . . . felicissimus: oxymoron. This villa had apparently belonged to some one who, like Sulla or Nerva, had been really happier in his private life than after he had obtained what was commonly considered the highest felicity.

5. in Tuscis: *on my Tuscan estate;* note that Pliny never says *in Tuscano*, but always uses this plural form. Horace, on the other hand, speaks of his Sabine farm both as *Sabinum* and *Sabini.* See note on *Marsi*, page 29, line 16.

6. interdum simul: cf. Ep. I. 6, to Tacitus, describing how Pliny combined hunting and study.

Letter 62. Pompeius Saturninus is addressed in Ep. I. 8. Saturninus simply, as here, in Epp. VII. 7; VII. 15; IX. 38; he was an advocate, and besides published speeches, history, and poetry.

11. nollem: *I wish it were not so.*

12. recitaturum: sc. *te.* **statim ut**: *as soon as.* **ago gratias quod expector**: *I thank you for waiting for me.*

13. Iulius Valens: see Crit. App. Iulius was a very common *nomen;* hence we cannot infer with safety that Valens was a kinsman of Avitus, line 17, below.

14. graviter iacet: *is seriously ill;* cf. Ep. II. 20. 2. **si illius . . . aestimetur**: *if you consider it from the point of view of his own advantage.* **utilitatibus**: abstract in plural; this is quite common, when it is intended to denote that the idea is exhibited in a variety of forms or instances.

16. inexplicabili: *incurable;* the metaphor is the same as in the ordinary phrase *morbo implicitus.*

17. Iulius Avitus: it is a question whether he is identical with Iunius Avitus mentioned in Ep. VIII. 23, with many particulars. He was, perhaps, a brother of Iulius Naso (Ep. VI. 6). Ep. II. 6 is addressed to Iulius (or Iunius) Avitus.

18. redit: i.e., from the province where he had been serving as quaestor.

19. Nihil . . . pertinent: *make no difference.*

21. Iam quod: for the predicate, refer to *Illud plane non*, etc., line 16, above.

Page 76. **3. sine fructu**, etc.: *without producing any lasting fame.*

BOOK VI

Page 77. Letter 63. Maturus Arrianus of Altinum is addressed in six letters besides this one; see introductory note to Ep. IV. 8. It is gratifying to find that in one respect Pliny felt obliged to approve of Regulus.

1. quaerere . . . desiderare: *to miss . . . to regret.*

3. studiis: the advocate's *profession.* **timebat, pallebat**: these words express the intensity of his interest in his professional efforts and the diligence with which he prepared his speeches. **quamvis . . . posset**: see Introduction, II. § 8. *d.*

4. ediscere: *commit to memory, learn by heart.*

5. circumlinebat: it was a trick of orators to blacken their faces round the eyes and to put a white patch on the forehead for theatrical effect. Regulus used to make up the side of his face which was next to the jury. **a petitore**: *for the plaintiff; a* = on the side of; cf. Livy I. 12. 2, *ab Sabinis Mettius Curtius, ab Romanis Hostius Hostilius.*

6. a possessore: *for the defendant* in a possessory suit.

7. candidum splenium: *white patch* over the eyebrow.

11. una dicentibus: *to those engaged as advocates in the same case.* **libera tempora**: *unlimited time for the speeches.* **audituros**: one would suppose his reputation sufficient to draw a crowd; moreover people flattered the powerful favorite by coming to hear him. Yet even he apparently found it necessary to send out invitations. On the substantive use of the future participle, see Introduction, II. § 2. *c.*

12. corrogabat: *got together by invitation;* on the practice of packing the audience, cf. Ep. II. 14.

13. invidia: i.e., the opposing counsel got the benefit of the allowance of unlimited time, without the odium of asking for it; the benefit, also, of the large audience. **auditorio**: as often in Pliny, not the place, but the people, *audience.*

14. deprehensum: *caught* by accident. **commode**: *at your ease.*

15. melius: sc. *fecisset.* **si ante**: sc. *mortuus esset;* see Introduction II. § 10. *h.*

17. eo principe: Trajan. **Ideo**: i.e., because he might now be living *sine malo publico*, it is not wrong to regret him.

19. binas vel singulas clepsydras: *two or one water-clock apiece,* say a half or a quarter of an hour, perhaps forty or twenty minutes. Cf. note on *clepsydra*, page 18, line 8, and see Class. Dict., article *Horologium.*

20. dandi et petendi: on the part of the court and of the advocates respectively.

21. qui dicunt: *advocates.*

22. qui audiunt: *iudices.*

23. studiorum: *for the profession.* **periculorum**: *suits.*

Page 78. **3. comperendinationes**: *adjournments,* in order that plenty of time might be afforded for the trial of causes.

5. paucioribus clepsydris: *in fewer quarter hours.*

7. qui ambitione . . . praestant: *who used to gain from everybody, by 'management,' what very few accord to conscientiousness.*

8. quotiens iudico: *whenever I am iudex.*

9. dico: *I speak as advocate in a cause.*

10. aquae: i.e., of time, measured by the water-clock. **temerarium**: *presumptuous.*

11. inaudita: *before you hear it.*

12. finire: *to limit.* **primam**: *as his first duty.*

14. At quaedam, etc.: the words of a supposed objector **Etiam**: **sed**: *True, but —.*

17. coram: *when I see you.*

18. communium: *of the common weal*, but see Crit. App.

19. emendari . . . corrigere: the former conveys a much less radical idea than the latter.

Letter 64. Verus is not otherwise known; he seems to be a tenant who has leased the farm in question.

25. centum milium nummum: genitive of quality = *worth* 100,000 *sesterces* = about $5000.

27. reparabit: *will recover.*

Page 79. 1. memineris: jussive subjunctive, but in 2d person, addressed to a definite individual, or optative; *modo* = only; as in English we say, 'If you would only remember!'

3. illius . . . mea: coördinate; construe both with *interest.* B. 211. 1. a; A. & G. 222. a; H. 406. 3; 408. 2; Roby 1284, 1285.

This letter shows Pliny's generosity to a dependent and his gratitude to an old servant; cf. Cic. *de Amic.* 74.

Letter 65. To Calpurnia, his third wife, Pliny addressed also Epp. VI. 7 and VII. 5. She appears to have lost both parents early, and to have been affectionately brought up by her aunt Calpurnia Hispulla; cf. Epp. IV. 19; V. 11; VI. 12. 3; VI. 30. 5; VIII. 11. 3. She was disappointed in the hope of children; see Epp. VIII. 10; VIII. 11; IV. 13. 5. After accompanying her husband to Bithynia, she returned to Italy, because of the death of her grandfather, Calpurnius Fabatus. See Introduction, page xviii.

5. occupationibus: probably professional engagements; possibly his official duties as *curator alvei Tiberis*, etc.

7. in Campaniam: this region was full of seashore resorts for health and fashion. Melmoth says Fabatus had a villa there. **prosequi**: *to escort.* **e vestigio**: *immediately.*

8. Nunc . . . cupiebam: epistolary past.

9. oculis . . . crederem: *believe my eyes* rather than reports; *see for myself.* **viribus . . . corpusculo**: *strength . . . flesh;* the diminutive is affectionate. **adparares**: *you are adding.*

10. ecquid . . . transmitteres: *whether, in short, you are enjoying, without injury to your health, the pleasures of that rich country;* for this use of *transmittere*, cf. page 17, line 3, and note.

11. etiam fortem: *even if you were well and strong.*

12. suspensum et anxium: note the causative force of these adjectives.

15. ratio: *consideration, thought.*

16. metuentum: for *metuentium.*

19. statimque, etc.: *-que* is adversative, — *though I shall be anxious again the minute I've finished reading.*

The ingenuity of the expressions of affection in this letter is no reason for doubting their sincerity; ingenuity was perfectly natural in Pliny, or, if not, it was second nature. And no man can be too polite to his wife.

Letter 66. About C. Minutius Fundanus, see introductory note to Ep. I. 9.

22. sis rogo: *I beg you to come.*

Page 80. **1. Petit honores**: *is a candidate for office.* **Iulius Naso**: to him is addressed Ep. IV. 6; cf. also Epp. V. 21. 3, and VI. 9. He was probably the brother of Julius Avitus.

3. consularem: Pliny's term as consul had been the months of September and October, 100.

4. omnium quae decucurri: *for all the offices which I have held. Omnium* is neuter and is substantively used; cf. Introduction II. § 2. c.

6. cum illo non sane paterna amicitia: *friendship with him, not indeed resulting from friendship with his father.* **neque . . . aetatem**: *for I am not old enough* to have been his father's friend.

11. frequentabam: *I attended.* **Quintilianum**: the great rhetorician, M. Fabius Quintilianus (A.D. 35–95); cf. Introduction, page xi. **Niceten Sacerdotem**: a famous rhetorician from Smyrna; but cf. Professor Gudeman's note on Tac. *Dial.* 15.

12. prodesse: i.e., those who remembered him would naturally be well disposed toward his son.

13. in senatu: where the elections were held from the time of Tiberius (Tac. *Ann.* I. 15). The name *comitia* was still used for election, though there was a mere announcement made to the popular assembly.

14. non nisi: these words, in the strict Latinity of the Ciceronian age, are usually separated by others intervening. **viventes**: accusative, object of *reverentur.*

15. omissa gloria patris: *giving up any dependence on his father's reputation.*

16. magnum ornamentum, gratia infirma: *a great distinction, but a feeble recommendation.*

19. permisit: *he permitted himself.*

20. Dicenti: *when I speak in court.*

21. cum maxime nascentibus: *at the beginning and very inception of my (literary) works.*

22. interest: *he takes an interest in.*

23. cum fratre: supposed to be the Julius Avitus of Ep. V. 21.

31. hoc etiam dignitas: see note on *coeperam etiam*, page 73, line 12.

Page 81. **2. repulsa**: this word is used especially of defeat at the polls.

Letter 67. About Tacitus, see introductory note on Ep. I. 6.

3. Iulium Nasonem: see Ep. VI. 6, and notes.

7. Tu . . . censeo, alios roges: *as for you, I recommend you to ask others. Roges* is the object of *censeo;* see Introduction II. § 8. *e;* cf. Cic. *de Amic.* 17, *ab eis censeo petatis.*

Letter 68. Lucceius Albinus may have been the son of the man of the same name mentioned by Tacitus (*Hist.* II. 58, 59), who died in A.D. 69 while procurator of Mauretania Caesariensis. Cf. Ep. IV. 9. 13, where Albinus was associated with Pliny in the prosecution of Caecilius Bassus in 103 or 104.

9. socrus meae: Pompeia Celerina. **Alsiensem**: Alsium was a seaside town of Etruria; cf. Ep. I. 4 for the list of Pompeia's different villas.

10. Rufi Vergini: in Silver Latin such inversions are common where the *praenomen* is omitted. Cf. Ep. II. 1 for a panegyric on Verginius; also the notes on that letter.

12. Hunc . . . secessum: *this retreat.*

13. nidulum: *the cosy little nest.* **contulissem**: iterative; for the mood, see Introduction II. § 8. *a.*

16. nec difficultas, etc.: *the difficulty of the undertaking is not the reason.* **modici ac potius exigui**: *modest or rather insignificant;* i.e., so small as to be petty or mean.

18. post decimum . . . annum: he died in A.D. 97; this fact dates this letter in 106 or 107. Prichard and Bernard say this is the latest letter that can be positively dated, except Ep. IX. 19.

19. titulo: *epitaph;* somewhat similar to Lucan's line (V. 664), *nulla meis aberit titulis Romana potestas.*

Page 82. **1. divinum . . . factum**: his refusal to take the empire for himself.

3. pulso . . . Vindice: Vindex led a revolt in Gaul against Nero in A.D. 68. His defeat was the first of the three occasions when Verginius refused the throne. Pliny, in Ep. IX. 19, considers whether the conduct of Verginius in regard to his tomb was more admirable than that of Frontinus, who forbade any monument at all.

6. conditoria: post-Augustan; *tombs.*

7. praesumere: *anticipate*, i.e., perform in advance.

8. cuius: objective genitive.

Letter 69. About Romanus, see introductory note to Ep. I. 5.

11. ne ego quidem: *nor I either.* **me recens fabula excepit**: *I had an early account.* (Melmoth.)

12. Passennus Paullus: cf. Ep. IX. 22; Smith, Dict. III. 157. He was greatly admired by Pliny. **splendidus eques**: cf. note on page 68, line 4.

14. Gentilicium: sc. *est; runs in the family.* **Properti**: Propertius was a native of Mevania, Ameria, Asisium or Hispellum, in Umbria, or of Perusia, in Etruria, most probably of Asisium.

16. Prisce, iubes: the first words of the poem recited by Passennus. **Iavolenus Priscus**: a noted jurist of the Sabinian school, cited two hundred times in the Digest of Justinian; see long article in Smith, Dict. II. 556. A man of this sort may easily have been bored at a 'recitation,' and his rather rude wit may have been some relief to his feelings. It would take more than this to prove that he was *dubiae sanitatis.*

19. interest . . . officiis: *is present at social functions*, or perhaps, *fulfils civil obligations;* cf. Ep. I. 9 for examples of *officia.*

20. adhibetur consiliis: is asked to act as assessor to praetors, to assist them with his advice. **ius civile**: even Cicero sometimes uses the simple accusative with *respondere* instead of *de iure.* **publice respondet**: he had the *ius respondendi*, the privilege granted by the emperors to certain jurists of giving under their seals opinions which would be binding upon *iudices* in suits at law. This was a quasi-delegation of imperial authority.

22. aliquantum frigoris attulit: *was somewhat chilling.*

23. recitaturis: for the free use of participles as substantives, see Introduction II. § 2. *c.*

Page 83. Letter 70. About Tacitus, see introductory note to Ep. I. 6.

1. avunculi: Pliny the Elder; cf. Introduction, pages ix and xii, and Ep. III. 5.

2. tradere posteris: Tacitus's account of the eruption of Vesuvius and of the elder Pliny's death was probably in one of the lost books of his Histories; cf. the expression of confidence in the immortality of Tacitus's work in Ep. VII. 33. 1. **morti . . . inmortalem**: cf. the similar oxymoron in *victurus occiderit* in the next sentence; see Introduction II. § 10. *k*. Cf. Lucret. III. 869.

3. propositam: *is in store for*.

4. pulcherrimarum . . . terrarum: the lovely country around the Bay of Naples.

5. urbes: Pompeii, Herculaneum, Stabiae. **semper victurus**: sc. *Plinius*.

7. scriptorum tuorum aeternitas: it is curious that Tacitus's account should have been lost, and that this one should have survived. The historian can hardly have given as detailed a narrative as this.

9. scribenda . . . legenda: *worth writing about . . . worth reading;* note the assonance; this is also an instance of substantival use of the gerundive.

11. Quo: *wherefore*.

12. deposco, etc.: *I ask that the task may be assigned me.* **Erat**: sc. *Plinius*.

13. Miseni: chief station of the Roman navy on the west coast, as Ravenna was the station on the Adriatic, from the time of Augustus; Suet. *Aug.* 49, *Classem Miseni et alteram Ravennae ad tutelam Superi et Inferi maris collocavit.* Misenum was ten or twelve miles from Neapolis, at the promontory forming the western point of the bay of Baiae. **imperio . . . regebat**: *was in command of. Imperium* is the proper word to designate military command. Pliny was *praefectus classi*, admiral, an equestrian function. See Egbert, *Latin Inscriptions*, page 176; Cagnat, 109 sqq.; Class. Dict., article *Honores*. **praesens**: *in person*. **Nonum Kal. Septembres**: i.e., *ante diem nonum*. August 24, one of the three days sacred to the *Manes*, when the '*Mundus*' in the *comitium* at Rome was opened and offerings to the infernal gods thrown in. The year was A.D. 79. The expression may be regarded as an indeclinable compound.

14. hora . . . septima: the hour beginning at noon and ending at that season, at 1.09 P.M. *Hora* means either the 12th part of the day, or the termination (not the beginning) of such a period. The reference here is to the end of the 7th hour. For a full discussion of this subject, in general, see Friedländer's Martial IV. 8, and note.

16. Usus ille sole: *he, having taken his sun-bath.* **frigida**: sc. *aqua; cold plunge;* cf. Ep. III. 5. 11, *plerumque frigida lavabatur.* **gustaverat**: *had lunched;* taken some slight refreshment, not going to a formal meal at table. **studebat**: absolute, as usual in our author; *was studying*.

17. poscit, etc.: the author of the Natural History was, of course, interested in this strange phenomenon. **soleas**: *sandals;* at Rome he would have called for *calceos*, 'boots' or 'shoes.' The Romans habitually went barefooted indoors.

19. Vesuvium: the previous eruptions of this mountain had been so long before that there was no record or tradition of them. The volcano was clothed with verdure to its summit. The present cone of Vesuvius proper did not then exist; what is called Monte Somma was then the highest peak.

21. pinus: the Italian pine is more umbrella-shaped than ours.

23. recenti spiritu evecta: *shot upward by the blast fresh from the crater.*

24. in latitudinem vanescebat: *it was going off sideways and getting thinner.*

27. eruditissimo viro: the language is well chosen; he was no naturalist in a modern sense, but an insatiable devourer of books. His knowledge of nature, as plainly appears from his writings, was chiefly at second hand.

Page 84. **1. Liburnicam**: a light swift galley, named from those of the Liburnian pirates of Dalmatia.

3. accipit codicillos: *a note was handed to him. Egrediebatur . . . accipit* may be considered an instance of parataxis; the former is logically the verb of a temporal clause.

4. Tasci: sc. *uxoris;* both this and *Rectinae* are probably misspelled in the course of Ms. transmission. Possibly we should read Bassi, as there was, according to a scholiast on Persius, a lyric poet, Caesius Bassus, who perished in his villa in an eruption of Vesuvius. The poor lady seems entirely forgotten in the sequel.

5. subiacebat: sc. *monti.*

6. discrimini: dative with *eriperet.* This usage, confined in earlier prose to the dative of persons, is in Silver Latin frequently extended to things; B. 188. 2. d; A. and G. 229; H. 386. 2. **Vertit . . . consilium**: i.e., from curiosity to the desire of lending aid — therefore he took the *quadriremes* instead of the *liburnica.*

7. studioso . . . maximo: *what he had begun through love of knowledge, he carried out in the spirit of a hero.*

9. erat . . . orae: *for the attractive shore was crowded with inhabitants.*

10. recta gubernacula: object of *tenet;* *he steered a straight* *course;* the steering was done with two large oars, one on each side of the stern.

12. figuras: *phases.*

14. quo propius accederent: *the nearer they approached;* connect with *calidior et densior.* The action is progressive, and in the older prose writers would have been expressed by the indicative, as would also an iterative action. The same construction occurs in Ep. VI. 1. 1.

15. pumices: *calcined stones.*

16. vadum: *shoaling* of the water in the bay. **ruinaque montis**: by the *débris* falling from the mountain. **obstantia**: *obstructed;* lit., *obstructing* those who tried to walk there.

18. fortes . . . fortuna iuvat: the proverb appears in Ter. *Phor.* 203 (*adiuvat* instead of *iuvat*), and different versions of it are found in Ennius, Cicero, Vergil, and Ovid; see Lexicon, under *fortis.* **Pomponianum pete**: *head her for Pomponianus's house.*

19. Stabiis: at Stabiae (Castellamare) on the south shore of the Bay of Naples. **diremptus sinu medio**: *separated* (from Pliny) *by the bay which lay between.*

21. quamquam . . . adpropinquante: see Introduction II. § 5. *j.*

22. cum cresceret, proximo: i.e., the danger would be immediate as soon as the shower of ashes, etc., from the mountain should extend itself. For the time being this was prevented by the wind blowing on shore. **contulerat**: sc. *Pomponianus.*

23. certus fugae: *determined to flee.* B. 204. 4; A. & G. 218. c; H. 399. III.; Roby 1318. **contrarius ventus**: *wind blowing toward the mountain;* this would keep back the falling ashes, etc., but would also prevent a ship from putting out from shore.

24. quo: sc. *vento.*

26. securitate: *unconcern, freedom from alarm.* **leniret**: imperfect because *iubet* is a historical present. **deferri**: sc. *se.*

27. accubat: *lies down at the dinner table.*

28. similis hilari: for the dative, see Introduction II. § 3. *f.*

30. excitabatur: *was intensified.*

31. per solitudinem: *by themselves;* this construction expresses 'attendant circumstance,' and is substantially equivalent to an adverb or modal ablative.

32. in remedium formidinis: *to allay their fears;* construe, of course, with *dictitabat.*

Page 85. **1. somno**: for this loose employment of the modal ablative, see Introduction II. § 3. *o.*

2. meatus animae: *respiration.* **amplitudinem**: *full habit.* All this is an extremely elegant way of saying that he snored abominably — a failing of many excellent people.

4. diaeta: *apartment;* he was probably sleeping in a large airy room, larger than the ordinary *cubiculum.* It may have been in a separate wing of the house, or even a summer house beyond a courtyard (*area*).

6. negaretur: *would have been impossible* (had he lingered longer there). We should have expected the pluperfect subjunctive. This is not merely a consecutive clause, but the apodosis of a conditional sentence (contrary to fact). The imperfect tense gives greater vividness to the expression, on the principle of *repraesentatio.*

12. quamquam: to be connected with the adjectives, not with the verb.

13. quod . . . elegit: *comparison of dangers led to a choice of this course,* i.e., to risk the consequences of exposure to the falling stones. The antecedent of *quod* is hopelessly vague in point of grammar, but the meaning is quite evident.

14. ratio rationem: *one argument prevailed over another;* note the repetition *ratio rationem . . . timorem timor*, combined with chiasmus.

15. Cervicalia: post-Augustan; *pillows.* **linteis**: *napkins, towels.*

20. ecquid . . . admitteret: *whether the sea would at all permit* (*the launching of their boat*). **vastum**: *wild, heavy.*

21. adversum: i.e., on shore. **linteum**: *a sail cloth* from his ship.

24. sulpuris: this appears to be a better spelling than *sulphuris.*

26. clausoque stomacho . . . angustus . . . aestuans: *closing the windpipe, which in his case was subject to chronic weakness, narrow, and often inflamed.* There is an apparent confusion between the windpipe and the œsophagus, the latter being properly designated by *stomacho.* But we must not be too severe upon Pliny's anatomy and physiology. He made no pretensions to scientific knowledge.

29. tertius: i.e., he arrived on the 24th, died on the 25th, was found on the 26th August; his '*novissimus dies*' was the day *before* he died.

30. habitus: *posture.*

31. ego et mater —— : aposiopesis.

The *vita Plinii*, ordinarily attributed to Suetonius, says that according to some accounts, feeling himself about to be suffocated, Pliny had himself killed by a slave. But Suetonius was a friend of the younger Pliny, and would have known better.

The eruption described in this letter overwhelmed Pompeii. Some modern authorities date it three months later. See Lanciani in Harper's Class. Dict., art. *Pompeii;* Mau-Kelsey, *Pompeii*, ch. iii.

Page 86. Letter 71. This letter to Tacitus is a continuation of Ep. VI. 16.

6. litteris quas . . . scripsi: the 16th of this book; the story is taken up from the sentence, *Interim Miseni ego et mater*, page 85, line 31.

8. id . . . ingressus: *after beginning upon that topic.*

9. Quamquam animus, etc.: Verg. *Aen.* II. 12, 13.

12. mox: in Silver Latin *afterward*, rather than *soon.* Note the ellipse of verb in this sentence; likewise in §§ 13, 16.

14. quia . . . solitus: cf. *quod frugi*, page 51, line 22, and note. **Campaniae**: dative of reference; *usual — for Campania.* **vero**: *however.*

15. verti: for *everti*, simple verb for compound.

16. surgebam: *I was just getting up.*

17. area: they went out of doors to avoid the danger of being crushed by a falling wall or roof; *area* is not the *atrium*, but a yard or court outside the house.

19. agebam, etc.: this sentence dates the author's birth, and indirectly helps to date that of Tacitus. See Ep. VII. 20, and notes.

21. excerpo: young Pliny was following his uncle's methods of work.

22. amicus . . . ex Hispania: Pliny the Elder had been a procurator in Spain from a time late in Nero's reign till the early part of Vespasian's.

23. ut . . . videt: note present tense with temporal *ut*, depending on historical present.

24. patientiam, securitatem: *apathy . . . unconcern.* **corripit**: *chides.*

25. hora . . . prima: if the sun rose at 5.06 A.M. on August 24, the first hour would be from then to 6.15.

26. languidus: *faint;* this adjective involves a poetic personification of *dies.* See Introduction II. § 10. *p.*

Page 87. **6. Egressi tecta**: *after getting beyond the houses;*

they had already gone out of doors. *Egredior* with the accusative is found in Caesar and Sallust, not in Cicero, but is especially common in the post-Augustan historians. See Introduction II. § 3. *i*.

10. Praeterea mare, etc.: a poetic coloring is given to this and the next two sentences by the use of verbs which suggest animate, rather than inanimate, subjects.

12. harenis: we should expect a preposition with this ablative of place, unless, possibly, the idea is instrumental.

13. nubes . . . dehiscebat: *a cloud, black and terrible, broken by quivering zigzag flashes of lightning, parted, revealing long masses of flame.*

15. fulguribus: *flashes of lightning* (sheet lightning). This is an instance of the construction known as ἀπὸ κοινοῦ, *fulguribus* being at once dative with *similes* and ablative with *maiores*, — *similar to and greater than.*

16. ille ex Hispania amicus: *ex Hispania* has the function of an adjective to *amicus.*

17. tuus, tuus: of course the first *tuus* agrees with *frater* and refers to Pliny's mother; the second agrees with *avunculus* and refers to Pliny himself.

20. non commissuros nos: *we would not allow ourselves. Nos* is subject, not object, of *commissuros.*

21. nostrae: sc. *saluti.*

23. descendere: notice the historical infinitives in §§ 11, 12, 15. **Capreas**: the island of Capri, at the south of the Bay of Naples.

24. Miseni quod procurrit: *the promontory of Misenum; Miseni* is partitive.

25. fugerem: this subjunctive in dependence on *iubere*, without *ut*, is both ante-classical and post-classical.

26. iuvenem: the context gives a causal force, — *since I was young.* **corpore gravem**: apparently she was like her brother in figure.

29. addere gradum: *to quicken her pace;* cf. Livy III. 27. 7; XXVI. 9. 5.

Page 88. **1. comitantium**: see note on *audientium*, page 50, line 7.

2. et nox: *when the darkness.*

4. Audires: *you might have heard*, if you had been there; B. 280. 3; A. & G. 311. a; H. 485. N. 1; Roby 1544.

5. quiritatus: *wailing cries;* derived, according to Varro, *de Ling. Lat.* V. 7, from the old appeal of the citizens, *Porro Quirites*,

'To the rescue, Quirites!' This is quoted also in Macrobius, *Sat.* II. 7. 4.

6. noscitabant: *were trying to indentify, to recognize.*

10. illam: the word implies something well known or commonly believed. Gierig, in his note on this passage, cites a number of passages showing the common belief that the world and the gods would one day fall back into chaos and night, out of which all things issued in the beginning.

12. Aderant qui . . . nuntiabant: note the indicative in the relative clause, as against *precarentur*, line 8, and *augerent*, line 12. **illud ruisse, illud ardere**: *this part had fallen, that part was on fire.*

13. falso sed credentibus: *falsely but to believing ears* (Lewis); a curious coördination of dissimilar constructions.

15. videbatur: *was seen*, not 'seemed.' **longius substitit**: *stopped some distance off.*

17. excutiebamus: *we (repeatedly) shook off*, so as not to be buried by them.

20. nisi me, etc.: *I might boast, if I had not believed*, etc. Pliny, of course, could not wish to survive the destruction of the universe. **omnibus**: neuter; *the universe.*

21. misero: construe with *solacio*, the construction of which is probably ablative of 'attendant circumstance' or 'manner.' For a similar thought, cf. Sen. *Troad.* 1024, *gaudet in multos sua fata mitti.*

24. luridus: *murky.* **cum deficit**: *when there is an eclipse;* the noun is *defectio.*

25. trepidantibus adhuc oculis: a very natural hypallage; *trepidantibus* properly should refer to the persons who were still trembling, not to their eyes. **mutata**: in predicate relation to *omnia.*

26. tamquam nive: the comparison need not include the point of color. **curatis utcumque corporibus**: i.e., *having bathed and eaten as well as we could.* **spe ac metu**: see note on *misero solacio*, line 21.

29. lymphati: *frenzied, crazed.*

Page 89. **2. non scripturus**: this letter does not, as the 16th does, purport to be material for Tacitus's history. Pliny's modesty about it seems exaggerated. It is a question whether he ever wrote anything finer; it is worthy, in style, of Tacitus himself.

Lord Lyttleton (1760), in his *Dialogues of the Dead* (No. 7), represents the elder Pliny as upbraiding his nephew for vanity and affectation in his style generally, and particularly in his conduct at the time of the eruption of Vesuvius.

Letter 72. About Fabatus, see introductory note to Ep. IV. 1.

4. natales: sc. *dies;* the Romans paid much attention to the celebration of anniversaries, especially the birthdays of their friends. Gifts were received and offerings made on birthdays, men sacrificing to their *genius*, women to Juno. Allusions in literature to such occasions are very frequent; e.g., Ep. III. 7. 8, where Silius celebrates Vergil's birthday. Martial VIII. 64; IX. 52; X. 24.

5. nostrorum: sc. *natalium.*

6. hic: *here*, i.e., at Pliny's home; it is immaterial from which house he happened to be writing. **istic securi**: *free from anxiety about the condition of things at your house*, or *on your behalf.*

7. Camilliana: so called, no doubt, because it had belonged to a person called Camillus, not necessarily a famous person of that name.

8. vexata: *damaged.*

9. Attendimus: *I am seeing to it.*

10. quam saluberrime: *as advantageously* (i.e., *cheaply*) *as possible.* Cf. *si praediolum . . . tam salubriter emerit*, page 19, line 6.

12. togati et urbani: the idea is the same in both words; the *toga* was rarely worn in the country; it was the formal garment of city life.

13. durum: *rough-and-ready.* (Lewis.)

15. honestissime cogitas: *your intentions are most creditable.*

Letter 73. About Voconius Romanus, see introductory note to Ep. I. 5.

19. Tollite cuncta, etc.: Verg. *Aen.* VIII. 439. These are the words of Vulcan, when, at Venus's request, he bids his Cyclopes clear away the work they have in hand for the gods and proceed to forge a suit of armor for Aeneas. The passage is, of course, an imitation of the story of the forging of arms for Achilles in *Iliad* XVIII.

22. ut inter meas: *considering that it is one of mine.*

Page 90. 5. quam = *postquam;* or, more precisely, we may say that *intra* has taken the place of *post*, *quam* remaining unchanged. Livy XXI. 15. 3 is merely a case of omission of *post.*

6. Sedebant centum et octoginta iudices: i.e., the court of the centumviri, all four chambers (*consilia*) together — a *quadruplex iudicium;* cf. Introduction, page xvi. This is a case of a will contested, by a *querela inofficiosi testamenti*, because of groundless disinheritance of a natural heir; cf. Ep. V. 1, and notes.

8. advocatio: the gathering of sympathizing friends and supporters. **numerosa**: in the sense of *crowded*, post-classical. **subsellia**: *benches* occupied by the spectators.

9. circumstantium: see Introduction II. § 2. c.

10. ambibat: note the less usual form of the imperfect. **tribunal**: the stage where sat the president of the court and the *iudices*.

11. superiore basilicae parte: the central space of the basilica was open to the roof, but the colonnades surrounding it were in two stories. It was from the upper gallery that women watched the proceedings in the court. **qua . . . qua**: *as well . . . as*.

12. audiendi, quod difficile, et quod facile, visendi: note this elaborate chiasmus.

13. imminebant: *were hanging over* the front of the galleries.

15. duobus . . . vicimus: it appears that the four sections of the court voted separately; we cannot be certain whether they all voted on the same question, or whether upon separate issues involved in the suit. The latter alternative is more easily reconciled with what follows. **Notabilis prorsus**: note the post-position of *prorsus*.

18. non quod casus videretur: *not that it really seemed accidental*. A *quod* clause embodying a real fact takes the indicative, but when the fact is stated merely to deny it, the subjunctive.

19. ex parte sexta: it was more usual to say *ex sextante* in referring to an estate. **Suberinus**: this person's connection with the case does not appear. The use of the word *inpudentia* indicates that he had been *exheredatus* by his own father for good reason, as does also *non ausus*. Gesner supposes him to have been the son of the *noverca*, step-son of the octogenarian testator.

20. vindicabat: *claimed;* the word is used of a 'real' action; i.e., one brought to recover a piece of property by a person who claims to be its rightful owner.

21. petere: the specific action claiming an inheritance was *hereditatis petitio*.

24. interesse iudicio: *to be present at the trial.* **quam**: sc. *orationem*.

25. gratiam brevissimae: i.e., because of its being very interesting.

26. copia rerum: *abundance of matter.* **arguta divisione**: *clear analysis*.

27. renovatur: *its freshness is preserved.* (Lewis.)

28. elata . . . pugnacia . . . subtilia: *elevated . . . argumentative . . . acute*.

29. Intervenit enim acribus, etc.: *in the midst of those strong and elevated passages there occurred*, etc.

30. calculos tabulamque: *counters and abacus*, with which calculations were performed. See Class. Dict., article *Abacus*.

31. privati iudicii: *a private inquiry*, like the audit of a servant's accounts by his master, or the like.

Page 91. **4. ὑπὲρ Κτησιφῶντος**: as Demosthenes's oration for Ctesiphon, better known as *De Corona*, was his masterpiece, so this was Pliny's. Sidonius Apollinaris eulogizes this speech for Attia Viriola in Ep. VIII. 10.

Letter 74. About Maximus, see introductory note to Ep. II. 14.

8. Recte fecisti: cf. a different view, expressed in Ep. IX. 6. **munus**: *exhibition;* so called because the expense was borne by the exhibitor, who thus made a present of the exhibition to the public. **Veronensibus nostris**: the people of Verona are called *nostri*, as being of the same province with Pliny, viz., *Gallia Cisalpina*. The amphitheatre of Verona, which would accommodate over 20,000 spectators, is in an excellent state of preservation to-day.

9. olim: in the sense of *iam diu;* cf. page 7, line 8, *olim mihi nullas epistulas mittis*. This sense is mostly post-Augustan.

11. cuius memoriae, etc.: gladiatorial shows seem to have originated in the funeral games, which were celebrated to honor the memory and appease the spirit of the departed. Beginning as an occasional event, they became at last a permanent institution for the amusement of the depraved city mobs. It is Pliny's obliging disposition, rather than a deliberate approval of such exhibitions, which finds expression in this letter. **opus**: *a building.*

16. Africanae: sc. *ferae*, *wild beasts*, especially *panthers*.

18. cessaverint: *failed to appear*.

19. ut acceptum . . . fieret: *to get the credit;* cf. *acceptum tibi fieri*, page 22, line 11, and note. **quod . . . stetit**: *that it was not your fault that you did not exhibit.*

BOOK VII

Page 92. Letter 75. Two other letters to his wife Calpurnia are Epp. VI. 4 and VI. 7.

1. In causa: cf. page 81, line 16.

3. Inde: in the sense of *ob eam causam*, mostly peculiar to Silver

Latin, but found in Cicero also. **in imagine tua**: *picturing you to myself.*

5. ad diaetam tuam: *to your sitting-room.* **ipsi**: *of themselves, of their own accord.* **pedes ducunt**: this expression was proverbial, as is implied by the words *ut . . . dicitur;* cf. Varro, *de Re Rust.* II. *pr.* 6.

8. conteror: *I am being worn out.*

9. cui requies in labore: i.e., his only relief is in hard work, which enables him to forget her while he is busy.

Letter 76. About Fabatus, grandfather of Calpurnia, read introductory note to Ep. IV. 1.

11. Hermes: Greek names are very common for superior slaves; freedmen generally continued in confidential relations with their former masters (*patroni*). **hereditarios**: forming part of an *hereditas.*

12. proscribi: *to be advertised for sale;* cf. page 98, line 10. **non exspectata**: *without waiting for.* **pro meo quincunce ex septingentis milibus**: *for my* $\frac{5}{12}$ *on the basis* (of a total for the whole estate) *of* 700,000 *sesterces;* thus Corellia got the land for less than its real value.

13. addixerit: *has sold.*

14. hos: sc. *agros.* **nongentis milibus**: i.e., this would be the price of the whole estate. Corellia, therefore, paid $\frac{5}{12}$ of 700,000 instead of $\frac{5}{12}$ of 900,000 sesterces.

15. ratum servem: *stand by, ratify.*

Page 93. **1. ut sororem . . . ut matri**: this *ut* (*as, as being*) expresses actual condition and then becomes causal.

3. Minicio Iusto: it is to him or to Fabius Iustus that Ep. VII. 2 is addressed. He is one of the legatees named in the will of Dasumius, A.D. 109; see introductory note to Ep. II. 6.

4. vetera iura: *friendly relations of long standing.*

5. praetore me: Pliny was praetor in A.D. 93; one of the duties of the praetors was the celebration of the *ludi Apollinares*, which occurred July 5, and, under the empire, of other public games. The expenses of these exhibitions they bore, wholly or in part. A man was judged by the style of the spectacles which he furnished to the people; but magistrates were no longer dependent on the popular favor for their election. Livy gives an account (XXVII. 23) of the institution of the *ludi Apollinares* in B.C. 208. **praesederit**: we should like to know why Pliny did not preside himself; it may have been owing to his contempt for the spectacle, expressed in Ep. IX. 6, but this is hardly likely.

6. cum . . . fui: note *cum* with perfect indicative to express the point of time at which the act occurred. **istic**: refers to the place where the recipient of the letter is; i.e., at, or near, Comum.

7. circa Larium nostrum: sc. *lacum*; the Lake of Como, on the shores of which Pliny had several villas, including 'Tragedy' and 'Comedy,' Ep. IX. 7.

9. his . . . cedere . . . Corelliae: *cedere* with both ablative and dative is not uncommon.

11. ei: i.e., to Corellia. **epistulas**: for *epistulam*; see note on page 70, line 3.

14. quod . . . meis moribus gessit: *what . . . has done in accordance with my wishes*; *moribus* is ablative; the sense is the same as that of *morem gerere mihi*.

16. omnino non vendere: *not to sell at all.*

18. iura: *relations, ties.*

Letter 77. Corellia was the sister of Corellius Rufus (cf. Ep. I. 12. 3) and the wife of Minicius Justus (cf. Ep. VII. 11).

20. honestissime: predicate omitted; sc. *facis*, *scribis*, or the like.

21. non ex septingentis: as in line 13, page 92, *on the basis of a valuation (for the whole estate) of* 700,000 *sesterces*; when Corellia finds out how cheap she has bought the land from Pliny, she wishes to increase the price to its real value, i.e., from $\frac{5}{12}$ of 700,000 sesterces to $\frac{5}{12}$ of 900,000. This Pliny refuses to allow.

23. partem vicesimam: $\frac{1}{20}$ or 5 per cent was the rate of the succession tax, on estates above a certain amount not derived from one's nearest relatives. It was first imposed by Augustus, A.D. 6 (Dio Cass. LV. 25), and was partly remitted by Trajan (*Paneg.* 37). In this case apparently the *publicani* had seized $\frac{1}{20}$ of the estate, and in redeeming it from them Corellia found that the whole was valued at 900,000 HS; or else the meaning is simply that she was obliged to pay her tax on the basis of that valuation. **emisti**: *you redeemed, bought back.*

25. in hoc uno . . . in omnibus: see Introduction II. § 2. *c*.

Page 94. Letter 78. About Caninius Rufus, of Comum, see introductory note to Ep. I. 3. The present letter, like Ep. IV. 13, is a good exhibition of Pliny's practical sense in regard to schemes of benevolence.

1. municipibus nostris: sc. *Comensibus.*

2. epulum: we find the account of a similar foundation by Pliny himself, in the Milan inscription; see Introduction, page xxvi.

3. non expedita sententia: *the answer is not easy.* **Numeres**: this is a quotation of a supposed question of Caninius, '*numerem?*' *Numeres . . . summam* and *Des agros*, line 5, are logically protases to *verendum est* and *neglegentur* respectively.

5. ut: construe with *publici*, not with *neglegentur;* on *ut*, see note on page 93, line 1.

7. ingenuorum ingenuarumque: *male and female children of free parents;* see *Paneg.* 28; Merivale, ch. 63. It had become necessary to induce poor parents not to expose their children in infancy. Therefore this charity was not confined to those whose parents were dead.

8. longe pluris: *worth a great deal more* (than 500,000 sesterces); *longe* is for *multo* of the classical age.

9. actori publico: *municipal clerk;* perhaps one having charge of revenues, analogous to a private *actor* or steward; or he was simply a public slave employed as the involuntary organ of acquisition for his owner, the municipal corporation. **mancipavi**: *I conveyed;* a merely formal sale, in order that the property might be conveyed back to Pliny subject to the mortgage. **vectigali inposito**: *with a rent charge imposed upon it.*

10. tricena, etc.: 30,000 *sesterces;* interest at 6 per cent on 500,000.

11. sors: *principal.*

12. vectigal: accusative; the value of the land largely exceeds the principal sum of which the rent charge is the interest. This was a safe but, as he proceeds to admit, a very expensive method, because to have an inextinguishable charge upon it rendered the estate very undesirable.

Letter 79. Ep. II. 13 is addressed to Priscus. Ep. III. 21 to Cornelius Priscus; Epp. VI. 8 and VII. 8 to Priscus. We cannot certainly identify the Priscus addressed in these letters, but probability favors Neratius Priscus, a prominent jurist, who was sometimes thought of by Trajan as his successor, instead of Hadrian. Helvidius the younger, son of Helvidius Priscus, is never spoken of as Priscus.

19. Fanniae: second wife of Helvidius Priscus, who twice accompanied him into exile. He was put to death under Vespasian some thirty or more years before the date of this letter. See note on page 17. line 10.

20. virgini: sc. *Vestali.* **adfinis**: *connected by marriage.*

21. pontificum: the Pontifex Maximus was the 'visitor' of the Vestal convent; cf. Lanciani, *Ancient Rome in the Light of Recent Discoveries*, ch. VI.

22. atrio: the existing remains of the Atrium Vestae, which was built for the most part in the reign of Hadrian, a few years later than the date of this letter, are about 100 feet S.E. of the temple of Castor and Pollux, near the Forum. For a full account of its excavation in 1883–84, see Lanciani, *loc. cit.*; cf. also Middleton, *Remains of Ancient Rome*, I. 307 sqq.

Page 95. 2. **hoc discrimine**, etc.: i.e., she caught the fever from the patient. **Insident**: *are continuous.*

3. defectio: *failure of strength.*

4. Helvidio: see note on page 45, line 5.

5. Thrasea: P. Thrasea Paetus, a noble Stoic of the reign of Nero, father-in-law of Helvidius, son-in-law of Caecina Paetus and Arria. As a senator he showed great boldness, in disapproving the wickedness of Nero, and was obliged by Nero to commit suicide in A.D. 66; see note on page 48, line 19. **reliqua labuntur**: *all else is breaking up.* (Lewis.)

7. Eripi oculis: for the dative, see Introduction II. § 3. *g.*

9. Bis: first, under Nero, to Macedonia; second, under Vespasian.

10. tertio: she was banished by Domitian for having persuaded Senecio to write a biography of her husband. **relegata**: *relegatio* was the mild form of banishment, not involving loss of *status*, i.e., of civil rights. *Deportatio*, on the other hand, amounted to the extinction of existence as a citizen.

13. Metio Caro: see note on page 3, line 10; Tac. *Agric.* 45. **an rogasset, respondit**: sc. *Fannia* for both.

14. commentarios: *note-books* of her husband.

15. matre: Arria the younger, daughter of Caecina Paetus.

16. libros . . . abolitos: cf. Tac. *Agric.* 2; they were burned by the executioners.

18. publicatis bonis: *when her property was confiscated.* **servavit**: i.e., at least one copy.

19. exsilium exsilii: intentional repetition of the word in another case; cf. Epp. VI. 16. 16; VII. 27. 6.

24. ut illas quae leguntur: the heroines of history; her grandmother, the elder Arria, was one of the most famous. Note the striking use of *lego* in the passive — ***are read about.***

26. licet adhuc posteros, etc.: a descendant of this family was consul in A.D. 196.

27. ut haec non novissima occiderit: i.e., to what a height of virtue they must rise to prevent the impression that she was the last of her house! Kraut calls *occiderit* a future perfect subjunctive in a consecutive clause.

32. rescisso vulnere: *an old wound torn open afresh.*

Page 96. **4. ultor**: cf. Ep. IX. 13. 1, *libros quos de Helvidi ultione composui.* **paria**: *equal to their deserts.*

5. solvendi: *of paying* my debt of gratitude.

6. eram: epistolary past; the epistolary tenses are comparatively little used by Pliny, because the letters are such in form rather than in substance; see Introduction II. § 7. *a.*

Letter 80. About Tacitus, see introductory note to Ep. I. 6.

8. Librum tuum: it would be interesting to know what the book in question was. Probably it was one of the earlier books of the Histories. It is evident from many other letters that the habit of sending one's literary productions to friends for criticism was very common.

12. librum meum: again we should like to know what book. Probably it was one of Pliny's speeches, on the revision of which he spent infinite pains. **adnotationibus**: a post-Augustan word.

16. aetate . . . propemodum aequales: it has been inferred from this expression, combined with others, and with facts otherwise known about Tacitus's career, that he was about eight years older than Pliny, and was born not far from A.D. 54.

17. non nullius . . . nominis: *not without some reputation.*

19. Equidem adulescentulus, etc.: this slightly favors the view which would put Tacitus's birth as early as A.D. 52.

21. longo sed proximus intervallo: quoted from Verg. *Aen.* V. 320; cf. Quint. X. 1. 53, *ut manifesto appareat quanto sit aliud proximum esse, aliud secundum.*

23. similitudo naturae: this likeness of the two friends is something very difficult for us to see, and *imitabilis* seems almost grotesque when applied to Tacitus.

Page 97. **1. nam mihi . . . proximus**, etc.: *for in my opinion to be next to you is to be first.* *Mihi* is a dative of the person judging; B. 188. 2. c; Roby 1148.

2. in testamentis: i.e., that our names are joined; still extant is the testament of Dasumius, where, if the text is correctly restored, and there seems little doubt of it, Tacitus and Pliny are mentioned together among the legatees. See introductory note to Ep. II. 6.

3. nisi . . . amicissimus: it was natural that they should both receive legacies from common friends, but they received them also from strangers. It seems to have been a practice, not uncommon, to leave legacies not only to emperors and their favorites, for prudential reasons, and to patrons and advocates, but also to distinguished men with whom the testators had no personal connection at all.

4. huc spectant: *have this significance.*

5. invicem: reciprocal in sense; this meaning is mostly post-Augustan, but common in Pliny.

Letter 81. L. Licinius Sura, a man of much culture, was of Spanish extraction. He is mentioned by Martial I. 49. 40, *Dum Sura lauaatur tuus;* VI. 64. 13; VII. 47. His third consulship was in A.D. 107. See Mommsen in Keil's *Pliny*. He was influential in recommending Trajan to Nerva as his successor, and Hadrian to Trajan. One other letter is addressed to Sura, Ep. IV. 30, about a wonderful spring near the Lake of Como.

9. phantasmata: Pliny is said to have been the first to introduce this word from the Greek. Terence uses *phasma* in this sense (*Eun.* 9), but merely as the title of a play of Menander.

10. numen: *supernatural power.*

13. Curtio Rufo: see Tac. *Ann.* XI. 21 for an account of Rufus and of the occurrence here related. **Tenuis**: *poor.* **obtinenti**: *the governor* (proconsul). Tacitus calls Rufus *sectator quaestoris.*

14. comes haeserat: *was a hanger-on.* **inclinato die**: in the afternoon. Tacitus makes it noon, the quietest time of day in that climate, the hour of the siesta. **in porticu**: this was at Hadrumetum, on the coast S.E. of Carthage.

15. offertur: reflexive; *presents itself;* cf. Introduction II. § 9. c.

16. perterrito: sc. *ei.* **Africam**: personification of the country

17. iturum: sc. *eum;* also with the other futures.

19. moriturum: he did die as proconsul in Africa.

26. pestilens: *unwholesome;* fright caused illness and death.

27. attenderes: B.356.3; A.&G.309.a; H.508.5.2); Roby 1544.

Page 98. **2. idolon**: this word, occurring in Cicero, is written as Greek. Pliny Latinizes a good many Greek terms.

4. inhabitantibus: another instance of the dative of agent with an uncompounded tense of the passive. The word is a neologism for *incolis* or *habitantibus;* cf. Ep. I. 6. 3, *inerrare.*

8. inerrabat: both the word and its construction with the dative are characteristic of Pliny and of Silver Latinity. **longior**: in point of time; = *diuturnior*. *Longus* gets this meaning apparently from being first used to qualify words of time like *vita*, *aetas*, etc. **timoris timor**: intentional repetition of word in different forms, a not infrequent stylistic trick of our author; see Introduction II. § 10. *m*.

9. solitudine: ablative with *damnata* instead of genitive; we also find *de* with ablative, and *in* and *ad* with accusative.

10. proscribebatur: *was advertised for sale, had a notice put on it.*

12. Athenodorus: of Tarsus, a Stoic; he is said to have been tutor to Augustus. Lucian tells the story with different names, and locates it in Corinth (Φιλοψευδής, 35). But he, of course, tells it to ridicule it.

13. omnia: *doceo*, taking two accusatives in the active, retains the second one in the passive.

15. prima . . . parte: in the atrium, or rather, as this is a Greek house, in the peristyle, near the outer entrance; *prima* is 'front.' The preposition *in* is omitted here as with *loco*.

16. pugillares stilum: see note on page 5, line 27.

18. audita simulacra: *the apparitions which had been reported;* on this force of *audita*, as well as *audio*, page 97, line 12, see Introduction II. § 3. *h*.

20. concuti: note the numerous historical infinitives in this passage of lively descriptive narrative.

22. auribusque praetendere: *animum* is object of this verb also; he closed his ears by fixing his attention upon his work. **crebrescere**: a poetic word, found often in Pliny and Tacitus.

23. iam . . . iam = *modo . . . modo*.

24. Stabat: sc. *effigies;* the imperfect beginning a sentence is particularly graphic; it paints a situation with one stroke.

25. hic: Athenodorus. **ut . . . exspectaret . . . significat**: the imperfect subjunctive properly depends upon the historical present.

27. illa: sc. *effigies.* **capiti . . . insonabat**: *kept clanking the chains over his head.*

28. idem . . . innuentem: *beckoning as before.*

29. illa: sc. *effigies.*

30. aream domus: *courtyard*, probably behind the house.

31. desertus: sc. *Athendorus; left alone.*

32. signum loco: *to mark the spot; loco* is dative, depending directly on *signum*, not on *ponit*.

Page 99. **3. exesa**: *corroded* by the rusty chains.

4. publice: *at the expense of the city.* **conditis manibus caruit**: *after the performance of funeral rites, was free from ghosts.* A harsh use of the ablative absolute; lit., when the ghost had been laid, was free. Collignon cites the ghost story of Tranio in Plautus's *Mostellaria* as very similar to this one.

5. haec . . . adfirmantibus credo: *the foregoing stories I believe on the word of those who tell them.*

7. eodem lecto: for the absence of the preposition, see Introduction II. § 3. *m.*

9. cultros: the plural seems to mean *scissors* (two blades).

11. Exiguum temporis: neuter adjective with partitive genitive, a favorite construction with Tacitus, sparingly used by Pliny.

13. in paedagogio: *in the pages' hall*, where young slaves were educated. The simplest explanation of the story which follows is that the young slaves were witty enough to hoax their learned master, or else that it was a practical joke at the expense of the boy whose hair was cut, an ancient instance of 'hazing.'

18. futurus: *though I should have been;* sc. *reus.*

19. scrinio: a box, usually cylindrical, to hold Ms. rolls. **Caro**: about the informer Metius Carus, see note on page 3, line 10. He and Pliny had become enemies in connection with the prosecution of Senecio and Fannia.

20. libellus: *an information.*

21. moris est: *it is usual.* **summittere**: *to allow to grow.* **recisos . . . capillos**: *the cutting of the hair.*

22. depulsi . . . periculi: *of the removal of the danger.*

23. intendas: *bring to bear on this subject.* For the absence of *ut* after *rogo*, see Introduction II. § 8. *e.*

25. copiam: *the benefit of.*

26. ex altera: sc. *disputa;* Pliny wishes an opinion or an argument on one side, rather than an impartial discussion. He evidently believes in ghosts or at least fears very much that they are real. Such belief was quite universal among his contemporaries.

Page 100. Letter 82. About Tacitus, see introductory note to Ep. I. 6. A very interesting parallel to this letter, in fact the model which it imitates, is one of Cicero's, of similar purport (*ad Fam.* V. 12), in which he goes so far as to ask Lucceius, on the ground of friendship, to say a little more in his favor than absolute historical truth would warrant.

The portion of Tacitus's Histories dealing with Pliny's time is lost, but Pliny's literary judgment was correct. It would have been interesting to see what Tacitus made of the matter involved in this letter. Lucceius's account of Cicero's consulship was promised, but never written.

4. exprimatur: *be portrayed.* This illustration from the art of painting is borrowed from Cicero's letter.

6. quamquam . . . possit: for the subjunctive, see Introduction II. § 8. *b.*

7. in publicis actis: *in the public records*, and therefore accessible to a historian. The *Acta* were a sort of official gazette; cf. Tac. *Ann.* III. 3; V. 4; XII. 24, etc. They were posted in the Forum, and copies were circulated in Italy and in the provinces.

9. cuius gratia periculo crevit: *the merit of which was heightened by its danger.*

11. Herennio: see note on page 3, line 9. **provinciae Baeticae**: cf. the cases of the same province against Gallus and Classicus, Ep. I. 7; III. 4; III. 9. This province (the modern Andalusia) was named from its principal river, the Baetis (Guadalquivir).

13. censuerat: *had passed a resolution.*

14. cum explorasset . . . vacaturos: *when he had learned* by inquiry *that the consuls would be ready to hear petitions.*

17. quorum esse in custodia debent: *in charge of which they ought to be.* It is probably better to refer *quorum* to *bona* than to *consules*, and to make *consules* rather than *bona* the subject of *debent.* For this use of *custodia* with objective genitive, Pr. & B. cite Cic. *pro Mur.* 31, and *de Repub.* VI. 15. Herennius feared that the property of Massa would be awarded to fictitious claimants of redress, who would then restore it quietly to him.

19. num, etc.: i.e., whether we have not done our part. **cognitione**: *investigation.*

21. necessitudo: *close relation, intimacy.* This is the fact early in Pliny's public life. In Ep. I. 7. 2, he speaks quite differently of a later time, when he had served the province more than once as its advocate.

22. quaestor: a quaestor was attached to each proconsul (i.e., governor of a senatorial province).

24. ut: sc. *sit.*

25. quae res ferebat: *what the occasion demanded.*

26. subiungo: ellipse of *ego*, which balances *Senecio.* **et**: has the sense of *when* as in Epp. V. 16. 2, and VI. 20. 14.

27. fidem: *the obligation.*

Page 101. **1. implesse**: zeugma; *fulfilled* (*fidem*), *vented* (*amaritudinem*). **impietatis reum postulat**: *accuses of disloyalty;* charges with reflecting on the emperor by the request which he had made. Massa was a notorious favorite of Domitian. Note the new sense of *impietas*, disloyalty to the person of the emperor, acquired in the imperial age. **Horror omnium**: sc. *fuit.*

2. clarissimi: this adjective was becoming stereotyped; in the later empire, it is the technical designation of a certain class in the civil hierarchy. It is here the title of a consul; in Ep. IX. 13, 19, of a consular.

3. ne mihi . . . obiecerit: *that he had exposed me to the suspicion of collusion.* Whatever derivation we assume, *praevaricatio* is 'crookedness,' especially that of an advocate who betrays his client through an understanding with the opposite party. Pliny uses the word also in Epp. I. 20. 2, and III. 9. 34.

6. Divus: *deified.* Very bad emperors, e.g., Nero, Domitian, do not enjoy this posthumous title in history. **Nerva**: he spent some time in exile under Domitian. **privatus quoque**: i.e., before he became emperor. **attendebat**: *used to take an interest in.*

9. simile antiquis: this phrase in Pliny is complimentary; cf. Epp. IV. 3. 1; V. 14. 3.

11. non exigo ut excedas: the sentence seems to imply a good deal, indirectly, as to the manner in which history was 'colored.' But this demand is decidedly more modest than Cicero's in the letter already cited. Pliny is a smaller man than his exemplar, even in vanity.

13. egredi: the use of this verb with the accusative is mainly post-classical, but it is found in Caesar and Sallust; cf. page 87, line 6. **honeste factis veritas sufficit**: cf. the remark of Verginius to Cluvius, page 113, lines 20–22.

BOOK VIII

Page 102. Letter 83. About C. Calvisius Rufus, see introductory note to Ep. II. 20.

2. vindemias: Masson thinks that these were the parts of the vintage received from tenants as rent; cf. Ep. IX. 37. 3.

3. certatim: *at auction.* **pretium**: *a bid,* if accusative, object of *invitabat;* or *the price*, if nominative, subject of *invitabat.*

4. et quod tunc, etc.: *the state of the vineyards at that time, and the prospects for the season;* or else, according to the second interpretation of *pretium*, *the present and the prospective price.*

5. expeditum . . . aecum: *easy . . . fair.*

8. paria peccata: referring to the maxim of the Stoics as to the equality of all bad deeds; cf. Cic. *pro Mur.* 29. 61, *omnia peccata esse paria;* Hor. *Sat.* I. 3. 96.

9. ne quis mihi, etc.: cf. Verg. *Aen.* V. 305, *Nemo ex hoc numero mihi non donatus abibit.*

11. concessi: *I remitted, threw off.*

12. occupaverant: *had invested.*

17. calculos ostendam: *I will explain the method of calculation.*

18. forte: *for instance.*

20. tulerunt: *carried away* (as a concession).

21. aliquantum . . . aliquid: *a considerable amount . . . something;* the former means more than the latter. **reposuisse**: *had paid* in cash on account of their purchase.

Page 103. **1. verum**: *just, right;* cf. Hor. *Ep.* I. 7. 98. **fides solutionis**: *conscientiousness in payment.*

7. Magno: sc. *pretio;* B. 225. 1; A. & G. 252; H. 422. **stetit**: *cost;* takes the ablative; in this sense mostly post-Augustan.

8. fuit tanti: *it was worth while, it paid.*

10. pertica: *measuring-pole, perch, rod.*

12. ἐν δὲ ἰῇ, etc.: Homer, *Il.* IX. 319, *In like honor are held both the coward and the brave.*

Letter 84. About Caninius Rufus of Comum, see introductory note to Ep. I. 3.

14. bellum Dacicum: the conquest of Dacia was one of the most important of the events of Trajan's reign, and is commemorated by the reliefs on the column of Trajan at Rome and on his triumphal arch at Beneventum; the country was made a Roman province after the second war, which began in 105 A.D. and ended in 106 or 107. See Merivale, ch. 63. Evidently Caninius was intending to write an epic poem on these wars.

17. inmissa terris nova flumina: *rivers made to flow in new channels*, referring, no doubt, especially to the burying of the treasure of Decebalus, the Dacian king, under the bed of a river, which was diverted a second time by Trajan, in order to find the treasure. This river is supposed to have been the Sargetia (Dio Cass. LXVIII. 14, in Xiphilinus). De la Berge suggests the identification of the Sargetia with the modern Schyul. There is an enumeration of these treasures in Joannes Lydus, *de Magistr.* II. 28. They were appropriated for the erection and decoration of the Forum and Column of Trajan. **novos pontes**, etc.: referring, perhaps, to the bridge of boats over the Danube in the first war, but more especially to the stupendous stone and wooden bridge over the same river. Extensive remains of the stone piers still exist at Turn Severin (ancient Drobetae). This bridge is represented on Trajan's column at Rome and on his arch at Beneventum.

18. montium abrupta: for the form of expression, cf. *reliqua rerum tuarum*, page 2, line 9; the subjugation of the country was more difficult because of the mountainous character of part of it; the ranges of Transylvania long sheltered the fugitive barbarians.

19. pulsum . . . regem: Decebalus was driven from his capital Sarmizegethusa when it was captured in the first war; in the second war he killed himself after the capture of his stronghold, in order to escape falling into the hands of the Romans.

20. bis triumphos: 102 and 106 or 107 A.D.

21. primus . . . novissimus: i.e., the first Dacian war ended in a triumph over a nation hitherto unconquered, the second finally completed their subjugation.

22. quod haec aequare dicendo: *to do justice by one's language to such achievements as these.*

26. regis: the king's name was Dĕcĕbălus. **Graecis versibus non resultent**: *that they may not refuse to fit Greek metres;* cf. the name in Horace's 'Journey to Brundisium,' which would not stand in a hexameter line: *Sat.* I. 5. 83, *mansuri oppidulo quod versu dicere non est.* Here *resultent* = *abhorreant.* Cf. also Ver. *Aen.* X. 330, *galea clipeoque resultant.*

Page 104. **2. ad lēvitatem versus**: *in order to secure smoothness of metre.*

3. non delicata, etc.: *not a matter of luxury, but of necessity.*

5. ipso: Trajan.

6. immitte rudentes: not 'slip your cables,' but *let out your sheets,* to get the full benefit of the fair wind.

9. mittito: *send* to me for perusal.

11. perinde carptim ut contexta: *in extracts as well as continuously; carptim* is used coördinately with the three participles.

14. extremamque limam: *finishing touches*, with the file. The metaphor is from the sculptor's art. Similarly we speak of literary 'polish.'

Letter 85. About Tacitus, see introductory note to Ep. I. 6.

23. atque adeo tu in scholam . . . extendo: *for you call me to school, while I am lengthening the holidays.*

24. Saturnalia: see note on page 33, line 19.

25. hyperbaton: *inversion;* i.e., the awkwardness of keeping the words *librum misisti* for the end of this long and involved sentence. This piece of wit is very laborious and not very funny.

27. personam: *the rôle.*

Page 105. **1. exseram**: *avail myself of.*

Letter 86. Concerning Romanus, consult introductory note to Ep. I. 5.

4. Clitumnum: this little Umbrian river flows into a tributary of the Tiber. Vergil speaks of the cattle and sheep along its banks, *Georg.* II. 146. Suetonius mentions a visit to it by the emperor Caligula, *Calig.* 43, and Claudian refers to it in his poem on the sixth consulship of Honorius, 506 sqq.:

> *Quin et Clitumni sacras victoribus undas*
> . . . .
> *Visere cura fuit.*

Cf. Macaulay, *Horatius* 54,

> Unwatched along Clitumnus
> Grazes the milk-white steer.

fontem: *source*, the proper name being in apposition, instead of the limiting genitive. But it is doubtful whether we should not read *Clitumni.*

6. proxime: *only lately.*

7. cupresso: collective, of course; see Introduction II. § 2. *b.* **Hunc**: sc. *collem.*

8. subter: cf. similar anastrophe, *quem contra*, page 18, line 12. **exprimitur**, etc.: *gushes forth in several streams.*

9. lato gremio: *broad basin.*

10. stipes: *small coins.* The reader is reminded of the custom of travellers' throwing copper coins into the fountain of Trevi at Rome 'to ensure their coming again to the city'; cf. Seneca *Nat. Quaest.* IV. 2, *In haec ora stipem sacerdotes et aurea dona praefecti, cum solemne venit sacrum, iaciunt.*

11. devexitate: *downward slope.*

12. sui: we should expect *sua.* **Fons adhuc**, etc.: the phrase expresses the rapid transition from a mere spring to a navigable stream.

15. transmittit : *allows to pass;* it is wide enough for vessels to pass in opposite directions. **perfert** : *supports on its bosom.* **illa qua properat ipse** : *in the direction of its own swift current.*

16. adiuvetur . . . superetur : the subject is *Clitumnus* or *flumen.*

20. fraxino . . . populo : *ash . . . poplar;* collective, like *cupresso*, line 7.

21. viridi imagine : *by the green reflection.* **adnumerat** : it is difficult to say whether this means *counts among its own charms* (Pr. and B.) or *increases, doubles by reflection.*

23. Clitumnus ipse : i.e., a statue of the river-god.

25. sortes : *responses* (of an oracle).

Page 106. **1. capite discreti** : *different in source.*

4. etiam natare : swimming was not allowed above the bridge, where the river was sacred. **Hispellates** : the town of Hispellum (modern Spello) lay a dozen miles from the head of the stream, at some distance from it.

6. hospitium : *place of entertainment for strangers, lodgings.* **secutae** : *attracted by;* informal personification of *villae.*

8. studebis quoque : i.e., deciphering inscriptions, etc.

11. quamquam : *rather, I should say.*

12. quae tua humanitas : *such is your kindliness.*

Letter 87. Besides this letter, Ep. I. 21 (to Plinius Paternus), and Epp. IV. 14 and IX. 27 are addressed to Paternus.

13. Confecerunt : *have deeply afflicted me.* **infirmitates** : *illnesses.* **meorum** : *of my slaves;* but he does not say *servorum;* they often became his *liberti* before their death.

15. facilitas manumittendi : manumission might be called easy because there were so many methods of accomplishing it. The formal methods were *vindictā*, by a fictitious suit before one of the higher magistrates; *censu*, by enrolment on the censor's list of citizens with the master's consent; *testamento*, by bequest. Besides these there were several informal methods, see Hunter, *Roman Law*, pp. 177 sqq.

17. servis : he is here speaking of their legal capacity and must use the word.

18. quasi testamenta : slaves had no legal capacity to make wills; freedmen were capable both of making wills and of inheriting. Pliny treated his slaves in this respect as if they had been emancipated, and gave practical effect to their last wishes. The quasi-property of slaves, who were legally incapable of ownership, but were often allowed by their masters to hold property as their own and sometimes to engage in trade, was called *peculium.*

19. quod visum : *as they think best.* **ut iussus** : *as if a binding command were laid upon me.*

20. relincunt : see note on *aecum*, page 5, line 20.

22. adquiescam : for the mood, see Introduction II. § 8. *b.*

26. damnum : *pecuniary loss.*

Page 107. **4. plura** : sc. *scripsi.*

5. dolendi voluptas : see Introduction II. § 9. *b.*

This letter shows Pliny's sympathetic nature in a very amiable light.

Letter 88. The person addressed is spoken of as Minicius Macrinus in Ep. I. 14. 5, elsewhere simply as Macrinus. He was a citizen of Brixia (Brescia), and was addressed in Epp. II. 7; III. 4; VII. 6; VII. 10; IX. 4. When he was by Vespasian *adlectus inter praetorios*, he declined the honor (Ep. I. 14. 5). His wife Acilia died after they had been married thirty-nine years (Ep. VIII. 5. 1).

8. istic : *where you are.*

9. alveum : for the accusative with *excedo*, cf. *annum . . . excessit*, page 43, line 26, and note.

11. fossa : ablative; *canal*, dug by Trajan, to carry off the overflow. **exhaustus** : *drained off* — but only partially.

13. pro : *instead of.*

16. delicatissimus amnium : *daintiest of rivers.*

18. decidentium : neuter plural; *débris.*

19. clausus : *dammed up.*

22. divitum apparatus : *appliances of luxury.*

23. instrumenta ruris : *farm implements.*

25. varie lateque : *varie* expresses the manifold character of the drifting objects; *late*, the extent of the flood which carried them.

Page 108. **1. turbines** : *waterspouts, torrents.*

2. opera quibus . . . cinguntur : *enclosures of that fertile country; pretiosa rura* might be translated *choice gardens* or *farms.*

4. luctibus : i.e., on account of the loss of friends who perished in the flood. **Ne quid simile** : sc. *sit.*

5. pro mensura periculi : *considering the extent of the catastrophe.*

6. consulas : *have pity upon, have regard for.*

Letter 89. About Gallus, see introductory notes to Epp. II. 17, and IV. 17.

13. comparatum: sc. *est.* **proximorum**: a striking instance of the substantive use of an adjective; see Introduction II. § 2. *c.* **incuriosi**: *indifferent.*

15. occasio: *access.*

16. datur: *it is possible.* **velis**: for the mood, see note on *moveris*, page 33, line 25.

18. auribus: *by hearsay.*

20. commendatrix: the idea is that the mere names of some countries lend an adventitious interest to what is found in them. **audita . . . haberemus**: *we should have heard of, read of, and gone to inspect;* here we see beginning the modern use of *habere* as an auxiliary verb.

22. pariter: *simultaneously.* **prosocer**: Calpurnius Fabatus; see introductory note to Ep. IV. 1.

23. Amerina: Ameria (now Amelia) is in Southern Umbria near the Tiber. **Haec**: sc. *praedia.*

24. subiacens: cf. *subiectus*, page 1, line 11. **Vadimonis**: nominative; now Laghetto di Bassano.

25. narrantur: *were told me*—by Fabatus, or by some one else who acted as Pliny's guide.

26. ipsum: sc. *lacum.* **circumscriptus**: *circular.*

27. aequalis: *regular.* **sinus, obliquitas**: *bay, irregularity.*

Page 109. **2. albidior**: *paler, lighter.* **viridior et pressior**: *greener and duller;* but the meaning of *pressior* is not clear.

3. medicatus: *medicinal;* Pliny appears to confuse two notions in one phrase; the *taste* and the *healing property.* **vis, qua fracta solidantur**: *efficacy in mending fractures.*

5. Nulla . . . navis: cf. Ep. VIII. 8. 6, and note.

6. herbidae: *overgrown.*

7. extremitas: *the border*, the lake being circular.

8. cuique: sc. *insulae.* **derasus**: *worn smooth.* **ut modus**: see Crit. App.

9. sibi: *against each other.*

11. humili: *hanging low.*

15. destitutae tranquillitate: *becalmed.*

19. promovent terram: i.e., apparently advance the shore line into the lake.

20. reddunt auferuntque: *enlarge and contract.* **cum medium tenuere**: *when they are in the middle* of the lake.

23. litori abrepta: for the dative, see Introduction II. § 3. *g.*

24. quasi inlata et inposita: *as if put on board a raft.*

25. egressa : *going ashore.*

26. descendisse . . . ascendisse : *disembarked . . . embarked.*

28. Specu : for the absence of the preposition, cf. *lecto*, page 99, line 7, and note. **si quid . . . accepit** : *whatever is thrown into it.*

BOOK IX

Page 110. Letter 90. Concerning Calvisius, see introductory note to Ep. II. 20.

1. Omne hoc tempus : apparently the period of the games.

3. Circenses : sc. *ludi;* any games celebrated in the Circus Maximus, especially the *ludi Romani*, which in the time of Augustus lasted from the 4th to the 19th of September, the last days being devoted to chariot racing, in which the chief interest of the spectators centred. But the occasion referred to in this letter may have been any of the numerous stated or extraordinary games.

4. teneor : *I am taken, attracted.* **Nihil novum** : Pr. and B. think this letter was suggested by Cic. *ad Fam.* VII. 1.

6. tot milia virorum : cf. Juvenal XI. 197,

Totam hodie Romam Circus capit.

After its restoration by Claudius, the Circus Maximus held 250,000 spectators; it was further enlarged by Constantine.

9. favent panno : *it is the colors that excite their interest. Pannus* means cloth, rag, garment; then especially the tunic of the charioteer (*auriga*), of the color of the *factio* to which he belonged. The colors were red (*russata*), white (*albata*), blue (*veneta*), green (*prasina*); Domitian added purple and gold (*purpurea et aurata*). The public became violent partisans of the different factions or colors, and under the later empire bloody riots were often the result. The *factiones* were companies of contractors who provided trained horses, drivers, and all the requisites for the races. See Class. Dict., art. *Circus.*

15. graves homines : precisely in the sense of *hommes sérieux.*

Page 111. Letter 91. About Romanus, see introductory note to Ep. I. 5.

1. patrocinium : *authority, example for my own conduct, defence against critics.* Romanus may have been building at Baiae. Pliny is enlarging his villas described in this letter.

3. Larium lacum : the Lake of Como.

4. duae : viz., 'Comedy' and 'Tragedy.'

5. delectant . . . exercent: *delight . . . keep busy;* i.e., he is forever adding improvements. **Altera inposita saxis**: on the cliffs, perhaps on the western shore of the lake.

6. altera . . . lacum tangit: perhaps at Bellagio.

8. cothurnis: high-heeled, thick-soled *buskins* worn by tragic actors.

9. socculis: low buskins worn by comic actors; *shoes, slippers, socks.*

10. possidenti: see Introduction II. § 2. c. **Haec . . . utitur**: *one enjoys a closer, the other a wider, view of the lake.*

12. duos: sc. *sinus.*

13. recta gestatio: *a straight promenade.* **longo limite**: *in a long stretch.* **super litus**: *along the shore;* this preposition is appropriate because the shore is high above the lake.

14. spatiosissimo xysto: ablative of quality limiting *gestatio* supplied from line 13; the phrase is coördinate with *recta* in line 13. The sentence means *here it gently curves in a spacious terrace-walk.* (Lewis.)

17. Hae mihi . . . supersunt: i.e., the charms which each possesses are my reasons for adding to each what it lacks.

19. quid . . . rationem: *why am I rendering an account;* i.e., justifying myself.

Letter 92. About Tacitus, the historian, consult note at the beginning of Ep. I. 6.

21. praeceptis tuis: what the advice was is shown by the rest of the sentence.

Page 112. 1. convenire non possit: *it is not possible to meet at the same time the demands of.*

7. unam alteram: *one or two;* the words are usually connected by *aut.*

Letter 93. About Falco, see introductory note to Ep. I. 23.

11. in Tuscos: *to my Tuscan estate;* see note on *Marsi*, page 29, line 16.

12. at hoc: *but this is possible.*

13. libellis . . . querulis: *petitions . . . grumbling ones;* the immemorial privilege of tenants.

14. meos: sc. *libellos; literary productions, papers* of a different sort from the *libellis* of line 13.

15. Retracto: *I am revising.* **actiunculas**: *my attempts at speeches in court;* modest diminutive of *actiones.*

16. frigidum et acerbum: *a dull and distasteful task.* **Rationes**: *the accounts* of the estate.

19. pro gestatione: *by way of a constitutional.*

Letter 94. In Ep. VI. 23 Pliny, in undertaking a law case, stipulates that Cremutius Ruso be engaged with him. It was his habit thus to assist young advocates just beginning their professional life.

22. legisse . . . in quadam epistula: manifestly a reference to Ep. VI. 10. 4. It thus appears that this collection of letters was published in parts, one or more books at a time.

23. Verginium Rufum: see Epp. II. 1, and VI. 10, and notes.

Page 113. **3. Reprehendis**, etc.: this discussion whether Verginius by his epitaph, or Frontinus by his refusal to have one, showed the more pride, is a good example of the academic character of the literature of the time. This letter does not even pretend to convey any information except an answer to a real or supposed question of Ruso, which sounds like a question proposed for a debating society.

4. Frontinum: S. Julius Frontinus (A.D 40–106) was governor of Britain (75–78), and was the author of two treatises still extant, one on military science, the other on the Roman aqueducts, of which he was made curator in 97. See also page 58, line 13, and note.

6. Utrumque dilexi: about Pliny's peculiarly intimate relations with Verginius Rufus, see Introduction, page xi.

11. victuri: agrees with *nominis; destined to live.*

12. supremis . . . titulis: i.e., the inscriptions on their graves.

14. in praedicando: *in talking about his deeds,* i.e., while he was alive; not referring to the inscription.

17. secum . . . locutum: *said to him,* i.e., to Verginius. **Cluvium**: M. Cluvius Rufus, governor of Hispania Tarraconensis in A.D. 69, is probably identical with this historian, who wrote an account of the times of Nero, Galba, Otho, and Vitellius. See Teuffel, *Roman Literature* (translated by Warr), 314. 2.

18. fides: *truthfulness, accuracy.*

23. parcior . . . et pressior: *more modest and self-restrained.*

26. per orbem . . . memoriam suam: *to give out, to be read all over the world, (the statement) that one's memory is destined to last.*

29. illum: Frontinus.

30. hunc: Verginius.

Page 114. Letter 95. We know nothing of Sabinianus, except that we learn from Ep. IX. 24 of the success of Pliny's intercession. This letter is often compared with St. Paul's epistle to Philemon. It exhibits the humanitarian spirit of one of the best Pagans beside the feeling of Christian brotherhood shown by the apostle.

14. **Remitte** : *pardon.*

16. **Torqueris** : reflexive; see Introduction II. § 9. c. **tam lenis** : *you who are so kindly.*

Page 115. Letter 96. About Maximus, see introductory note to Ep. II. 14.

1. **agenti** : *speaking in court* as advocate. **centumviri** : cf. Introduction, page xvi.

2. **auctoritatem gravitatemque** : *dignity and solemnity.*

6. **Corneli Taciti** : the historian.

7. **sedisse se cum quodam** : see Crit. App. **Circensibus** : sc. *ludis*; cf. note on Ep. IX. 6. 1.

9. **se** : i.e., Tacitus. **nosti me** : the vanity of this on the part of Tacitus is lessened by the previous conversation.

10. **ex studiis** : *from your reading*; or, *from my studies*, i.e., *works.*

12. **litterarum propria** : *belonging to literature.* **non hominum** : *not merely of individuals.*

13. **litteris redduntur** : *are associated with, are assigned to, the branches of literature which we pursue.*

15. **Recumbebat** : i.e., at a dinner table.

16. **Fadius Rufinus** : Fadia was the name of a family of Arpinum, which appeared in history about Cicero's time; the cognomina which occur in it are Gallus and Rufus. **super eum** : if Pliny had, as was likely, the place of honor (*locus consularis*), he would have been *imus in lecto medio;* then, if Fadius was next him (which is not certain, for we are not sure that *mecum* means next above Pliny), the man *super eum* would be *summus in medio.*

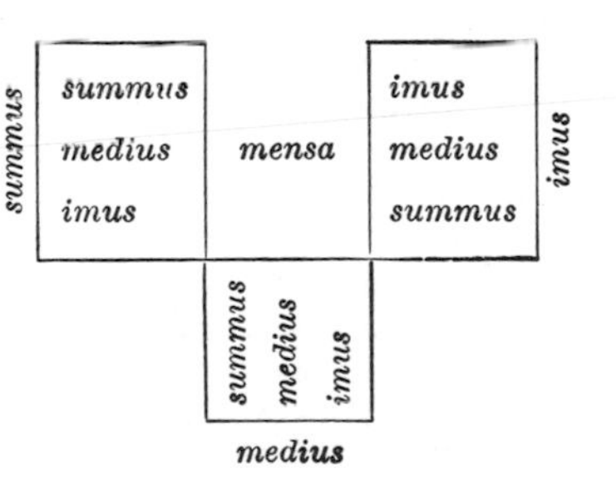

18. **vides hunc** : sc. *inquit.*

19. ille: i.e., the *municeps.*

22. οὗτός ἐστι Δημοσθένης: this anecdote is related by Cicero (*Tusc.* V. 36. 103).

Page 116. Letter 97. This letter is the sequel of Ep. IX. 21 addressed to Sabinianus.

Letter 98. As Caninius was a poet and man of letters, it is appropriate that the letters to him are on literary subjects, or at least are such as to imply his interest in literary pursuits. For details about him and a list of the letters addressed to him, see introductory note to Ep. I. 3.

9. materiam: *subject.*

10. isto: *your.* **laetissimo, altissimo**: *lively, elevated.*

11. super cenam: *during dinner*; we say 'the gentlemen lingered *over* their wine.' Cf. page 40, line 16, and note.

12. auctori: *the teller of the tale.* **fides**: *credibility.* **quid poetae**: sc. *rei est; what business has a poet with credibility?*

14. Hipponensis colonia: *the colony of Hippo;* this was Hippo Diarrhytus or Zaritus on the coast of the former Carthaginian territory, west of Utica, now Bizerta.

15. stagnum: *lagoon.*

17. prout aestus . . . inpulit: *as the tide ebbs and flows.*

18. Omnis . . . aetas: *all ages, old and young.*

20. sollicitat: *tempts.*

21. altissime provehi: *to swim out into the deepest water.*

22. natantes: accusative. **certamine**: ablative of time.

Page 117. 1. Delphinus, etc.: Pliny the Elder, *N. H.* IX. 8. 26, tells same story; he dates it *intra hos annos.*

3. subire: *picks up and carries*, lit., *gets under.*

5. aequalibus: *to his comrades, playfellows.* **Serpit . . . fama**: *the story spreads;* the verb indicates slow progress. *Rumor* and *Fama* usually *fly* in the poets.

9. si quid est mari simile: i.e., the lagoon and the inlet.

12. variosque . . . expeditque: *described all sorts of convolutions.*

14. donec . . . subiret: the use of the subjunctive here is post-Augustan. There is no notion of expectancy or purpose involved. B. 293. III. 1. *a*; A. & G. 328. 2. *a.* N.; H. 519. II. 2. N. 1; Roby 1670. **innutritos mari**: *accustomed from birth to the sea.*

15. tangunt . . . praebentem: *while he also allowed himself to be touched and stroked.*

19. huius . . . illius: i.e., *the boy's . . . the dolphin's.*

26. conlusorem: *playmate.*

27. extrahi . . . revolvi: reflexive passives: see Introduction II. § 9. *c.*

28. Octavium Avitum: not otherwise known.

29. legatum pro consule: the elder Pliny in his version of the story ascribes the act to *Flavianus, proconsul Africae.* **educto**: dative; sc. *delphino.* **religione prava**: *superstition;* he evidently took the dolphin for a sea-god. It was usual to anoint statues of gods.

30. cuius . . . refugisse: infinitive in a subordinate clause of *oratio obliqua;* B. 314. 4; A. & G. 336. 2. *b*; H. 524. 1. 1); Roby 1784. *b.*

Page 118. **3. mora modica**: *short stay.*

5. occulte: construe with *interfici.*

7. est opus adfingas: Kühner, *Ausführliche Grammatik*, II. page 808, cites this as the only instance in Latin literature of *opus est* with the simple subjunctive. See Introduction II. § 8. *e.*

Letter 99. Cn. Pedanius Fuscus Salinator is addressed also in Epp. VII. 9 and IX. 40. He was a patrician (Ep. VI. 26. 1). Pliny instructed him or advised him in his professional studies, and was interested in his *début* as a pleader (Ep. VI. 11; VII. 9). He married the daughter of Julius Servianus, had a son born in A.D. 118, in which year he was *consul ordinarius.* See Mommsen in Keil's *Pliny,* page 421.

9. in Tuscis: *on my Tuscan estate;* see note on page 112, line 11.

10. horam primam: the first hour after sunrise. The length of the hour, one-twelfth of the time from sunrise to sunset, varied with the season; see note on page 37, line 12.

11. clausae . . . manent: i.e., to keep out the daylight.

12. ab eis: substantive use of the neuter pronoun, as, e.g., page 60, line 13.

16. ad verbum . . . similis: *like one actually writing and correcting.*

18. Notarium: *short-hand writer; notae* were the stenographic characters. Those of the system invented by Cicero's freedman were called *notae Tironianae;* then the proper name became a general one for any stenographic signs. **die admisso**: i.e., by opening a shutter.

21. xystum . . . cryptoporticum: see notes on page 32, lines 11 and 16.

24. intentio: *concentration of mind.*

26. non tam vocis . . . stomachi: *not so much for the sake of my voice as of my digestion.* Pliny, *N. H.* XXVIII. 4, and Celsus I. 8, recommend the practice of vigorous speaking as assisting the functions of digestion.

Page 119. **1. exerceor**: reflexive; see Introduction II. § 9. *c.*

3. comoedus: *a recitation* by an actor. **lyristes**: *music.*

4. meis: i.e., the members of his family, including guests.

6. conditur: poetic; *is laid to rest.*

12. non sine pugillaribus: on this point cf. Ep. I. 6. **ut . . . non**: this is a clause not of result but of purpose; the clause is affirmative; *non* modifies *nihil.*

13. colonis: *tenants;* see page 51, line 20, and note.

Letter 100. Mustius, judging especially from the last sentence of this letter, seems to be Pliny's architect. This is the only letter in the collection that is addressed to him.

16. Haruspicum monitu: *by the advice of the haruspices.* Their function was to interpret the will of the gods, chiefly from the entrails of sacrificial victims. They were at first Etruscans, but the emperor Claudius established a regular collegium of Roman haruspices.

17. in praediis: *on my property, land.* **in melius . . . in maius**: rather favorite locutions in the Silver Age; cf. Ep. III. 11. 1.

18. cum . . . alioqui: *though in fact.* **stato die**: *on the stated day.* **frequentissima**: Ceres is the goddess of crops, and the region is an agricultural one; naturally her temple is crowded. **Idibus Septembribus**: this festival, apparently connected with the harvest, is not to be confused with the *Cerealia,* which occurred on April 10.

21. suffugium: *shelter;* i.e., a means of escaping from the rain. This, being a substantive of transitive signification, is properly followed by objective genitives *imbris* and *solis;* one might say *suffugere imbrem,* etc. Cf. *tactum suffugit et ictum,* Lucr. V. 150.

24. Velim ergo emas: *therefore please buy; velim* simply softens the abruptness of the command. On the absence of *ut*, see Introduction II. § 8. *e.*

Page 120. **1. excolantur**: *should be adorned.*

2. signum: *statue.*

4. quod videatur . . . repetendum: *which it seems necessary for you to send;* lit., 'which it seems ought to be procured from where you are.' This does not satisfactorily render the *re* in *repetendum.* But Pr. & B.'s rendering, 'nothing occurs to me that seems desirable to be taken up into consideration from the spot,' i.e., where the temple is, necessitates, as they admit, taking *istinc* in the sense of *illinc.*

5. **nisi tamen . . . scribas** : *unless you sketch a plan*, etc.

6. **circumdari templo** : *be built around the temple.*

9. **explicabuntur** : *may be conveniently located;* this word is used on account of the extent of the portico.

CORRESPONDENCE WITH TRAJAN.

Page 121. Letter 101. 1. **imperator** : Trajan succeeded his adoptive father, Nerva, as emperor, Jan. 23, A.D. 98. This letter must have been written very soon after. Trajan was in Germany commanding the armies along the Rhine. It was at Cologne in the Lower Province that the news of his accession reached him. It was more than a year before he went to Rome — some time in A.D. 99. **sanctissime** : *most sacred;* such words as this were fast becoming, or had already become, conventional, as applied to the emperors. Later the word *sacer* is used of the emperor's palace, functionaries, occupations, etc., quite as a matter of course. *Sanctus* was used in quite a different sense of private individuals, indicating purity of character.

3. **festinaverunt** : Nerva's reign had been short, only from Sept. 18, A.D. 96, to Jan. 23, A.D. 98. **gubernacula** : for plural, see note on page 84, line 10.

4. **susceperas** : pluperfect, referring back to the time of his association with Nerva as colleague and presumptive successor. His adoption had occurred on Oct. 27, A.D. 97, while he was absent in Upper Germany.

6. **Fortem et hilarem** : *well and happy.*

Letter 102. 8. **domine** : this word was used in polite address to all classes of persons, sometimes even by superiors to inferiors. The early tendency to make it an official title of the emperors was checked by Augustus and Tiberius, and it seems to have been a couple of centuries before it became a regular official title. Hardy's note (*Pliny: Correspondence with Trajan*) on this word is exhaustive and interesting.

9. **iure trium liberorum** : *the rights of a father of three children.* From the time of Augustus the unmarried and the childless were placed by law under certain disabilities and disadvantages as compared with those who were married and had children (*Lex Iulia et Papia*

Poppaea, A.D. 9). Hardy's note gives a convenient enumeration of the privileges attached to the *ius trium liberorum:* (1) inheritance of legacies left to *caelibes*, which the latter were forbidden to take (*caduca*); (2) preference *in petendis honoribus;* (3) holding offices before the legal age or without the legal interval; (4) preference in the assignment of provinces; (5) precedence before equals and colleagues; (6) exemption from the duties of *tutor* and *iudex;* (7) mitigation of punishment in certain cases. Wise emperors granted the *ius trium liberorum* sparingly, others more freely, to childless persons. The grant was strictly personal, and did not benefit the heirs of the persons concerned, nor was it in any way assignable.

10. Iuli Serviani: brother-in-law of Hadrian, born about A.D. 47. He held many important official positions, and was one of the persons mentioned in the will of Dasumius, already referred to; see introductory note to Ep. II. 6. For details, see Mommsen in Keil's *Pliny*. At the time of this letter he was legate of Upper Germany. Pliny addressed him in Epp. III. 17 and VI. 26.

Page 122. **1. rescripto**: a *rescriptum*, sometimes called *epistula*, was the technical name for the emperor's official reply to a petition or to the inquiry of a magistrate asking for instructions or advice.

2. summam voti: *the height of my desires.*

4. peculiarem: *personal.*

5. illo tristissimo saeculo: Domitian's reign.

6. duobus matrimoniis: this evidently means two marriages in Domitian's reign. On the other hand, the letters about Calpurnia seem to refer to a recent marriage, and are evidently to be dated well on in Trajan's reign. Hence we infer that Calpurnia was the third wife of Pliny; see Introduction, page xviii.

8. patrem fieri: i.e., obtain the privileges of a father, become a *pater* in the eye of the law. With the general sentiment of this sentence, cf. *Paneg.* 26, *Super omnia est tamen quod talis es, ut sub te liberos tollere libeat, expediat.*

Letter 103. This and the following letters were written from Pliny's province, Pontus and Bithynia; see Introduction, page xviii.

11. socrui meae: Pompeia Celerina, mother of Pliny's second wife, who had died in A.D. 97, as we may infer with strong probability from Ep. IX. 13. 4 and 13. Concerning Pompeia, see Epp. I. 4; III. 19. 8; VI. 10. 1; and notes.

12. in hanc provinciam: Bithynia.

16. ne audeo quidem: his gratitude is so great that he shrinks from the attempt to express it adequately in act; besides, that might be treating the emperor too much as an equal. **quamvis maxime possim**: this seems to mean *(and I should not dare) were I never so able*. The sentence reminds one of *nec . . . scio, nec, si sciam, dicere ausim*, Livy, *Praef.* 1.

17. ut . . . non indignus: *non* is, of course, to be connected with *indignus*, not with *ut*; see note on page 118, line 12.

Letter 104. **20. de condicione**: i.e., whether they were to be considered as free or as slaves.

Page 123. **1. θρεπτούς**: *foundlings*, deserted children brought up at the public expense; lit., 'nourished.' **constitutionibus principum**: Gaius I. 5, *Constitutio principis est quod imperator decreto vel edicto vel epistula constituit; nec umquam dubitatum est quin id legis vicem obtineat, cum ipse imperator per legem imperium accipiat.*

2. proprium aut universale: *personal or general.* General decisions were regarded as precedents, personal ones were not. Ulp. *Dig.* I. 4. 1. 2, (*Constitutiones*) *personales nec ad exemplum trahuntur.*

5. exemplo: *with a mere precedent.*

7. Anniam: see Crit. App.

8. epistulae: specimens of *epistulae* of emperors may be seen in Bruns, *Fontes Juris Romani Antiqui*[6], 233; 241–243; 246.

9. ad eosdem et ad Achaeos: see Crit. App. **Domitiani**: on the omission of *divi*, see note on page 101, line 6.

10. proconsules: of Achaia.

11. parum emendata: *not in correct form;* the copy was not accurate.

12. fidei: *authenticity.*

13. scriniis: cases for books and papers; he means those in the official bureaux, containing the archives.

Letter 105. **15. sublati**: *rescued.* **in servitute**: i.e., in *de facto* slavery. This did not affect their position *de iure*, which might be asserted successfully at any time if it could be proved.

16. commentariis: *records.*

20. intra eas provincias, etc.: see Crit. App.

22. adsertionem: *claim of liberty by suit.* Such a suit was called *causa liberalis.* The plaintiff who maintained the liberty of the alleged slave was called *adsertor libertatis;* he was said *adserere* or *vindicare in libertatem*, the object of the infinitive being, of course, the individual whose liberty was to be established. **denegandam**: it was the magistrate's business to decide whether a claim was to be submitted to actual trial; in other words, he either granted an action (*dedit actionem*) or refused it (*negavit*, *denegavit*).

23. neque . . . pretio alimentorum: they were not to be required to pay for their previous support in order to gain the freedom to which they were entitled.

Page 124. Letter 106. **1. in statione Nicomedensi**: *on duty at Nicomedīa*, the capital of Bithynia, afterwards the capital residence of Diocletian, when he divided the empire into four administrative parts. Pliny, as we learn from Ep. *ad Trai* 21, had several cohorts of soldiers under his command in Bithynia, no doubt 'auxiliary' troops, rather than detachments from some legions.

3. pistoribus: *millers*, and probably also *bakers*, as it was usual to combine the two trades.

4. operas . . . locaverat: *had let his services for hire, had contracted to work.* The contract of *locatio-conductio* might be for work (*operarum*) as well as for the use of property (*rei*); e.g., rent of a house. The lessor was the *locator*, the lessee (hirer) was the *conductor*; see Sohm, *Institutes*, page 311; Hunter, *Roman Law*, pages 505–514. **confugisse**: a right of sanctuary attached to the statues of emperors.

6. Laberio Maximo: consul for the second time in A.D. 103, general in the Dacian wars. **Susago**: probably a Dacian leader or an ally of Decebalus. **Moesia**: the country north of Macedonia and Thrace, and south of the Danube.

7. Decebalo: king of the Dacians about twenty years, died in A.D. 105; the name was not personal, but official, like Pharaoh, Caesar, Arsaces, etc. **Pacŏro**: otherwise called Arsaces XXIV., succeeded his father Vologeses I. (Arsaces XXIII.), was contemporary with Domitian and Trajan, and an ally of their enemy Decebalus. The statement here made is interesting as evidence of the latter's attempt to secure the alliance of the Parthians. **pluribusque annis**: this throws some light on the date of Pliny's administration of Bithynia. Hardy observes that Callidromus was probably taken prisoner in the first Dacian War and sent to Pacorus in the interval between it and the second war, i.e., A.D. 102–104; then he was several years in Parthia.

8. ministerio: *service.*

10. mittendum . . . putavi: because he might be able to give valuable information about Dacia and Parthia.

12. sibi: construe with *subtractam*. **et quibus**, etc.: the construction is (*habentem ea*) *quibus* (*Pacorus*) *ornatus fuisset.*

14. glebulam: *ingot*, probably of gold.

15. Signata: *sealed*, in a closed package.

16. aposphragisma (ἀπό, σφραγίζω): the impression of a seal, or of the figure engraved on a signet-ring; a very rare word. Pliny was rather fond, as we have already noticed, of Latinizing Greek words.

Letter 107. **17. et hunc natalem**: apparently Sept. 17, A.D. 112, exactly a year after Pliny's arrival in Bithynia, which is stated in Ep. *ad Trai.* 17 A. to have been XV. Kal. Oct., the emperor's birthday.

19. aliis super alia operibus: cf. Ep. VII. 8. 1, *aliis super alias epistulis; Paneg.* 14, *aliis super alias expeditionibus.*

Page 125. Letter 108. **1. mi Secunde carissime**: if the emperor uses Pliny's name at all, it is always Secundus; he says, *mi Secunde*, *Secunde carissime*, *mi Secunde carissime.*

Letter 109. **4. Sollemne**: *customary.*

6. Cognitionibus: *trials*, at Rome. It appears that there had been such trials, but they had not been important enough for Pliny to have become acquainted with the procedure followed in such cases. The contrary of Orosius's statement that Trajan had issued a general edict against Christians is implied in what Pliny says here. The Christians were much confounded with the Jews in the popular mind.

7. quid, etc.: i.e., whether the mere name or profession of Christian or some overt acts beside.

10. tenĕri: adjective, not the verb *tenēri*. **paenitentiae**: this made no difference in regard to the prosecution of crimes in general.

11. prosit: *desisse* is the subject.

12. nomen ipsum: *the mere profession.* The emperor's answer, which follows, implies an affirmative reply to this point. It was the secession from the state religion which was punished; the object of the government was not theological, but political.

14. modum: *method.*

17. duci: sc. *ad supplicium; to execution.* **dubitabam . . . debere**: the accusative and infinitive with *dubito* is frequent only after the Augustan age, and generally it is negative.

20. cives Romani: all will remember St. Paul's appeal from Felix to Caesar, which was allowed because of his citizenship. **in urbem**: sc. *Romam.*

Page 126. **1. ipso tractatu**: *by the very fact of judicial procedure* (Hardy); *simply from the matter being dealt with* (Pr. & B.). He means that informers were encouraged to report further cases, when they found that cognizance was taken of them.

2. plures species inciderunt: *more cases have occurred.* **Propositus est libellus**: *an information was lodged.*

3. sine auctore: *anonymously.*

4. praeeunte me: *repeating the words after me.*

5. imagini tuae: an act of adoration of the emperor's statue was regarded as tantamount to a declaration of allegiance to the empire. But to the Christians it was, of course, an act of idolatry, involving the most vital religious considerations, not merely an expression of political obedience.

6. ture ac vino supplicarent: the test was to scatter a few grains of incense upon the altar fire and pour a few drops of wine as a libation. Christians who consented to do so were called in the church, as a reproach, *turificati;* Cyprian, Ep. 55.

7. male dicerent: *to curse* or *revile*, as an act of renunciation of Christianity.

11. non nemo: *at least one.*

15. stato die: presumably he means on Sunday, *dies solis*, *dies dominica* (French, *dimanche*). **ante lucem**: both because the Christians were for the most part poor folk, often slaves, who had to work for their living, and also because it was safer.

16. carmen: *form of prayer*, *liturgy.* **secum invicem**: *to each other*, *in turn;* in the post-Augustan writers *invicem* is often used to reinforce the reciprocal pronoun.

17. sacramento: *by an oath;* this was Pliny's understanding of the word; it is doubtful whether it had at this date acquired, even among Christians, the sense of 'sacrament,' meaning the eucharist. **aliquod**: notice its occurrence in a negative sentence.

19. appellati: *when called upon to restore it.* Making a deposit with a man was an appeal to his good faith, a breach of which under these circumstances was regarded by the Romans with especial abhorrence.

20. rursus: later in the day, perhaps at evening, when their labors were over.

21. ad capiendum cibum: this does not refer to the eucharist, but to the ἀγάπη, or love-feast, a meal which the early Christians used to eat in common. **promiscuum**: *common*, *ordinary.*

22. desisse: sc. *se.*

23. hetaerias: *associations.*

25. ministrae: *deaconesses;* the Latin word is evidently a translation of διάκονος. It was not ordinary to examine slaves to elicit testimony against their masters.

26. superstitionem pravam inmodicam: this seems a sudden burst of prejudice, like that of the ignorant public, after a fair and temperate account of the situation. *Superstitio* was a religion not authorized by the Roman state.

31. civitates: in the sense of *urbes;* a late use of the word.

32. vicos: *villages* or smaller towns subordinated, *attributi,* to the government of the *civitates.*

Page 127. **2. desolata templa**: strong evidence of the extent to which Christianity had prevailed.

4. venire: from *veneo, to be sold.*

This letter and the next are referred to by Orosius VII. 12, in connection with a general mention of Trajan's persecution of Christians.

Letter 110. In this reply Trajan seems to refuse to enact any general edict for the empire at large.

8. Actum: *course, procedure, method.* **in excutiendis causis**: *in investigating the cases.*

11. Conquirendi non sunt: Pliny was not to seek out Christians in order to bring them to punishment; but if they were duly and formally accused before him, he was not to be at liberty to overlook their violation of the law.

12. puniendi: i.e., for the *nomen ipsum* (page 125, line 12),— by the sword.

15. veniam . . . inpetret: this answers the question in the last letter, *detur paenitentiae venia*, etc., page 125, lines 10 sqq.

16. libelli: *accusations, informations.*

17. pessimi . . . saeculi: *very bad as a precedent, and not in accordance with the spirit of our age.*

APPENDIX

I

THE CHRONOLOGY OF THE LETTERS

JOH. MASSON published at Amsterdam, in 1709, his *Plinii Secundi Iunioris vita ordine chronologico sic digesta ut varia dilucidentur historiae Romanae puncta quae Flavianos Imperatores uti Nervam et Traianum spectant.* (Prefixed to Arntzen's edition of the Panegyric, Amst. 1738.)

The most important contribution in recent times to this subject is Mommsen's article in Hermes, III. pp. 31–139, *Zur Lebensgeschichte des jüngeren Plinius.*

Mommsen minimizes the significance of the phrase in Ep. I. 1, *non servato temporis ordine*, and concludes that upon the whole, though not in every particular, the arrangement of the letters is chronological, and also that Pliny himself issued all nine books at successive dates. The latter point may be inferred not merely from the well known practice of publishing literary works in instalments, but also from Ep. IX. 19, *significas legisse te in quadam epistula mea*, referring to Ep. VI. 10, and from Ep. VII. 28, addressed to the same person as Ep. I. 1, justifying the author's praising of his friends. Mommsen argues that letters on the same subject, or otherwise evidently synchronous, are found in the same book or in consecutive books, and conversely that two certainly synchronous letters are never far separated, and that of a pair of letters the later one never comes first in the collection. A similar chronological order is traced in the references to certain persons, e.g., M. Regulus and Calestrius Tiro, in the references to Pliny's marriages and to the relatives of his wives. A gradual change is observed in the list of Pliny's correspondents, older men appearing in the earlier books, younger in the later ones, while men of the author's own age appear all through the collection.

Mommsen then proceeds to assign a probable date for the publication of each book.

Book I.	97	Book V.	106
Book II.	100 (beginning)	Book VI.	106 or 107
Book III.	101, or perhaps 102	Book VII.	107
Book IV.	105 (beginning)	Book VIII.	109

Book IX., perhaps at same time as Book VIII.

The Bithynian correspondence with Trajan, from 111, September, to 113, after January.

Book I.

Ep. 5 was written before the return of Junius Mauricus from exile, which occurred after Jan. 1, 97, but probably not long after Nerve's accession, and certainly in his reign.

Ep. 12. The death of Corellius Rufus seems to have taken place not long after that of Domitian, but he was still alive when Pliny appeared in the Senate against the accusers of Helvidius (Ep. IX. 13. 6).

Ep. 10. At the date of this letter Pliny was in an office which may have been the *praefectura* of the *aerarium militare* (94–96 or 95–97) or of the *aerarium Saturni* (98 on).

Book II., Mommsen thinks, contains letters of the years 97–100.

Ep. 1, about the death of Verginius, belongs to the end of 97 or the beginning of 98.

Ep. 13 contains a reference to Nerva's death. The Priscus there addressed was probably the legate of Pannonia, perhaps in 98 or 99.

Epp. 11 and 12 are of certain date, for the decision about Marius Priscus was in January, 100.

Ep. 7. The emperor who honored Spurinna was probably not Trajan, but Nerva.

Book III.

Epp. 13 and 18, in which Pliny sends a copy of his oration of thanks (September, 100), are unquestionably of 101.

Epp. 4 and 9, about the trial of Classicus, Mommsen thinks must have been written in the autumn of 101. This is a mooted point. It is discussed by him at length, but his conclusions are combated by other writers.

Ep. 8. He cites the military *diploma* (Henzen, 5442), in which L. Neratius Marcellus appears as *legatus Britanniae* on 19 Jan., 103, and infers that the business referred to in this letter would naturally be dated back in 101, confirming his inference by the age of Suetonius at that time, at the time of Ep. I. 18, and at other known dates.

Ep. 21. Upon the basis of this letter and what has preceded, he fixes the death of Martial in 101.

Ep. 7. Silius Italicus died in his 75th year in 101.

BOOK IV.

Mommsen infers by a combination of Ep. 29. 2 with Epp. V. 4. 2; 9; 13; VI. 5 and a *diploma* (Henzen, 6857), concerning the date of the consulship of Licinius Nepos and Afranius Dexter, that this book was issued in the beginning of 105. He finds it consistent with this date that Pliny no longer appears as *praefectus aerarii* (Ep. 12), but as a consular (Epp. 8. 5; 17. 3), and receives the augurship (Ep. 8; *ad Trai.* 13). All this suits 103 and 104. So does the fact that Trajan is at Rome, for he returned from the first Dacian war in 102 and went to the second in 105.

BOOK V.

It is inferred from allusions to Afranius Dexter, to Licinius Nepos, that this book was issued the year after the 4th (106). The last five books seem to have appeared in more rapid succession than the first four. This may be inferred from the references to the trials of Bassus and Varenus and to the proconsulate of Tiro. The rest of the contents of the book are consistent with its issue in 106. Pliny again appears as holding an office, and soon after this Cornutus becomes his colleague by receiving the *cura* of the *Via Aemilia.* Trajan is never spoken of as at Rome; this is the time of the second Dacian war (105–106 or 107).

BOOK VI.

The monument of Verginius Rufus (Ep. 10) is not finished ten years after his death. He died at the end of 97.

Pliny seems still in office (Ep. 4. 1). Trajan is at first absent in Dacia, then back in Rome after great deeds.

Other allusions favor 106 or 107.

BOOKS VII., VIII., IX., treat less of public matters, and afford less basis for chronological inference.

BOOK VII.

The date is inferred with some probability from the references to Cornutus, Varenus, Calestrius Tiro, and Pompeius Faleo.

Book VIII.

Ep. 23 cannot have been written before 108 or 109 if Avitus is the one mentioned in the testament of Dasumius.

Book IX.

This is the poorest of all in dates. Possibly VIII. and IX. were issued together; all we can be sure of is that they were not issued before 108 or 109.

The correspondence with Trajan is independent of the chief collection, which never had more than nine books.

Epp. 1 and 2 come at the beginning of Trajan's reign.

Epp. 3–14 fall in the period before Pliny's *legatio* in Bithynia.

Epp. 15–121 all concern that *legatio*, so far as they admit any inference as to date, place, and circumstance. Few of them can have been written anywhere else.

Mommsen points out the important datum for this series. Pliny mentions several times a Calpurnius Macer, a contemporary governor, his nearest neighbor, a commander of legions. His province must have been Lower Moesia (C.I.L. III. 777). Consideration of this and other known facts leads Mommsen to date the *legatio* from 111, September, to 113, January.

Mommsen's chronology of Pliny's life is followed in the biographical portion of the Introduction.

H. F. Stobbe (*Zur Chronologie der Briefe des Plinius*, Philologus, XXX. 347–393) embodies the results of his own investigation, which was independent of Mommsen's. The conclusions which he reaches are somewhat different.

His discussion involves many of the same points as that of Peter (see below), and his objections are mainly directed against Mommsen's dating of the proceedings against Classicus in 101. He thinks that Pliny undertook the case in the autumn of 99, while that of Priscus was still pending. If this was so, it would not be necessary to assume, as Mommsen does, that the 8th and 9th letters in the correspondence with Trajan are out of place in the group 3–11, where all the others are in strict order of time.

The principal distinctive feature of Stobbe's dissertation is an elaborate consideration of the times and distances involved in the correspondence supposed to have been carried on, by means of the state couriers, between Pliny in Italy and Trajan in Pannonia, in the summer of 99.

Another important contribution to the subject is that of C. Peter (*Zur Chronologie der Briefe des jüngeren Plinius*, Philologus, XXXII. 698 sqq.).

Peter criticises Mommsen's view that it is always true that letters whose dates can be fixed fit into the chronological order and that the others are not inconsistent with it, and especially the opinion that no letters were written before the death of Domitian. He thinks but little weight is to be attached to the fact that wherever two letters have a connection the later one always stands later in the collection, that letters about the same subject or of the same period come in the same book or in two consecutive books. In the same light he regards the argument of Mommsen about the age of the correspondents, observing that most correspondents get but a single letter.

Then follow the positive inferences which Peter draws. In the letters of the 4th and 5th books Pliny appears as a poet, and a lyric poet at that. But in Ep. VII. 4 he says that he has *nunc primum* made an essay in hendecasyllabics, while in Ep. VIII. 21 he calls the collection of his poems *musteus liber*, and in Ep. IX. 34 himself a *novus poeta.* Hence these letters must have been written earlier than those in books 4 and 5.

He finds that Epp. IV. 3, IV. 18, and V. 15, to Arrius Antonius are not in the right order; also that the same is true of Epp. VIII. 1 and IX. 34, and of Epp. II. 11, II. 12; compared with Epp. III. 4, III. 9.

With reference to Ep. II. 9, he argues that it disproves the idea that the letters of the 2d book go only to the beginning of 100, on account of chronological considerations, which, he states, render it impossible that Erucius should have been a candidate for the tribuneship in 100.

The most careful attention is devoted to the date of the trial of Classicus, which Mommsen places in 101, forgetting, as Peter claims, the fact that the case of Marius (Ep. II. 11) was twice under discussion, — once about May, 99, and again in January, 100. The decision on the first occasion was that civil proceedings should go on first, and meantime co-defendants and witnesses for the criminal proceedings should be brought from the province. Peter's opinion is as follows:

The trial of Classicus is to be dated in September, 99, for

1. Both Marius Priscus and Classicus governed provinces in the same year.

2. Mommsen is obliged to assume that Pliny was *praefectus aerarii Saturni* for four years, which is without example.

3. He is therefore obliged to consider Epp. *ad Trai.* 8 and 9 as out of the chronological order in which all the other letters of the group stand.

4. In Ep. VI. 29, where Pliny names the five great cases in which he had been counsel, that of Classicus, with regard to its second main discussion, is named before that of Marius Priscus.

The expression *ante memoriam meam*, in Ep. II. 14. 3, and the general tone of that letter mark Pliny as advanced in life.

Thus Peter goes through the books in order, finding a number of letters which seem to him inconsistent with the chronological arrangement of Mommsen, his final conclusion being that we cannot accept Mommsen's scheme of arrangement — a purely negative conclusion.

Summing up, our verdict would be as follows : The scheme arranged by Mommsen commends itself in its main features. Certain points may be considered as insufficiently established, but they do not invalidate the conclusions as a whole. The argument is a constructive one, in which the different parts, leading to a common object, have cumulative force. Destructive argument is relatively easier. Conclusions may be attacked, or even refuted, and nothing put in their place. Some of the objections to Mommsen's positions are undoubtedly fanciful or unsound, some may be admitted to be convincing in detail. In one important particular the case against Mommsen's view is very strongly supported ; that is, in the matter of the date of the trial of Classicus and all that is involved therein. We may modify our acceptance of Mommsen's chronology to the extent of adopting the conclusions of Stobbe and Peter in this respect, while believing it to be substantially correct as a whole.

II

CRITICAL

Page 1, line 11. *subiectus et serviens lacus : serviens* is untranslatable. An estate which was burdened with an 'easement' for the benefit of another estate was called *serviens.* Thus the lake lying below the villa, and lending itself to the view, was a permanent enhancement of its charm.

2, 8. *exclude* MVD ; *excude* pςa ; *excute* Fr Riccard. The metaphor of the first is embodied in the note, that of the second (and third, which appears merely a wrong transcription of the second) seems to be borrowed from the forge or the sculptor's studio.

4, 9. *suppliciter*] *simpliciter* V Riccard, in the latter corrected by later hand to *suppliciter; subtiliter* D.

6, 4. *ipsumque illud*] *ipsum illud* MV Monacensis.

8, 8. *ut ipsum audiebam*] *ut ipsum praedicantem audiebam* Sichardus. But Pliny constantly omits *verba dicendi.*

9, 10. *firmissimi* MV ; *fortissimi* F Riccard pra.

11, 3. *ut iuvenis iuvenem*] *ut iuvenem iuvenis* would seem a better order, though there seems to be no Ms. authority for it. Then *ut iuvenem* would match *ut senem* in line 5, and the parenthesis in line 4 would immediately follow *iuvenis*, to which (and not to *iuvenem*) it refers.

15, 20. *scirem sponte te facturum* Riccard. Professor Merrill says there is no *te* before *facturum* in Riccard. *Te* after *sponte* would easily be omitted in copying.

16, 8. *discere* MVDrςa ; *doceri* F Riccard p.

18, 8. *indici*] *indicere* MV.

22, 5. *cumque ego nubenti tibi* MV. Keil *ed. maior* has *cumque vivente eo nubenti tibi.*

22, 11. *acceptum tibi fieri;* perhaps we should read *ferri* with F.

25, 15. *Enotuerunt* FDpa ; *enituerunt* MV.

26, 18. *Mater e primis citerioris* M ; *mater e primis ipse citerioris* VFDpr Cataneus a ; *mater e primis ipsa citerioris* ς. One Ms., according to Cataneus, omitted *mater*. Mommsen proposes to read : *pater . . . clarus : clarior vitricus . . . mater e primis. Ipse citerioris Hispaniae* (*scis quod iudicium provinciae, quanta sit gravitas*) *flamen proxime fuit*, which is at least intelligible. He argues that *flamen*, used absolutely, is impossible, and that the *iudicium provinciae* could not be shown in regard to Voconius's mother, but to himself.

29, 7. *teneris* MVFDpra. Mommsen's emendation *taetris* is quite unnecessary.

30, 15. *in D litterae*] *in O litterae* pra ; *in d litterae* F ; *inde litterae* MVD Riccard.

31, 6. *qui suspensus et tubulatus*] *qui suspensus et subulatus* F Riccard ; *qui suspensus et turbulatus* D ; *quod suspensum et tabula tum* MVς.

32, 14. *ventis inquietus* MVD ; *ventus inquietus* Fpa Riccard.

34, 20. *multis* MVD ; *multi* F Riccard pra. It is hard to choose between *iocabantur* FD Riccard and *loquebantur* MVς.

39, 19. *erectius* Fpra ; *rectius* MVD.

40, 31. *studiis* Cellarius ; *studii* MVFDpra.

46, 6. *fuerit* FD Riccard ςa ; *fuerat* MVr.

48, 17. *et vivis*]; it is likely enough that *tu* has dropped out in copying; ETTVVIVIS could easily be changed to ETTVIVIS and then to ETVIVIS.

48, 26. *ut non moriar* MVD; *ne moriar* Fpra.

51, 14. *inter sua* MVD Riccard r; *intersita* Fpςa.

51, 20. *colonorum*; the explanation of this word by Pr. & B. seems to assign to Pliny's time facts in regard to the *status* of tenants, which properly apply only to a considerably later date; see Sohm's *Institutes* (translation), page 115; Sandars's *Justinian*, pages 78, 179; and especially Hunter's *Roman Law*, page 162.

55, 10. *tiferni tiberini* MVς; *tifernium tiberinum* F Riccard; *tiferali tiberini* D; Sc. *cui nomen est* or the like.

56, 5. *mancipatum* Fpa; *emancipatum* MVrς; *emancipatur* D.

57, 20. *ut orator* MVD; *ut plurimis orator* F Riccard pr.

58, 23. *possim* FDpa; *possem* MVς.

59, 19. *qui sorte* F Beroaldus a (*forte* Riccard); *cui sorti* MV; *cui sorte* Dς.

60, 3. *aerari populo* MVς; *aerario populo* D; *aerario populoque* F Riccard pra.

61, 11. *omnia autem peregre emuntur* MVς; omitted in FD Riccard pra.

61, 30. *finitimis* MV; *in finitimis* FDpa; *a finitimis* rς.

65, 10. *loco*] *vice* MVς.

65, 11. *verereris me*] *venereris me* F Riccard; *venerere me* pra; *verere me* D; *dilexeris meque* MV.

65, 27. *hoc a Maurico* MV; *hoc Maurico* Fςa.

66, 4. *orbatus* Fa; *orbus* Dpr; *captus* MVς.

66, 24. *decesserunt exulant alii* Dpra; *recesserunt exulant alii* F Riccard; *decesserunt alii exulant alii* MV.

67, 22. *tabellam* MV; *tabellas* D Riccard pra; *tabulas* F.

69, 17. *omniaque me usu cepisse*] *omniaque mea suscepisse* F Riccard; omitted in M.

71, 10. *resedisse* MDpr; *sedisse* F Riccard a.

72, 18. *exemplar*] *exemplum* M.

72, 26. *aerarii fuit, fuit et* Ma; *aerarii* (*aerari* D) *fuit et* Dpr.

73, 21. *impleverat* Ma; *expleverat* Dpr.

74, 15. *margarita* M; *margaritas* Dpra.

74, 16. *tus* M; *tura* Dpr.

75, 13. *Iulius*] *silvius* M.

77, 9. *a nimia superstitione*] *animi*[a] *superstitione* M; *animi superstitione* Dpra; *anili superstitione* Casaubon.

78, 18. *amore communium* MDpa ; *amore communium civium* ς ; *amore communi* Sichardus ; *in more communi* Casaubon ; *amore communi omnium* Mommsen. The sense of *communium* in this passage is so unusual that the temptation is strong to accept Mommsen's emendation.

79, 9. *adparares* M ; *adquireres* Dpς.

80, 21. *primis* M ; *primus* Dpra.

81, 10. *aliquando* Dpra ; *aliquandiu* M Monacensis.

82, 15. *non interfuisti ne ego quidem* Ma ; *interfuistine ? ego quidem* Dpr.

83, 22. *elata* Ma ; *flata* Dp ; *eflata* r ; *efflata* ς.

84, 4. *recline tasci* (*rectine casci* D, *Rectinae Nasci* a) *imminenti periculo exterritę* MDa.

85, 21. *viderat*] Mommsen and Keil add *erat*.

86, 14. *quia . . . crederentur*] *quia campaniae solitus illa* (*ille* Dp) *vero nocte ita* (*iam* D) *invaluit ut non moveri omnia sed verti* (*sed everti* a) *crederentur* Dpra ; *q* (i.e. *quia*) *campanię non solum castella verum etiam oppida non moveri omnia sed verti credebantur* M.

91, 8. *gladiatorum* Mςa ; *gladiatorium* Dpra.

93, 2. *deinde ut matri* Keil pra ; *deinde matri* M ; *deinde mihi ut matri* D.

95, 17. *quamquam*] *quos* M.

95, 21. *Eritne quam* Keil ; *erit quam* M ; *erit ne quam* Dpr.

103, 2. *aequare* Mr ; *aequari* Keil a.

103, 15. *Nam quae*] *namque* Mr ; Keil follows a in inserting *quae* after *denique*.

104, 5. *inter eos ipso* M ; *inter deos ipso* Beroald. a Keil ; *inter deos ipsos* r.

105, 4. *clitumnum fontem* Mra ; *Clitumni* Keil.

105, 21. *ut* M ; *velut* Keil.

107, 25. *trabes*] a Keil add *atque culmina*.

108, 7. *paulum* M ; *parvulum* Keil.

109, 3. *color . . . medicatus*] so Gesner ; *viridior et pressior* M ; *viridior et preciosior* r ; *et pressior* (omitting *viridior*) a ; *viridiore pressior* Barthius.

109, 8. *ut* a ; *vel* M ; *ac* Keil.

115, 6. *narrabat sedisse se cum Circensibus proximis equitem Ro. hunc* a ; *narrabat sedisse circensibus proximis eq. R.* (*proximis equi. ro.* p. *proximum eq. R.* r.) *hunc* Dpr ; *narrabat sedisse se cum quodam circensibus proximis hunc* M ; *narrabat enim Circensibus* *sedisse proximum equiti Ro. hunc* ς; *narrabat sedisse secum circensibus proximis equitem Romanum: hunc* Keil.

115, 9. *me et quidem*] *me equidem* M.

116, 7. *ut te erroribus*] *ut terroribus* D; *uter erroribus* M.

117, 11. *venit*] omitted by Keil.

117, 16. *praebentem* a; *praebentem se* Mommsen; *praeeuntem* Dpr.

117, 17. *adnatat nanti insilit tergo* a; *adnatanti insiliit tergo* rς; *adnatanti* (*-di* D) *insiliit ergo* Dp; *adnatantis insilit tergo* Sichardus; *adnatat natanti insilit tergo* Cortius.

117, 29. *proconsulis* ςa; *proconsulem* D.

123, 7. *ad Anniam*] Hardy substitutes *ad Asiam*.

123, 9. *ad eosdem acheos* A (Avantius 1502); *ad eosdem dein ad Achaeos* a (Aldus 1508); *ad eosdem et Achaeos* Budaeus.

123, 20. *intra eas* Keil; *inter eas* Aa.

123, 21. *rescripsit non est Bithynia* a; *rescripsit intermissa est Bithynia* Orelli; *rescripsit praeterita est Bithynia* Mommsen.

124, 12. *et quibus insignibus ornatus fuisset* Cataneus; *et cuius ornatus fuisset* Orelli; *cum aliis quibus ornatus fuisset* Mommsen.

124, 20. *augeas* Cataneus; *augebis* Aa.

INDEX

I

PERSONS TO WHOM THE LETTERS ARE ADDRESSED

The Roman figures refer to the letters in the complete books; the heavy-faced figures to the consecutive numbers of this volume.

II

PROPER NAMES OCCURRING IN THE LETTERS

The references are by page and line of the text.

III

GRAMMATICAL AND LEXICAL

The references are to the notes, by page and line of the text to which the notes apply.

IV

MISCELLANEOUS

MATTERS OTHER THAN GRAMMATICAL TREATED IN THE NOTES

References are by page and line of text treated in the notes.

This edition of *Selected Letters of Pliny* has been printed on paper having a life expectancy of three hundred years.

UNIVERSITY OF OKLAHOMA PRESS
NORMAN